Classic Stories from the Lives of Our Prophets

Classic Stories from the Lives of Our Prophets

Compiled by
Leon R.
Hartshorn

Deseret Book Company
Salt Lake City, Utah

©1971 Deseret Book Company
©1988 Leon R. Hartshorn

Deseret Book is a registered trademark of Deseret Book Company.

Library of Congress Catalog Card No. 73-155235

ISBN 0-87579-196-4

Printed in the United States of America

Contents

John Taylor

Wilford Woodruff

Lorenzo Snow

Joseph F. Smith

Heber J. Grant

George Albert Smith

David O. McKay

Joseph Fielding Smith

Harold B. Lee

Spencer W. Kimball

Ezra Taft Benson

Biographical Sketch

JOSEPH SMITH

Joseph Smith occupies a unique place among the prophets —his birth and his name, Joseph, were known nearly four thousand years before he came to the earth. Joseph who was sold into Egypt said of the great latter-day prophet:

Yea, Joseph truly said: Thus saith the Lord unto me; a choice seer will I raise up. . . .

. . . Behold; that seer will the Lord bless. . . .

And his name shall be called after me; and it shall be after the name of his father. And he shall be like unto me; for the thing, which the Lord shall bring forth by his hand, by the power of the Lord shall bring my people unto salvation.

Yea, thus prophesied Joseph: I am sure of this thing. . . . (Nephi 3:7, 14-16; italics added.)

Not only was the Prophet Joseph's birth known, but after his death, the Lord caused to have written and included as scripture the following:

Joseph Smith, the Prophet and Seer of the Lord, has done more, save Jesus only, for the salvation of men in this world, than any other man that ever lived in it. (D&C 135:3.)

1

Joseph Smith had bestowed upon him all of the priesthood authority needed to preside over the dispensation of the fulness of times, the dispensation in which all things that have been are gathered into one.

Joseph Smith, because of the magnitude of his mission, received authority from, and was intimately acquainted with, numerous immortal beings. In addition to God the Father and his Son Jesus Christ, he received visitations from Moroni, Peter, James, John, John the Baptist, Moses, Elias, Elijah, and many others.

Joseph Smith is also somewhat unique among the great latter-day prophets in that he served the Lord on the earth as a prophet while yet in his youth. The Prophet has recorded the following experience in his life which occurred when he was just fourteen years old:

. . . I saw a pillar of light exactly over my head, above the brightness of the sun, which descended gradually until it fell upon me.

. . . When the light rested upon me I saw two Personages, whose brightness and glory defy all description, standing above me in the air. (Joseph Smith 2:16, 17.)

Later Joseph Smith had the great privilege of having a heavenly teacher to help prepare him to accomplish his assigned task of translating an ancient volume of holy scripture. He published his inspired translation of the sacred record when he was just twenty-four years old, and at the same age he became the leader of the Restored Church.

Joseph Smith was a strong, vigorous, highly motivated prophet. He was greatly persecuted, but he never lost his eternal perspective, and he never ceased to be grateful and joyful.

Joseph Smith was born on December 23, 1805, and just thirty-eight years later, in June of 1844, the initial latter-day prophet was faced with death. He had moved with his faithful followers four times to seek safety, but without success. The Prophet said, "If I go to Carthage I am a dead man." He did not want to leave his wife and four children; he wanted to see his unborn child. But it was not to be. On June 27, 1844, the first prophet of the last dispensation was killed by a mob of men with blackened faces.

The bodies of Joseph and Hyrum lay side by side as they were returned to Nauvoo. Joseph Smith was dead at the early age of thirty-eight, but his life was a phenomenal success, and his deeds will be remembered and millions would be better because of him.

Joseph Smith was the epitome of the whole, well-rounded man. He was an intense prophet, a devoted father, a capable leader, and an excellent scholar. But with it all, he had a love for athletics and possessed a delightfully keen sense of humor. He was totally unpretenious and was completely without guile. He was in very deed what he said he was—a prophet of the Living God.

JOSEPH SMITH

"Oh Father! The Pain Is So Severe"

The following is told by Joseph Smith's mother, Lucy Mack Smith.

Joseph, our third son, having recovered from the typhus fever, after something like two weeks' sickness, one day screamed out while sitting in a chair, with a pain in his shoulder.°And, in a very short time he appeared to be in such agony that we feared the consequence would prove to be something very serious. We immediately sent for a doctor. When he arrived and had examined the patient, he said that it was his opinion that this pain was occasioned by a sprain. But the child declared this could not be the case as he had received no injury in any way whatever, but that a severe pain had seized him all at once, of the cause of which he was entirely ignorant.

Notwithstanding the child's protestations, still the physician insisted that it must be a sprain, and consequently he anointed his shoulder with some bone liniment, but this was of no advantage to him, for the pain continued the same after the anointing as before.

When two weeks of extreme suffering had elapsed, the attendant physician concluded to make closer examination,

---

°Joseph Smith was eight years old at the time of this illness.

whereupon he found that a large fever sore had gathered between his breast and shoulder. He immediately lanced it. . . .

As soon as the sore had discharged itself, the pain left it and shot like lightning (using his own terms) down his side into the marrow of the bone of his leg and soon became very severe. My poor boy, at this, was almost in despair, and he cried out, "Oh, father! the pain is so severe, how can I bear it!"

His leg soon began to swell, and he continued to suffer the greatest agony for the space of two weeks longer. During this period I carried him much of the time in my arms in order to mitigate his suffering as much as possible; in consequence of which I was taken very ill myself. The anxiety of mind that I experienced, together with physical overexertion, was too much for my constitution, and my nature sank under it.

Hyrum, who was rather remarkable for his tenderness and sympathy, now desired that he might take my place. As he was a good, trusty boy, we let him do so, and, in order to make the task as easy for him as possible, we laid Joseph upon a low bed and Hyrum sat beside him, almost day and night for some considerable length of time, holding the affected part of his leg in his hands and pressing it between them, so that his afflicted brother might be enabled to endure the pain which was so excruciating that he was scarcely able to bear it.

At the end of three weeks, we thought it advisable to send for the surgeon. When he came he made an incision of eight inches on the front side of the leg, between the knee and ankle. This relieved the pain in a great measure, and the patient was quite comfortable until the wound began to heal, when the pain became as violent as ever.

The surgeon was called again, and he this time enlarged the wound, cutting the leg even to the bone. It commenced healing the second time, and as soon as it began to heal it also began to swell again, which swelling continued to rise till we deemed it wisdom to call a council of surgeons; and when they met in consultation they decided that amputation was the only remedy.

Soon after coming to this conclusion, they rode up to the door and were invited into a room apart from the one in which Joseph lay. They being seated; I addressed them thus: "Gentlemen, what can you do to save my boy's leg?" They answered, "We can do nothing; we have cut it open to the bone and find it so affected that we consider his leg incurable and that amputation is absolutely necessary in order to save his life."

This was like a thunderbolt to me. I appealed to the principal surgeon, saying, "Dr. Stone, can you not make another trial? Can you not, by cutting around the bone, take out the diseased part, and perhaps that which is sound will heal over, and by this means you will save his leg? You will not, you must not, take off his leg, until you try once more. I will not consent to let you enter his room until you make me this promise."

After consulting a short time with each other, they agreed to do as I had requested, then went to see my suffering son. One of the doctors, on approaching his bed, said, "My poor boy, we have come again." "Yes," said Joseph, "I see you have; but you have not come to take off my leg, have you, sir?" "No," replied the surgeon, "it is your mother's request that we make one more effort, and that is what we have now come for."

The principal surgeon, after a moment's conversation, ordered cords to be brought to bind Joseph fast to a bedstead; but to this Joseph objected. The doctor, however, insisted that he must be confined, upon which Joseph said very decidedly, "No, doctor, I will not be bound, for I can bear the operation much better if I have my liberty." "Then," said Dr. Stone, "will you drink some brandy?"

"No," said Joseph, "not one drop."

"Will you take some wine?" rejoined the doctor. "You must take something, or you can never endure the severe operation to which you must be subjected."

"No," exclaimed Joseph, "I will not touch one particle of liquor, neither will I be tied down; but I will tell you what I will do—I will have my father sit on the bed and hold me in his arms, and then I will do whatever is necessary in order to have the bone taken out." Looking at me, he said, "Mother, I want you to leave the room, for I know you cannot bear to see me suffer so; father can stand it, but you have carried me so much, and watched over me so long, you are almost worn out."

Then looking up into my face, his eyes swimming in tears, he continued. "Now, mother, promise me that you will not stay, will you? The Lord will help me, and I shall get through with it."

To this request I consented, and getting a number of folded sheets, and laying them under his leg, I retired, going several hundred yards from the house in order to be out of hearing.

The surgeons commenced operating by boring into the bone of his leg, first on one side of the bone where it was affected, then on the other side, after which they broke it off with a pair of forceps or pincers. They thus took away large pieces of the bone. When they broke off the first piece, Joseph screamed out so loudly, that I could not forbear running to him. On my entering the room, he cried out, "Oh, mother, go back, go back; I do not want you to come in. I will try to tough it out, if you will go away."

When the third piece was taken away, I burst into the room again—and oh, my God! What a spectacle for a mother's eye! The wound torn open, the blood still gushing from it, and the bed literally covered with blood. Joseph was pale as a corpse, and large drops of sweat were rolling down his face, whilst upon every feature was depicted the utmost agony!

I was immediately forced from the room, and detained until the operation was completed; but when the act was accomplished, Joseph put upon a clean bed, the room cleared of every appearance of blood, and the instruments which were used in the operation removed, I was permitted again to enter.

Joseph immediately commenced getting better, and from this onward, continued to mend until he became strong and healthy. When he had so far recovered as to be able to travel, he went with his uncle Jesse Smith to Salem, for the benefit of his health, hoping the sea breezes would be of service to him, and in this he was not disappointed.

Having passed through about a year of sickness and distress, health again returned to our family, and we most assuredly realized the blessing. And indeed, we felt to acknowledge the hand of God more in preserving our lives through such a tremendous scene of affliction, than if we had, during this time, seen nothing but health and prosperity.

Lucy Mack Smith, *History of Joseph Smith* (Salt Lake City: Bookcraft, 1958), pp. 54-58.

———◆———

JOSEPH SMITH

"A Burden Has Been Lifted from Me This Day"

Finally a long-awaited day came. The translation (of the Book of Mormon Plates) was completed. Joseph Smith wanted those who cared for him to be present at the Whitmer farm in Fayette. His father was there, his mother, Oliver Cowdery, Martin Harris, and the Whitmers. He must have electrified the small group when he told them that this was the day when three others would behold the plates besides himself. He told Oliver Cowdery he would be one of the witnesses and David Whitmer would be another. And then, approaching Martin Harris, in essence he said, "Martin, you have got to humble yourself before God this day. If you do, you will also be privileged to be one of the witnesses."

The four left the house and went to the woods. They knelt and began to pray, praying vocally in turn. After each one had prayed twice, Martin Harris arose and said, "It is my fault that our prayers are not answered," and then he left. Shortly after his departure, a brilliant light appeared and an angel stood before them holding the plates and turning some of the leaves. They all heard the voice of God speak from the heavens bearing witness that the translation was correct. As the vision closed, Joseph Smith went to find Martin Harris. He found him praying. He knelt with him, and they prayed together. The same vision was opened to them. They beheld an angel, saw the plates, and they heard the voice of God. Martin Harris was soon so overcome with joy that he cried out, " 'Tis enough. 'Tis enough. Mine eyes have beheld. Mine eyes have beheld."

Joseph had been gone from the Whitmer home for a long time. As he entered the house, he did not speak. He sat down by his mother. He laid his head on his mother's breast. So much had happened to the young prophet in the past decade, though he was not yet twenty-four years old. He in essence said, quietly, reflectively: "Mother, you don't know what a burden has been lifted from me this day. Now people will know that I don't go around to deceive them. The Lord has caused that the plates have been shown to three others besides myself, and they must be witnesses with me."

Leon R. Hartshorn, *Joseph Smith: Prophet of the Restoration* (Salt Lake City: Deseret Book Co., 1970), pp. 13-14.

JOSEPH SMITH

"I Feel Sorry for This Brother to the Amount of Five Dollars"

When the Saints had been driven from Missouri and began to settle in Illinois, Joseph went to Quincy, where "he visited around from house to house among the Saints to see how they were situated, and gave words of strength and encouragement to them." When informed some time later that a brother who lived some distance from Nauvoo had had his house burned down, nearly everyone present expressed sympathy for the man. But Joseph put his hand in his pocket, took out five dollars, and said: "I feel sorry for this brother to the amount of five dollars; how much do you feel sorry?"

Hyrum L. Andrus, *Joseph Smith, the Man and the Seer* (Salt Lake City: Deseret Book Co., 1960), p. 32.

JOSEPH SMITH

"It Makes Them Happy"

On another occasion Joseph Smith had indulged in playing a game of ball with some of the young men in Nauvoo. When his brother Hyrum saw it he wished to correct the Prophet and even rebuked him, saying that such conduct was not becoming in a prophet of the Lord. The Prophet answered in a mild voice, "Brother Hyrum, my mingling with the boys in a harmless sport like this does not injure me in any way, but on the other hand it makes them happy and draws their hearts nearer to mine; and who knows but there may be young men among them who may sometime lay down their lives for me!"

Edwin F. Parry, *Stories About Joseph Smith the Prophet* (Salt Lake City, 1934), p. 97.

JOSEPH SMITH

"We Passed on Without Interruption"

Towards the latter end of August, in company with John and David Whitmer, and my brother Hyrum Smith, I visited the Church at Colesville, New York. Well knowing the determined hostility of our enemies in that quarter, and also knowing that it was our duty to visit the Church, we had called upon our Heavenly Father, in mighty prayer, that he would grant us an opportunity of meeting with them, that he would blind the eyes of our enemies so that they would not know us, and that we might on this occasion return unmolested. Our prayers were not in vain, for when within a little distance of Mr. Knight's place, we encountered a large company at work upon the public road, amongst whom were several of our most bitter enemies. They looked earnestly at us, but not knowing us; we passed on without interruption. That evening we assembled the Church, and confirmed them, partook of the Sacrament, and held a happy meeting, having much reason to rejoice in the God of our salvation and sing hosannas to his holy name. Next morning we set out on our return home, and although our enemies had offered a reward of five dollars to any one who would give them information of our arrival, yet did we get out of the neighborhood, without the least annoyance, and arrived home in safety. Some few days afterwards, however, Newel Knight came to my place, and from him we learned that, very shortly after our departure, the mob came to know of our having been there, when they immediately collected together, and threatened the brethren, and very much annoyed them during all that day.

Joseph Smith, *History of the Church.* Period 1 (Salt Lake City: Deseret Book Co., 1963), 1:108-9.

————◆——◆——

JOSEPH SMITH

"I Got Both Feet in the Mud"

Margaret McIntyre Burgess, who, as a child, lived with her parents in Nauvoo, Illinois, related this incident of her cherished recollections of the Prophet Joseph.

My older brother and I were going to school, near to the building which was known as Joseph's brick store. It had been raining the previous day, causing the ground to be very muddy, especially along that street. My brother Wallace and I got both feet in the mud and could not get out, and, of course, child-like, we began to cry, for we thought we would have to stay there. But looking up, I beheld the loving friend of children, the Prophet Joseph coming to us. He soon had us on high and dry ground. Then he stooped down and cleaned the mud from our little heavy-laden shoes, took his handkerchief from his pocket, and wiped our tear-stained faces. He spoke kind and cheering words to us and sent us on our way to school rejoicing.

Parry, *Stories About Joseph Smith the Prophet*, pp. 23-25.

JOSEPH SMITH

"One of the Wagon Wheels Came Off"

We had appointed a meeting for this evening, for the purpose of attending to the confirmation of those who had been the same morning baptized. The time appointed had arrived and our friends had nearly all collected together, when to my surprise I was visited by a constable and arrested by him on a warrant, on the charge of being a disorderly person, of setting the country in an uproar by preaching the Book of Mormon, etc. The constable informed me, soon after I had been arrested, that the plan of those who had got out the warrant was to get me into the hands of the mob, who were now lying in ambush for me, but that he was determined to save me from them, as he had found me to be a different sort of person from what I had been represented to him. I soon found that he had told me the truth in this matter, for not far from Mr. Knight's house the wagon in which we had set out was surrounded by a mob, who seemed only to await some signal from the constable. But to their great disappointment, he gave the horse the whip and drove me out of their reach.

Whilst driving in great haste one of the wagon wheels came off, which left us once more very nearly surrounded by them, as they had come on in close pursuit. However, we managed to replace the wheel and again left them behind us. He drove on to the town of South Bainbridge, Chenango County, where he lodged me for the time being in an upper room of a tavern; and in order that all might be right with himself and with me also, he slept during the night with his feet against the door, and a loaded musket by his side, whilst I occupied a bed which was in the room, he having declared that if we were interrupted unlawfully, he would fight for me and defend me as far as it was in his power.

Joseph Smith, *History of the Church*, 1:88-89.

JOSEPH SMITH

"I Was Healed in an Instant"

On the sixth of May I gave the parting hand to the brethren in Independence and, in company with Brothers Rigdon and Whitney, commenced a return to Kirtland, by stage to St. Louis, from thence to Vincennes, Indiana, and from thence to New Albany, near the falls of the Ohio River. Before we arrived at the latter place, the horses became frightened, and while going at full speed Bishop Whitney attempted to jump out of the coach, but having his coat fast, caught his foot in the wheel, and had his leg and foot broken in several places; at the same time I jumped out unhurt. We put up at Mr. Porter's public house, in Greenville, for four weeks, while Elder Rigdon went directly forward to Kirtland. During all this time, Brother Whitney lost not a meal of victuals or a night's sleep, and Dr. Porter, our landlord's brother, who attended him, said it was a pity we had not got some "Mormon" there, as they could set broken bones or do anything else. I tarried with Brother Whitney and administered to him till he was able to be moved. While at this place I frequently walked out in the woods, where I saw several fresh graves, and one day when I rose from the dinner table, I walked directly to the door and commenced vomiting most profusely. I raised large quantities of blood and poisonous matter, and so great were the muscular contortions of my system, that my jaw in a few moments was dislocated. This I succeeded in replacing with my own hands and made my way to Brother Whitney (who was on the bed), as speedily as possible; he laid his hands on me and administered to me in the name of the Lord, and I was healed in an instant, although the effect of the poison was so powerful as to cause much of the hair to become loosened from my head. Thanks be to my Heavenly Father for his inter-

ference in my behalf at this critical moment, in the name of
Jesus Christ. Amen.

Joseph Smith, *History of the Church*, 1:271.

———◆—◆—◆———

JOSEPH SMITH

_____

"When I Am with the Boys"

**Bishop Calvin W. Moore, a veteran of the Mormon Battalion, tells this incident that
happened in Nauvoo.**

It was at the time Porter Rockwell
(a friend of the Prophet) was in jail in Missouri. His mother went
to see him at the jail, and the Missourians told her that if she
would raise a certain amount of money and give them, they
would let her son go. Joseph started out to get the money. He
came to a large crowd of young men who were wrestling, that
being the popular sport in those days. Among the boys there
was a bully, from La Harpe, I believe. He had thrown every one
on the ground who took hold of him. When Joseph came to the
crowd he told them what he wanted, passed around the hat,
raised what money he could, and then went into the ring to
take part with the boys in their games. He was invited to wres-
tle with this bully. The man was eager to have a tussle with the
Prophet, so Joseph stepped forward and took hold of the man.
The first pass he made Joseph whirled him around and took him
by the collar and seat of his trousers and walked out to a ditch
and threw him in. Then, taking him by the arm, he helped him
up and said, "You must not mind this. When I am with the boys
I make all the fun I can for them."

Parry, *Stories About Joseph Smith the Prophet*, pp. 27-29.

———◆—◆—◆———

JOSEPH SMITH

It Was Just So With His Mind

Elder William M. Allred says he once heard the Prophet justify himself for playing with the young people by relating this story:

"**A** certain prophet was sitting under the shade of a tree amusing himself in some way, when a hunter came along with his bow and arrow and reproved him. The prophet asked him if he kept his bow strung up all the time. The hunter answered that he did not. The prophet asked him why, and he said it would lose its elasticity if he did. The Prophet said it was just so with his mind; he did not want it strung up all the time."

Parry, *Stories About Joseph Smith the Prophet,* pp. 27-29.

JOSEPH SMITH

"You Can Thank Joseph Smith for Being Alive"

At the time the Prophet Joseph Smith and some of his brethren were betrayed into the hands of the mob from Missouri, there was one of the mobocrats, . . . Moses Wilson, who was trying to get a little state evidence against the Mormon leaders because the mob in whose power they were held wanted to shoot them the next morning. In fact, Joseph and others were court-martialed by the mob . . . when they were civilians, and had never so much as carried a sword. The Mormon leaders were out in the rain while the mob was

17

decreeing their destruction. Wilson came to Lyman Wight. Lyman Wight was a rough and ready fellow. . . . He was the type of man the Missourians feared. In fact, they had called him "the wild ram of the mountains." . . . Moses Wilson came up to Wight and he said to him, "We have nothing against you other than you are too friendly to Joe Smith, and we believe him to be a d—— rascal. . . . Now if you'll just bring a little evidence against Joe, we will give you your release. You can have any office you want in the state militia. But," he said, "if you don't, you'll be shot tomorrow morning at nine o'clock."

Lyman Wight looked Wilson squarely in the eye, and said, "General, you have your men wrong, both in myself and in Joseph Smith. Joseph Smith is the best friend you've got. In fact," he said, "if it hadn't been for Joseph Smith, you would have been in hell long ago, and I would have put you there myself by slitting your throat; and Joseph Smith is the only man who could stop me from doing it. So you can just thank Joseph Smith for being alive."

Ivan J. Barrett, *Seminar on the Prophet Joseph Smith*, 1964, "Joseph Smith's Personality" (Brigham Young University, 1965), pp. 53-54.

———◆—◆—◆———

JOSEPH SMITH

"One of the Most Daring and Heroic Deeds"

While on the mountains some distance from Washington, our coachman stepped into a public house to take his grog, when the horses took fright and ran down the hill at full speed. I persuaded my fellow travelers to be quiet and retain their seats, but had to hold one woman to prevent her from throwing her infant out of the coach. The passengers were exceedingly agitated, but I used every persuasion to calm their feelings, and opening the door, I secured my hold on the side of the coach the best way I could, and succeeded in placing myself in the coachman's seat and reining up the horses, after they had run some two or three miles. And neither coach, horses, or passengers received any injury. My course was spoken of in the highest terms of commendation as being one of the most daring and heroic deeds, and no language could express the gratitude of the passengers when they found themselves safe and the horses quiet. There were some members of Congress with us, who proposed naming the incident to that body, believing they would reward such conduct by some public act; but on inquiring my name to mention as the author of their safety, and finding it to be Joseph Smith the "Mormon Prophet," as they called me, I heard no more of their praise, gratitude, or reward.

Joseph Smith, *History of the Church,* 1:271.

———◆—◆———

JOSEPH SMITH

"Did You Feel Strangely When Smith Took You by the Hand?"

Shortly after the family of Joseph Smith, Sr., moved to Far West, Missouri, in the summer of 1838, difficulties arose between the Saints and the mob element in that area. It started at an election held at Gallatin, the county seat of Daviess County, Missouri, when a group of non-Mormons attempted to prevent certain of the brethren from voting. The Prophet was not present at the time. A struggle occurred in which several non-Mormons were hurt, and the report was afterward circulated that Joseph Smith had himself killed seven men and intended to organize the Saints and exterminate all who were not of the Mormon faith.

A few days thereafter, Joseph was at the home of his parents, writing a letter, when a large body of armed men came to the door. Eight of their officers dismounted and entered the house, stating that they had come "to kill Joe Smith and all the 'Mormons'." When Mother Smith informed them that her son had not been in Daviess County, one of the officers rejoined, "There is no doubt that the report is perfectly correct; it came straight to us, and I believe it; and we were sent to kill the Prophet and all who believe in him, and I'll be d——d if I don't execute my orders." After some further comments, Joseph arose from his writing table and was introduced by his mother. As they stared at him, "he smiled, and, stepping towards them, gave each of them his hand, in a manner which convinced them that he was neither a guilty criminal nor yet a hypocrite." He then sat down and explained to them the attitude of the Saints and what their course had been amid the difficulties that had been heaped upon them. After talking to them for some time, he turned and said, "Mother I believe I will go home now. Emma will be expecting me." At this, two of the officers sprang to their feet and suggested that he should not go alone and that they would attend him in order to protect him. As the three men left the house, Mother Smith overheard the following conversation among the officers who remained at the door:

1st Officer: "Did you not feel strangely when Smith took you by the hand? I never felt so in my life."

2nd Officer: "I could not move. I would not harm a hair of that man's head for the whole world."

3rd Officer: "This is the last time you will catch me coming to kill Joe Smith, or the 'Mormons' either."

1st Officer: "I guess this is about my last expedition against this place. I never saw a more harmless, innocent-appearing man than the 'Mormon' Prophet."

2nd Officer: "That story about his killing those men is all a d——d lie, there is no doubt of it; and we have had all this trouble for nothing; but they will never fool me in this way again; I'll warrant them."

Lucy Mack Smith, *History of Joseph Smith*, pp. 254-56.

JOSEPH SMITH

"This Is Not My Little Mary"

The following story was told by Margaret McIntyre Burgess.

Joseph's wife, Emma, had lost a young babe. My mother had twin baby girls. The Prophet came to see if she would let him have one of them. Of course it was rather against her feelings, but she finally consented for him to take one of them, providing he would bring it home each night. This he did punctually himself and also came after it each morning.

One evening he did not come with it at the usual time and mother went down to the Mansion to see what was the matter; and there sat the Prophet with the baby wrapped up in a little silk quilt. He was trotting it on his knee and singing to it to get it quiet before starting out, as it had been fretting. The child soon became quiet, when my mother took it and the Prophet came up home with her.

Next morning when he came after the baby, Mother handed him Sarah, the other baby. They looked so much alike that strangers could not tell them apart; but as Mother passed him the other baby he shook his head and said, "This is not my little Mary." Then she took Mary from the cradle and gave her to him, and he smilingly carried her home with him. After his wife became better in health, he did not take our baby away any more, but often came in to caress her and play with her.

Parry, *Stories About Joseph Smith the Prophet*, pp. 25-27.

JOSEPH SMITH

"How Do You Know He Wasn't Baptized Before He Became a Thief?"

Josiah Quincy, along with other guests, was dining at the Mansion House at Nauvoo one evening.

As he (Josiah Quincy) and others finished dining in the Mansion House at Nauvoo, the request was made that Joseph Smith preach to the group. To this request he readily complied, emphasizing in his discourse that baptism for the remission of sins was essential to salvation. "Stop!" interrupted a Methodist minister who was present among the listeners. "What do you say to the case of the penitent thief?"

"What do you mean?" inquired the Prophet.

The minister explained, "You know our Savior said to the thief, 'This day shalt thou be with me in paradise,' which shows he could not have been baptized before his admission."

To this the Prophet quipped, "How do you know he wasn't baptized before he became a thief?" When the spontaneous outburst of mirth that followed had subsided, he continued on a more serious note: "But that is not the true answer. In the original Greek, as this gentleman (turning to Quincy) will inform you, the word that has been translated 'paradise' means simply 'a place of departed spirits.' To that place the penitent thief was conveyed, and there, doubtless, he received (vicariously) the baptism necessary for his admission to the heavenly kingdom."

Andrus, *Joseph Smith, the Man and the Seer*, pp. 27-28.

JOSEPH SMITH

"Did You Say Joe Smith in a Sermon?"

As written by Josiah Quincy.

While the Prophet escorted his visitors about the city, the minister continued the contest on one issue after another. As they stopped in a beautiful grove, Joseph commented, pointing to a platform and a number of seats, "When the weather permits we hold our services in this place, but shall cease to do so when the Temple is finished."

The minister remarked with a note of sarcasm, "I suppose none but Mormon preachers are allowed in Nauvoo."

"On the contrary," replied the Prophet, "I shall be very happy to have you address my people next Sunday, and I will insure you a most attentive congregation."

"What! Do you mean that I may say anything I please and that you will make no reply?" inquired the minister.

To this the Mormon leader replied, "You may certainly say anything you please; but I must reserve the right of adding a word or two, if I judge best. I promise to speak of you in the most respectful manner."

As they rode on the dispute continued. "Come," said the Prophet as he slapped his antagonist on the knee to emphasize his production of a triumphant test, "if you can't argue better than that, you shall say all you want to say to my people and I will promise to hold my tongue. For there's not a Mormon among them who would need any assistance to answer you."

The minister later sought to even things up by referring to some point of doctrine which he considered erroneous. "Why, I told my congregation the other Sunday that they might as well believe Joe Smith as such theology as that," he declared.

"Did you say 'Joe Smith' in a sermon?" inquired the Mormon leader.

"Of course I did. Why not?" rejoined the minister.

The Prophet's reply was given with a quiet superiority that was overwhelming: "Considering only the day and place, it would have been more respectful to have said Lieutenant-general Joseph Smith."

Clearly the worthy minister was no match for the head of the Mormon church.

Andrus, *Joseph Smith, the Man and the Seer,* pp. 28-29.

◄—◄—►

J O S E P H   S M I T H

"Remember, I'm a Prophet"

Josiah Quincy comments on his visit with the Prophet as follows:

I should not say quite all that struck me about Smith if I did not mention that he seemed to have a keen sense of the humorous aspect of his position.

"It seems to me, General," I said, as he was driving us to the river, about sunset, "that you have too much power to be safely trusted to one man."

"In your hands or that of any other person," was the reply, "so much power would, no doubt, be dangerous. I am the only one man in the world whom it would be safe to trust with it. Remember, I'm a prophet!"

The last five words were spoken in a rich, comical aside, as if in hearty recognition of the ridiculous sound they might have in the ears of a Gentile. I asked him to test his powers by naming the successful candidate in the approaching presidential election.

"Well, I will prophesy that John Tyler will not be the next

president, for some things are possible and some things are probable; but Tyler's election is neither the one nor the other!"

Parry, *Stories About Joseph Smith the Prophet*, pp. 119-23.

JOSEPH SMITH

"I Preached a Sermon and Baptized Three"

The year was 1832. Joseph Smith was living in Hiram, Ohio. Although he was a prophet, he was not insulated from nor isolated from hardship, suffering, or sorrow. In the year 1828, Emma Smith had given birth to a child while she and the Prophet were living in Harmony, Pennsylvania. The child, a son, died the same day. In 1831, a year prior to our 1832 setting, Emma had given birth to twins—a boy and a girl. What joy there must have been in the Smith household that day, but how shortlived was that joy. Before the sun had set, both infants were dead. Strangely enough, on that very same day, Sister John Murdock, who lived nearby, also gave birth to twins; and they also were a boy and a girl. The twins lived, but Sister Murdock died. Can you picture in your mind the Prophet—a young man, a large man, a sorrowing man—visiting with John Murdock. They exchange sympathetic expressions. If you have never read the story, you can guess the outcome. When John Murdock's twins were nine days old, they were brought to Emma—a boy and a girl. These babies, adopted by the Prophet and his wife, would in a measure replace those buried. These babies would ease Emma Smith's aching heart.

That same year . . . John Johnson invited the Prophet and his family to come to live with him in his spacious farm house at Hiram. The Prophet gladly accepted the invitation. At the time he was engaged in revising the Bible, and this assistance was most welcome.

The Prophet's children were subject to illness as were other children; and in March, 1832, both of the infants had the measles. This necessitated not just one but both parents' being up with the babies for several nights. Finally, near midnight one night, the Prophet insisted that his wife go into an adjoining room to get some rest. She was reluctant, but he was persistent. He assured her that he would listen for any outcry from their little son, who was the sicker of the two infants. She consented and retired to the next room. Joseph lay down on a small bed next to the crib of the little boy Joseph. He had intended to listen, but soon fatigue overcame him, and he was asleep.

Unknown to him, a mob of some forty men had gathered in the woods a short distance from the house where they waited patiently for the lamps to be extinguished. After the house became dark, they continued to wait until they were certain that all of its occupants were asleep. They approached quietly and opened the door; and the Prophet, sleeping very soundly, was in their grasp and raised from his bed before the screams of his wife, Emma, awoke him. He fought desperately to free himself. He was an athletic man, powerfully built, six feet tall and weighing over 200 pounds. He managed to free one leg and kicked one of the mobsters with tremendous force. The mobster reeled back, landed on the frozen earth, and cried out, in essence, "Don't let loose of him, don't let loose of him. If you let loose of him, he'll run over the lot of us." He then choked the Prophet Joseph. The Prophet was carried several hundred feet from the house. His clothing was torn from him, and the mob tried to force acid into his mouth. He clenched his teeth and resisted. They cursed him and slammed the bottle against his teeth until they chipped one of his front teeth and spilled the acid on the ground. As they called for the bucket of tar, one of the mobsters was so filled with hate that he could not contain himself, and he fell upon the unprotected body of Joseph Smith and said, "G—D—— you, I'll show you how the Holy Ghost falls on a person." He then began to scratch the flesh of the Prophet.

Joseph Smith was covered with the hot tar and left on the ground.

Eventually, he partially recovered his strength and started toward the house. In the meantime Emma had gathered up her sick babies and taken them out into the cold night to hide them, fearing the mob would return and do them harm. She returned to the house before Joseph did and was there to open the door when he called to her. As she looked upon her husband covered with tar and blood, she thought that he was completely covered with blood. The shock was more than she could stand, and she fainted. Joseph called out again, and Brother Johnson appeared with a blanket. Joseph wrapped it around himself and went into the house. The remainder of the night was spent removing the tar. The washing and scraping was done under the direction of Dr. Fredrick G. Williams with others assisting.

Joseph recorded the events of the night in a concise, objective, factual way. Then he said that with the rising of the sun it was the Sabbath day, and records very simply, "I preached a sermon and baptized three."

Hartshorn, *Joseph Smith: Prophet of the Restoration:* pp. 1-3.

JOSEPH SMITH

"Joseph Had to Bear with Us, Like Children"

The Prophet's cousin George A. Smith observed Joseph on the Zion's Camp march and wrote:

The Prophet took a full share of the fatigues of the entire journey. In addition to the care of providing for the Camp and presiding over it, he walked most of the time and had a full proportion of blistered, bloody, and sore feet, which was the natural result of walking from twenty-five to forty miles a day in the hot season of the year.

But during the entire trip he never uttered a murmur, while most of the men in the Camp complained to him of sore toes, blistered feet, long drives, scanty provisions, poor quality of bread, bad corn dodger, frowzy butter, strong honey, maggoty bacon and cheese, etc. Even a dog could not bark at some men without their murmuring at Joseph. If they had to camp with bad water, it nearly caused a rebellion. Yet we were the Camp of Zion, and many of us were prayerless, thoughtless, careless, heedless, foolish, or devilish, and we did not know it. Joseph had to bear with us and tutor us like children. There were many, however, in the Camp who never murmured and who were always ready and willing to do as our leaders desired.

John Henry Evans, *Joseph Smith, An American Prophet* (New York: McMillan, 1946), pp. 117-18.

JOSEPH SMITH

"It Is Cold-blooded Murder"

. . . **D**estruction came at Far West, and the Prophet was betrayed into the hands of his enemies by Colonel George Hinkle, a trusted associate. Joseph was one of the several Church leaders to be so betrayed. Parley Pratt wrote of that first abusive night when he, Joseph Smith, and others were prisoners:

We were placed under a strong guard, and were without shelter during the night, lying on the ground in the open air, in the midst of a great rain. The guards during the whole night kept up a constant tirade of mockery, and the most obscene blackguardism and abuse. They blasphemed God;

mocked Jesus Christ; swore the most dreadful oaths; taunted Brother Joseph and others; demanded miracles; wanted signs, such as "Come Mr. Smith, show us an angel." "Give us one of your revelations." "Show us a miracle." "Come, there is one of your brethren here in camp whom we took prisoner yesterday in his own house, and knocked his brains out with his own rifle, which we found over his fireplace; he lays speechless and dying; speak the word and heal him, and then we will all believe." "Or, if you are Apostles or men of God, deliver yourselves, and then we will be Mormons." Next would be a volley of oaths and blasphemies; then a tumultuous tirade of lewd boastings of having defiled virgins and wives by force, etc., much of which I dare not write; and, indeed, language would fail me to attempt more than a faint description. Thus passed this dreadful night, and before morning several other captives were added to our number. . . .

The Prophet's life was spared only by the courageous act of Alexander Doniphan. Brigadier General Doniphan received an illegal order from his commanding officer Major General Samuel D. Lucas to take Joseph Smith and the other prisoners into the public square at 9:00 the next morning and shoot them. General Doniphan wasted no time in sending the following bold reply to his superior officer:

It is cold-blooded murder. I will not obey your order. My brigade shall march for Liberty tomorrow morning at 8:00; and if you execute these men, I will hold you responsible before an earthly tribunal, so help me God. (HC 3:190-191)

Hartshorn, *Joseph Smith: Prophet of the Restoration*, p. 24.

◄——►

JOSEPH SMITH

"Majesty Have I Seen But Once"

In one of those tedious nights we had lain as if in sleep till the hour of midnight had passed, and our ears and hearts had been pained, while we had listened for hours to the obscene jests, the horrid oaths, the dreadful blasphemies and filthy language of our guards, Colonel Price at their head, as they recounted to each other their deeds of rapine, murder, robbery, etc., which they had committed among the *"Mormons"* while at Far West and vicinity. They even boasted of defiling by force wives, daughters, and virgins, and of shooting or dashing out the brains of men, women, and children.

I had listened till I became so disgusted, shocked, horrified, and so filled with the spirit of indignant justice that I could scarcely refrain from rising upon my feet and rebuking the guards; but had said nothing to Joseph, or anyone else, although I lay next to him and knew he was awake. On a sudden he arose to his feet, and spoke in a voice of thunder, or as the roaring lion, uttering, as nearly as I can recollect, the following words:

"Silence, ye fiends of the infernal pit! In the name of Jesus Christ I rebuke you, and command you to be still; I will not live another minute and hear such language. Cease such talk, or you or I die this instant!"

He ceased to speak. He stood erect in terrible majesty. Chained, and without a weapon; calm, unruffled and dignified as an angel, he looked upon the quailing guards, whose weapons were lowered or dropped to the ground, whose knees smote together, and who, slinking into a corner, or crouching at his feet, begged his pardon and remained quiet till a change of guards.

I have seen the ministers of justice, clothed in magisterial robes, and criminals arraigned before them, while life was suspended on a breath, in the courts of England; I have witnessed a Congress in solemn session to give laws to nations; I have tried to conceive of kings, of royal courts, of thrones and crowns, and of emperors assembled to decide the fate of kingdoms; but dignity and majesty have I seen but once, as it stood in chains, at midnight, in a dungeon, in an obscure village of Missouri.

Parley P. Pratt, *Autobiography of Parley P. Pratt* (Salt Lake City: Deseret Book Co., 1966), pp. 228-30.

JOSEPH SMITH

"Judge, You Will Aspire to the Presidency of the United States"

Joseph Smith was dining at Carthage, Illinois, with Judge Stephen A. Douglas and others. After dinner, Judge Douglas asked the Prophet to give him an account of the persecutions of the Saints in Missouri. Joseph did so, talking for almost three hours.

At that time the judge seemed to be very friendly towards the Prophet. When Joseph had told him all that the Saints had passed through, he looked straight into Mr. Douglas' face and said: "Judge, you will aspire to the presidency of the United States; and if you ever turn your hand against me or the Latter-day Saints, you will feel the weight of the hand of the Almighty upon you; and you will live to see and know that I have testified the truth to you; for the conversation of this day will stick to you through life."

Seventeen years afterwards Mr. Douglas was named for president of the United States. It was firmly believed that he would be elected, for he was looked upon as a great man. But, in order to make friends of those who were opposed to the Saints, he turned against the Latter-day Saints, and said many things about them which were false and wicked.

Well, the day of the election came, and Judge Douglas was defeated; he was voted down in every State in the Union except one. It was at that time that Abraham Lincoln was made president.

In less than a year Judge Douglas died at his home in Chicago, a disappointed and almost broken-hearted man.

William A. Morton, *From Plowboy to Prophet* (Salt Lake City: Deseret Book, 1938), pp. 122-23.

———◆———

JOSEPH SMITH

"Brother Fordham Arose from His Bed"

As told by Wilford Woodruff.

Before starting on our missions to England, we were under the necessity of settling our families. A place called Commerce, afterwards named Nauvoo, was selected as the place at which our people should settle.

I left Quincy in company with Brother Brigham Young and our families, on the fifteenth of May, and arrived in Commerce on the eighteenth. After an interview with Joseph we crossed the river at Montrose, Iowa. President Brigham Young and myself, with our families, occupied one room about fourteen feet square. Finally Brother Young obtained another room and moved his family into it. Then Brother Orson Pratt and family moved into the same room with myself and family.

While I was living in this cabin in the old barracks, we experienced a day of God's power with the Prophet Joseph. It was a very sickly time, and Joseph had given up his home in Commerce to the sick, and had a tent pitched in his door-yard and was living in that himself. The large number of Saints who had been driven out of Missouri were flocking into Commerce, but had no homes to go into, and were living in wagons, in tents, and on the ground. Many, therefore, were sick through the exposure they were subjected to. Brother Joseph had waited on the sick until he was worn out and nearly sick himself.

On the morning of the twenty-second of July, 1839, he arose, reflecting upon the situation of the Saints of God in their persecutions and afflictions. And he called upon the Lord in prayer, and the power of God rested upon him mightily. And as Jesus healed all the sick around him in his day, so Joseph, the prophet of God, healed all around on this occasion. He healed all in his house and door-yard, then, in company with

Sidney Rigdon and several of the twelve, he went among the sick lying on the bank of the river and he commanded them in a loud voice, in the name of Jesus Christ, to come up and be made whole, and they were all healed. When he healed all that were sick on the east side of the river, they crossed the Mississippi river in a ferry-boat to the west side, to Montrose, where we were. The first house they went into was President Brigham Young's. He was sick on his bed at the time. The Prophet went into his house and healed him, and they all came out together. As they were passing by my door, Brother Joseph said: "Brother Woodruff, follow me." These were the only words spoken by any of the company from the time they left Brother Brigham's house till we crossed the public square, and entered Brother Fordham's house. Brother Fordham had been dying for an hour, and we expected each minute would be his last.

I felt the power of God that was overwhelming his prophet.

When we entered the house, Brother Joseph walked up to Brother Fordham, and took him by the right hand; in his left hand he held his hat.

He saw that Brother Fordham's eyes were glazed, and that he was speechless and unconscious.

After taking hold of his hand, he looked down into the dying man's face and said: "Brother Fordham, do you not know me?" At first he made no reply; but we could all see the effect of the Spirit of God resting upon him.

He again said: "Elijah, do you not know me?"

With a low whisper, Brother Fordham answered, "Yes!"

The Prophet then said, "Have you not faith to be healed?"

The answer, which was a little plainer than before, was: "I am afraid it is too late. If you had come sooner, I think I might have been."

He had the appearance of a man waking from sleep. It was the sleep of death.

Joseph then said: "Do you believe that Jesus is the Christ?"

"I do, Brother Joseph," was the response.

Then the Prophet of God spoke with a loud voice, as in the majesty of the Godhead: "Elijah, I command you, in the name of the Jesus of Nazareth, to arise and be made whole!"

The words of the Prophet were not like the words of man, but like the voice of God. It seemed to me that the house shook from its foundation.

Elijah Fordham leaped from his bed like a man raised from the dead. A healthy color came to his face, and life was manifested in every act. . . .

He then called for his clothes and put them on. He asked for a bowl of bread and milk, and ate it, then put on his hat and followed us into the street to visit others who were sick.

As soon as we left Brother Fordham's house, we went into the house of Joseph B. Noble, who was very low and dangerously sick.

When we entered the house, Brother Joseph took him by the hand, and commanded him, in the name of Jesus Christ, to arise and be made whole. He did arise and was immediately healed.

This case of Brother Noble's was the last one of healing upon that day. It was the greatest day for the manifestation of the power of God through the gift of healing since the organization of the Church.

When we left Brother Noble, the Prophet Joseph went with those who accompanied him from the other side to the banks of the river, to return home.

While waiting for the ferry-boat, a man of the world, knowing of the miracles which had been performed, came to him and asked him if he would not go and heal two twin children of his, about five months old, who were both lying sick nigh unto death.

They were some two miles from Montrose.

The Prophet said he could not go; but, after pausing some time, he said he would send one to heal them; and he turned to me and said: "You go with the man and heal his children."

I went with the man, and did as the Prophet commanded me, and the children were healed.

Wilford Woodruff, *Leaves from My Journal* (Salt Lake City: The Deseret News, 1909), pp. 67-71.

"I Am Gazing upon the Valleys of Those mountains"

. . . I had a conversation with a number of brethren in the shade of the building on the subject of our persecutions in Missouri and the constant annoyance which has followed us since we were driven from that state. I prophesied that the Saints would continue to suffer much affliction and would be driven to the Rocky Mountains; many would apostatize, others would be put to death by our persecutors or lose their lives in consequence of exposure or disease, and some of you will live to go and assist in making settlements and build cities and see the Saints become a mighty people in the heart of the Rocky Mountains.

[Among those present when this prediction was uttered was Elder Anson Call, who has left on record additional details respecting this remarkable prediction. He says that in the shade of the building mentioned was a barrel of ice water, and the men were drinking it to quench their thirst on the hot August day. Following is Anson's account:]

"With the tumbler still in his hand he prophesied that the Saints would go to the Rocky Mountains: and, said he, 'this water tastes much like that of the crystal streams that are running from the snowcapped mountains. . . .' I had before seen him in a vision and now saw while he was talking his countenance changed to white, not the deadly white of a bloodless face, but a living brilliant white. He seemed absorbed in gazing at something at a great distance and said: 'I am gazing upon the valleys of those mountains.' This was followed by a vivid description of the scenery of these mountains as I have since become acquainted with it.

"Pointing to Shadrach Roundy and others he said: 'There are some men here who shall do a great work in that land.'

Pointing to me, he said: 'There is Anson, he shall go and shall assist in building up cities from one end of the country to the other and you,' rather extending the idea to all those he had spoken of, 'shall perform as great a work as has been done by man; so that the nations of the earth shall be astonished; and many of them will be gathered in that land and assist in building cities and temples and Israel shall be made to rejoice.'

"It was impossible to represent in words this scene, which is still vivid in my mind, of the grandeur of Joseph's appearance, his beautiful descriptions of this land and his wonderful prophetic utterances as they emanated from the glorious inspiration that overshadowed him.

Joseph Smith, *History of the Church,* 5:85-86.

━━◆━━◆━━◆━━

JOSEPH SMITH

"I Have Taken Them to Myself"

The following was told by the Prophet's mother, Lucy Mack Smith:

He [Samuel Smith] succeeded the next day in getting to Nauvoo in season to go out and meet the procession with the bodies of Hyrum and Joseph, as the mob had the kindness to allow us the privilege of bringing them home and burying them in Nauvoo, notwithstanding the immense reward which was offered by the Missourians for Joseph's head.

Their bodies were attended home by only two persons, save those that went from this place. These were Brother Willard Richards and a Mr. Hamilton, Brother John Taylor having been shot in prison, and nearly killed. . . .

After the corpses were washed and dressed in their burial clothes, we were allowed to see them. I had for a long time braced every nerve, roused every energy of my soul, and called upon God to strengthen me, but when I entered and saw my murdered sons extended both at once before my eyes and heard the sobs and groans of my family and cries of "Father! Husband! Brothers!" from the lips of their wives, children, brothers, and sisters, it was too much; I sank back, crying to the Lord in agony of my soul, "My God, my God, why hast thou forsaken this family!" A voice replied, "I have taken them to myself, that they might have rest."

Lucy Mack Smith, *History of Joseph Smith,* p. 324.

Biographical Sketch

After the Prophet's death, Sidney Rigdon, Joseph Smith's wavering former counselor, had returned from Pittsburg to plead with the people to make him the guardian of the Church. He called a meeting of the Saints and addressed them. When he concluded, Brigham Young, President of the Council of the Twelve, stood and said, "Here is Brigham. Have his knees ever faltered?" Every honest person in that congregation was compelled in his heart to reply, "No, Brother Brigham. You have never faltered. From the moment you first heard the gospel fourteen years ago, your course has been an undeviating course of righteousness and truth, and you have pursued it with astonishing zeal."

As the people watched and listened to Brigham Young, the mantel of Joseph fell upon him and he looked and sounded like the martyred prophet. Brigham Young asked all those who wanted Sidney Rigdon to lead them to manifest it. No one raised his hand. He then asked for a show of hands of those who would sustain the Twelve, with Brigham Young as the president of the Quorum, the presiding body in the Church. The voting was unanimous.

Brigham Young had been sustained as an original member of the Quorum of the Twelve in this dispensation in 1835. The death of David W. Patton and the apostasy of Thomas B. Marsh brought Brigham Young to the presidency of that quorum. He was a tireless worker in the cause of truth. Under his leadership the temple at Nauvoo was completed as a monument to the Lord Jesus Christ and the beloved Prophet, Joseph Smith. Brigham Young was the leader of the mass exodus to the West and looked over Salt Lake Valley and declared, "This is the right place." He was loved of his people. He was a man of faith and a man of vision. Under his inspired leadership, more than three hundred communities were colonized. The missionary efforts of the Church became world-wide and tens of thousands of converts came to Zion. He was universally loved and respected by his people, and when he came to a community, it was a great occasion. No one had to encourage the Saints to provide a warm welcome for their Prophet. The greeting was spontaneous and joyous. The bands played, banners waved, people cheered, and little girls dressed in starched dresses threw flowers in the roadway before the Prophet's carriage. Brigham Young led his people for more than thirty years, and under his inspired leadership, the forbidding wilderness literally blossomed as a rose.

Brigham Young was born on June 1, 1801, in Whittingham, Vermont. In 1829 he moved to Mendon, New York, just fifteen miles from Palmyra. In 1830 a missionary of the Restored Church came to Mendon. He approached the home of a family named Tomlinson. Phinehas Young, a brother of Brigham Young, was having lunch with the Tomlinsons. The missionary said:

" 'There is a book, sir, I wish you to read.' The thing appeared so novel to me, [said Phinehas] that for a moment I hesitated, saying—'Pray, sir, what book have you?' 'The Book of Mormon, or, as it is called by some, the Golden Bible.' 'Ah, sir, then it purports to be a revelation?' 'Yes,' said he, 'it is a revelation from God.' I took the book, and by his request looked at the testimony of the witnesses [which in that day, in the first editions, was in the back of the book] . . . Said he—'If you will read this book with a prayerful heart and ask God to give you a witness you will know of the truth of this work.' I told him I would do so, and then asked him his name. He said his name was Samuel H. Smith. 'Ah,' said I, 'you are one of the witnesses.' 'Yes,' said he, 'I know the book to be a revelation from God, translated by the gift and power of the Holy Ghost, and that my brother, Joseph Smith, Jun., is a Prophet, Seer and Revelator.' "[1]

The book was read by Phinehas, his father, John Young, and by Brigham Young. Brigham Young had little opportunity to meet Mormon missionaries, and it wasn't until April 14, 1832, that he was baptized. He was ordained an elder the same day and his soul was filled with the "fire" of the gospel. He yearned to meet the Prophet Joseph, and in company with his brother, Joseph Young, and his close friend, Heber C. Kimball, he traveled to Kirtland, Ohio, to meet Joseph Smith. He dedicated himself to the Prophet, moved to Kirtland to be near him and to follow his example and direction.

From the time Brigham Young heard the gospel in 1830 until 1837, he traveled thousands of miles—mostly on foot—for the sake of the gospel. His loyalty and zeal from his introduction to the gospel to the time of his death is legend.

Four years before the end of his life, President Young wrote the following to the editor of the *New York Herald:*

My whole life is devoted to the Almighty's service, and while I regret that my mission is not better understood by the world, the time will come when I will be understood, and I leave to futurity the judgment of my labors and their result as they shall become manifest.[2]

At the age of seventy-six, Brigham Young lay near death. He had lived a full, exemplary life. His eyelids were shut; he appeared to be unconscious. Suddenly his eyes opened, and in a strong voice he uttered one word three times: "Joseph. Joseph. Joseph." He closed his eyes, and the great prophet Brigham Young was dead. The date—August 29, 1877.

Preston Nibley, who wrote extensively of Brigham Young, said:

If I were to point out the principle thing, which, more than all others, made President Young the great man he was, I think I should reply, without

---

[1]S. Dilworth Young, *Brigham Young—His Life* (First Half), Brigham Young University, Speeches of the Year (Provo, 1964), p. 3.

[2]Preston Nibley, *The Presidents of the Church* (Salt Lake City: Deseret Book Co., 1941), pp. 82-83.

hesitation, that it was his ability to believe—his great faith. First, faith in a living God, to whom he felt personally responsible and to whom he felt obligated to render up an accounting for all the deeds done in the flesh. Second, faith in every principle and doctrine revealed and taught by the Prophet Joseph Smith, and a firm and unyielding determination to shape his life according to those principles. Third, faith in himself, and in his ability to carry on the great work of establishing the Kingdom of God, the leadership of which had come to him after the death of the Prophet. Time and time again, in this history, I have been astounded by the strength of this man's faith; such faith I never encountered in any other person. On his tombstone one might well have written, HE BELIEVED. Yes, he believed his religion, this great man, and he shaped his life to its principles, to his dying day.

Brigham Young carried on the work commenced by Joseph Smith in a remarkable manner. Those who were concerned about the future of the Church at Joseph's death, those who thought it was Joseph Smith's church, quickly learned that the leader of the Church was the Lord Jesus Christ, and that Brigham Young had been prepared to assume leadership of the Church under the direction of the head of the Church. What a great leader the second prophet of the dispensation of the fulness of times was!

BRIGHAM YOUNG

"He Talked to the Lord"

Heber J. Grant seems to have gained inspiration and encouragement from President Brigham Young whom he met in a rather unusual way:

Fifty-four years ago [1863], as a little child, I took a sleigh ride with President Brigham Young, that is, I ran out and took hold of the back of the sleigh, intending to ride a block and then drop off and walk home; but President Young was driving such a fine team, or at least his driver was, that I dared not let go, hence rode on till we reached the Cottonwood, and then when the sleigh slowed up, to pass through the stream, I jumped off, and the president saw me. He said, "Stop, Brother Isaac, stop. The little boy is nearly frozen. Put him under the buffalo robe and get him warm." Isaac Wilson was his driver. After I got warm he inquired my name, and told me about my father, and his love for him. He told me to tell my mother that he wanted her to send me up to his office in six months to have a visit with him; and in six months I went for the visit. From that time, fifty-four years ago, until the day of his death, I was intimately acquainted with President Young. . . .

I was almost as familiar in the homes of President Brigham Young as I was in the home of my own mother. . . . I have spent hours and hours, as a child, in the rooms of Eliza R. Snow, listening to her counsel and advice, and hearing her relate incidents in the life of Joseph Smith the Prophet, and bearing witness of the wonderful blessings of God to Brigham Young. As I say, I was familiar with the Prophet Brigham Young. I knelt down time and time again in his home in the Lion House at family prayers, as a child and as a young man; and I bear witness that as a little child, upon more than one occasion, because of the inspiration of the Lord to Brigham Young while he was supplicating God for guidance, I have lifted my head, turned and looked at the place where Brigham Young was praying, to see if the Lord was not there. It seemed to me that he talked to the Lord as one man would talk to another.

Church History, Student Supplement (Provo: Seminaries and Institutes of Religion, 1969), pp. 61-62.

BRIGHAM YOUNG

"Brother Brigham Will Preside over the Church"

No mortal man affected the life of Brigham Young as deeply as did the Prophet Joseph Smith. The meeting of these two famous men occurred in September of 1832, just five months after Brigham's baptism. Just weeks before, Elder Young had experienced the deep sorrow which accompanies the loss of a loved one—his wife died, leaving him the father of two little girls. Shortly after the burial of his wife, Brigham Young— with this tragedy fresh in his mind—found a home for his daughters in the home of his friend, Heber C. Kimball, and journeyed to Kirtland, Ohio, to meet the Prophet. Brigham Young recorded his thoughts concerning this initial meeting thusly:

. . . **W**e found the Prophet, and two or three of his brothers, chopping and hauling wood. Here my joy was full at the privilege of shaking the hand of the prophet of God, and receiving the sure testimony, by the spirit of prophecy, that he was all that any man could believe him to be, as a true Prophet.

In the evening a few of the brethren came in, and we conversed together upon the things of the kingdom. He called upon me to pray; in my prayer I spoke in tongues. As soon as we arose from our knees the brethren flocked around him, and asked his opinion concerning the gift of tongues that was upon me. He told them it was the pure Adamic language. Some said to him they expected he would condemn the gift brother Brigham had, but he said, "No, it is of God, and the time will come when brother Brigham Young will preside over this Church." The latter part of this conversation was in my absence.

[As far as is known this was the first time the Prophet Joseph had heard the gift of tongues.]

Church History, Student Supplement, pp. 7-8.

━━━◄━►━━━

BRIGHAM YOUNG

"Hurrah, Hurrah for Israel"

As told by Heber C. Kimball.

September 14, President Brigham Young left his home at Montrose to start on the mission to England. He was so sick that he was unable to go to the Mississippi, a distance of thirty rods, without assistance. After he had crossed the river he rode behind Israel Barlow on his horse to my house, where he continued sick until the eighteenth. He left his wife sick with a babe only three weeks old, and all his other children were sick and unable to wait upon each other. Not one soul of

45

them was able to go to the well for a pail of water, and they were without a second suit on their backs, for the mob in Missouri had taken nearly all he had. On the seventeenth Sister Mary Ann Young got a boy to carry her up in his wagon to my house, that she might nurse and comfort Brother Brigham to the hour of starting.

September 18, Charles Hubbard sent his boy with a wagon and span of horses to my house; our trunks were put into the wagon by some brethren; I went to my . . . wife who was then shaking with a chill, having two children lying sick by her side; I embraced her and my children, and bade them farewell. My only well child was little Heber P., and it was with difficulty he could carry a couple of quarts of water at a time, to assist in quenching their thirst.

It was with difficulty we got into the wagon, and started down the hill about ten rods; it appeared to me as though my very inmost parts would melt within me at leaving my family in such a condition, as it were almost in the arms of death. I felt as though I could not endure it. I asked the teamster to stop, and said to Brother Brigham, "This is pretty tough, isn't it; let's rise up and give them a cheer." We arose, and swinging our hats three times over our heads, shouted: "Hurrah, hurrah for Israel." Vilate, hearing the noise, arose from her bed and came to the door. She had a smile on her face. Vilate and Mary Ann Young cried out to us: "Good-bye, God bless you." We returned the compliment, and then told the good driver to go ahead. After this I felt a spirit of joy and gratitude, having had the satisfaction of seeing my wife standing upon her feet, instead of leaving her in bed, knowing well that I should not see them again for two or three years.

Orson F. Whitney, *The Life of Heber C. Kimball* (Salt Lake City: Bookcraft, 1945), pp. 265-66.

BRIGHAM YOUNG

"One York Shilling"

As Brigham Young and Heber C. Kimball arrived in Kirtland, Ohio on their way to England, Elder Kimball recorded the following.

Brother Brigham had one York shilling left, and on looking over our expenses we found we had paid out over $87.00 out of the $13.50 we had at Pleasant Garden, which is all the money we had to pay our passages with. We had traveled over four hundred miles by stage, for which we paid from eight to ten cents a mile, and had eaten three meals a day, for each of which we were charged fifty cents, also fifty cents for our lodgings. Brother Brigham often suspected that I put money in his trunk, or clothes, thinking that I had a purse of money which I had not acquainted him with; but this was not so. The money could only have been put in his trunk by some heavenly messenger, who thus administered to our necessities daily as he knew we needed.

Whitney, *Life of Heber C. Kimball,* p. 273.

BRIGHAM YOUNG

"Bogus Brigham"

As told by Brigham Young.

While brother George A. Smith was referring to the circumstance of William Miller going to Carthage, it brought to my mind reflections of the past. Perhaps to relate the circumstances as it occurred would be interesting.

I do not profess to be much of a joker, but I do think this to be one of the best jokes ever perpetrated. By the time we were at work in the Nauvoo Temple, officiating in the ordinances, the mob had learned that Mormonism was not dead, as they had supposed. We had completed the walls of the temple, and the attic story from about half-way up of the first windows, in about fifteen months. It went up like magic, and we commenced officiating in the ordinances. Then the mob commenced to hunt for other victims; they had already killed the Prophets Joseph and Hyrum in Carthage jail, while under the pledge of the State for their safety, and now they wanted Brigham, the president of the Twelve Apostles who were then acting as the presidency of the Church.

I was in my room in the temple; it was in the southeast corner of the upper story. I learned that a posse was lurking around the temple, and that the United States Marshal was waiting for me to come down, whereupon I knelt down and asked my Father in heaven, in the name of Jesus, to guide and protect me that I might live to prove advantageous to the Saints. Just as I arose from my knees and sat down in my chair, there came a rap at my door. I said, "Come in," and brother George D. Grant, who was then engaged driving my carriage and doing chores for me, entered the room. Said he, "Brother Young, do you know that a posse and the United States Marshal are here?" I told him I had heard so. On entering the room brother Grant left the door open. Nothing came into my mind what to do, until looking directly across the hall I saw brother William Miller leaning against the wall. As I stepped towards the door I beckoned to him; he came. Said I to him, "Brother William, the marshal is here for me; will you go and do just as I tell you? If you will, I will serve them a trick." I knew that brother Miller was an excellent man, perfectly reliable and capable of carrying out my project. Said I, "Here, take my cloak," but it happened to be brother Heber C. Kimball's; our cloaks were alike in color, fashion and size. I threw it around his shoulders and told him to wear my hat and accompany brother George D. Grant. He did so. I said to brother Grant, "George, you step into the carriage and look towards brother Miller, and say to him, as though you were addressing me, 'Are you ready to ride?' You can do this, and they will suppose brother Miller to be me, and proceed accordingly," which they did.

Just as brother Miller was entering the carriage, the marshal stepped up to him, and, placing his hand upon his shoulder, said, "You are my prisoner." Brother William entered the carriage and said to the marshal, "I am going to the Mansion House, won't you ride with me?" They both went to the Mansion House. There were my sons Joseph A., Brigham, jun., and brother Heber C. Kimball's boys, and others who were looking on, and all seemed at once to understand and partake of the joke. They followed the carriage to the Mansion House and gathered around brother Miller, with tears in their eyes, saying, "Father (or President Young) where are you going?" Brother Miller looked at them kindly, but made no reply; and the marshal really thought he had got "Brother Brigham."

Lawyer Edmonds, who was then staying at the Mansion House, appreciating the joke, volunteered to brother Miller to go to Carthage with him. . . . When they arrived within two or three miles of Carthage, the marshal with his posse stopped. They arose in their carriages, buggies, and wagons, and, like a tribe of Indians going into battle, or as if they were a pack of demons, yelling and shouting, they exclaimed, "We've got him! We've got him! We've got him!" When they reached Carthage the marshal took the supposed Brigham into an upper room of the hotel and placed a guard over him, at the same time telling those around that he had got him. Brother Miller remained in the room until they bid him come to supper. While there, parties came in, one after the other, and asked for Brigham. Brother Miller was pointed out to them. So it continued, until an apostate Mormon, by the name of Thatcher, who had lived in Nauvoo, came in, sat down and asked the landlord where Brigham Young was. The landlord, pointing across the table to brother Miller, said, "That is Mr. Young." Thatcher replied, "Where? I can't see any one that looks like Brigham." The landlord told him it was that fat, fleshy man eating. "Oh, h—!" exclaimed Thatcher, "that's not Brigham; that is William Miller, one of my old neighbors." Upon hearing this the landlord went, and, tapping the sheriff on the shoulder, took him a few steps to one side, and said, "You have made a mistake, that is not Brigham Young; it is William Miller, of Nauvoo." The marshal, very much astonished, exclaimed, "Good heavens! and *he* passed for Brigham." He then took brother Miller into a room, and, turning to him, said, "What in h— is the reason you did not tell me your name?" Brother Miller replied, "You have not asked me my name." "Well," said the sheriff, with another oath, "What is your name?" "My name," he replied, "is William Miller." Said the marshal, "I thought your name was Brigham Young. Do you say this for a fact?" "Certainly I do," said brother Miller. "Then," said the marshal, "why did you not tell me this before?" "I was under no obligations to tell you," replied brother Miller, "as you did not ask me." Then the marshal, in a rage, walked out of the room, followed by brother Miller, who walked off in company with Lawyer Edmonds, Sheriff Backenstos, and others, who took him . . . to a place of safety; and this is the real . . . story of "Bogus" Brigham, as far as I can recollect.

Brigham Young in *Journal of Discourses,* 14:218-19.

◆━━◆━━◆

BRIGHAM YOUNG

"The Fever Left Me on the Eighteenth Day"

I was suddenly . . . attacked with the most violent fever I ever experienced. The Prophet Joseph and Elder Willard Richards visited and administered unto me; the Prophet prophesied that I should live and recover from my sickness. He sat by me for six hours, and directed my attendants what to do for me. In about thirty hours from the time of my being attacked by the fever, the skin began to peel from my body, and I was skinned all over. I desired to be baptized in the river, but it was not until the fourteenth day that Brother Joseph would give his consent for me to be showered with cold water, when my fever began to break, and it left me on the 18th day. I laid upon my back, and was not turned upon my side for eighteen days.

I laid in a log house, which was rather open; it was so very cold during my sickness, that Brother Isaac Decker, my attendant, froze his fingers and toes while fanning me, with boots, great coat and mittens on, and with a fire in the house, from which I was shielded by a blanket.

When the fever left me on the 18th day, I was bolstered up in my chair, but was so near gone that I could not close my eyes, which were set in my head—my chin dropped down and my breath stopped. My wife, seeing my situation, threw some cold water in my face; that having no effect, she dashed a handful of strong camphor into my face and eyes, which I did not feel in the least, neither did I move a muscle. She then held my nostrils between her thumb and finger, placing her mouth directly over mine, blew into my lungs until she filled them with air. This set my lungs in motion, and I again began to breathe. While this was going on I was perfectly conscious of all that was passing around me; my spirit was as vivid as it ever was in my life, but I had no feeling in my body.

Preston Nibley, *Brigham Young—The Man and His Work* (Salt Lake City: Deseret News Press, 1936), pp. 44-45.

BRIGHAM YOUNG

"You Shall Have Money in Plenty to Pursue Your Journey"

At Dublin, Indiana, the Church leaders and their families remained nine days. The Prophet was destitute of money to pursue his journey and sought employment chopping wood or splitting rails. Being unsuccessful in his search for work, he went to Brigham Young, who had been in Dublin for three weeks. "Brother Young," he said, "You are one of the twelve who have charge of the kingdom in all the world; I believe I shall throw myself upon you and look to you for counsel in this case." His devoted disciple replied, "If you will take my counsel it will be that you rest yourself, and be assured you shall have money in plenty to pursue your journey."

A Brother Tomlinson living in Dublin had tried to sell his farm so that he could move with the Saints to Missouri. He had asked Brigham Young's counsel on the matter and was told by Elder Young that the Lord had manifested to him that he should sell his farm and assist the Prophet on his way to Missouri. He immediately complied with this advice and gave Joseph four hundred dollars, which made possible the continuance of the Prophet's journey.

When the Prophet and his company were within one hundred and twenty miles of Far West, they were met by some of their Missouri brethren who brought teams, supplies, and money to help the Prophet to further his journey to the newly-formed city of the Saints. Eight miles east of Far West, Thomas B. Marsh, John Corrill, Elias Higbee and others welcomed their Prophet and his associates. After driving into Far West, Joseph and his family were kindly received by George W. Harris, where they were refreshed after their long and tedious travels.

Brigham Young in *Journal of Discourses,* 18:252.

BRIGHAM YOUNG

"I Saw a Tear Rolling down His Cheek"

The following story was related by B. F. Grant, son of Jedediah M. Grant.

My father died when I was only a few weeks old. Mother made moccasins out of deer skins, and sold them to stores at a very 'small margin of revenue to her. She did housework for different families when it was obtainable. When I was two years old, mother married outside the Mormon Church. As she was going to Denver, Colorado, to live, grandmother persuaded her to leave me in her care. Grandmother was a cripple. It was difficult for her to care for a little boy, and so after a time, she gave me to Beason Lewis, who lived in Richmond, Cache Valley. I remained with this family until I was between eleven and twelve years old. About this time mines were discovered in Montana, and trains passed through Utah buying flour, butter eggs, etc., to be carried to the Montana mines. One of these trains stopped at the Lewis place to make repairs to their wagons. I made arrangements to run away from home and go with this train to Montana. I remained there until I was fourteen. The terminus of the Union Pacific was located at Corinne, where the freight from Montana was delivered. I met one of the freighters, who, learning that I was a son of Jedediah M. Grant, invited me to go back to Utah with him. I returned to Salt Lake City when I was between fourteen and fifteen years of age. I went to work in a coal and wood yard.

I had been in Salt Lake City only a short time when in some way President Young learned where I was and what I was doing. President Young's son Feramorz and my brother, Heber, at the request of President Young, searched me out and informed me that President Young wanted to see me.

The next day I called on him at his office, and he happened

to be alone. I told him who I was, and he did not merely reach out his hand to shake mine, but he arose from his chair and gave me a father's handshake. In so doing he discovered that the callouses on my hands were hard and thick, and he remarked, "My boy, what kind of work are you doing?" I replied, "I am unloading coal and chopping wood."

He then resumed his seat and continued his inquiry regarding my past life and what I had been doing. He remarked, "Isn't it pretty heavy work, shoveling coal and chopping wood, for a boy of your age?"

I replied, "No, sir, I have been used to hard work all my life."

He answered, "Wouldn't you like to have something easier than your present work, for instance, a position in a store?"

I replied, "I haven't got sense enough to work in a store."

He said, "What do you mean by that?"

I replied, "I can neither read, nor write."

I discovered this good and great man's heart was touched by this remark. I saw a tear rolling down his cheek, and he took his handkerchief and wiped them off and said, "My boy, come and live with me; I will give you a home; I will clothe you; I will send you to school; and you can work during the vacation for me."

I accepted his kind offer. He became a father to me. He furnished a home; he clothed me and provided an opportunity for me to attend school; and he gave me five dollars a week for spending money, which was a very princely allowance in those days of hardship and trial. His own sons would laughingly tell me they thought I was their father's pet.

Soon after I went to live with President Young, I was given a team and was doing general work on his farm and performing other duties incident to pioneer life. Many a time I have passed him on the road with a load of gravel, sand or other materials, and I don't remember an instance in my life that this great man, if he saw me, ever failed to recognize me by waving his hand. I cannot help but think, where in the world could you find another man of his importance and busy life who would condescend to recognize or speak of a boy such as I?

During the vacation when I was driving a team, at times breakfast would be served a little late. There was a certain time when every team was supposed to be hooked up and going to its work. When breakfast was late I would not always be on time with my team. The foreman complained to me about this and I told him that I milked the cows and fed the pigs and did the chores, but could not go to work without breakfast. One morning he became angry and told me if I couldn't get out on time to quit. I, boy-like, took his advice without calling on President Young, left, and went to work in the coal yard again.

President Young was soon informed of this and sent for me. When I went into his office he shook hands and wanted to know why I left home. I told him the boss had discharged me.

"Oh," he said, "the boss? Who is he?" I gave the foreman's name.

He laughed and said, "No, my boy, I am the boss. Didn't I make arrangements for you to come and live with me?"

I replied, "Yes, sir."

He then said, "Remember, when you are discharged I will attend to it myself; now go back, get your team and go to work."

"I don't know whether ——— will allow me to go to work now."

"Never mind, my boy," he assured me, "I'll attend to it myself."

B. F. Grant, "Church Section," Salt Lake *Deseret News*, May 30, 1942, p. 4.

BRIGHAM YOUNG

"It Appeared to Be Joseph Smith"

As told by John Taylor.

After the martyrdom of the Prophet, the Twelve soon returned to Nauvoo and learned of the aspirations of Sidney Rigdon. He had claimed that the Church needed a guardian, and that he was that guardian. He had appointed the day for the guardian to be selected, and of course was present at the meeting, which was held in the open air. The wind was blowing toward the stand so strongly at the time that an improvised stand was made out of a wagon, which was drawn up at the back part of the congregation, and which he, William Marks, and some others occupied. He attempted to speak, but was much embarrassed. He had been the orator of the Church; but, on this occasion his oratory failed him, and his talk fell very flat. In the meantime President Young and some of his brethren came and entered the stand. The wind by this time had ceased to blow. After Sidney Rigdon had spoken, President Young arose and addressed the congregation, which faced around to see and hear him, turning their backs towards the wagon occupied by Sidney.

. . . It was necessary that there should be some manifestation of the power of God. . . . No sooner did President Young arise than the power of God rested down upon him in the face of the people. It did not appear to be Brigham Young; it appeared to be Joseph Smith that spoke to the people—Joseph in his looks, in his manner, and in his voice; even his figure was transformed so that it looked like that of Joseph, and everybody present, who had the Spirit of God, saw that he was the man who God had chosen to hold the keys now that the Prophet Joseph had gone behind the veil, and that he had given him power to exercise them. And from that time forward, notwithstanding the claims of Sidney Rigdon . . . God has borne testimony to the acts and teachings of His servant Brigham, and those of his servants, the apostles, who received the keys in connection with him. God sustained him and upheld him, and he blessed all those that listened to his counsel.

John Taylor in *Journal of Discourses*, 23:363-64.

BRIGHAM YOUNG

Visited by Joseph Smith

One morning, while we were at Winter Quarters, Brother Brigham Young said to me and the brethren that he had had a visitation the night previous from Joseph Smith. I asked him what he said to him. He replied that Joseph had told him to tell the people to labor to obtain the Spirit of God; that they needed that to sustain them and to give them power to go through their work in the earth.

Wilford Woodruff, *Deseret Weekly News*, 53:21.

BRIGHAM YOUNG

"We Met Mr. Bridger"

We had to have faith to come here. When we met Mr. Bridger on the Big Sandy River, said he, "Mr. Young, I would give a thousand dollars if I knew an ear of corn could be ripened in the Great Basin." Said I, "Wait eighteen months and I will show you many of them." Did I say this from knowledge? No, it was my faith; but we had not the least encouragement—from natural reasoning and all that we could learn of this country—of its sterility, its cold and frost, to believe that we could ever raise anything. But we traveled on, breaking the road through the mountains and building bridges until we arrived here, and then we did everything we could to sustain ourselves. We had faith that we could raise grain; was there any harm in this? Not at all. If we had not had faith, what would have become of us? We would have gone down in unbelief, have closed up every resource for our sustenance and should never have raised anything. I ask the whole world, is there any harm in having faith in God?

Brigham Young in *Journal of Discourses*, 23:173.

BRIGHAM YOUNG

"I Am Going to Build a City Here"

As told by Wilford Woodruff.

President Young was inspired to come here, and he was inspired to work after he got here. And when Samuel Brannan, who took the ship *Brooklyn* from New York to San Francisco, loaded with Latter-day Saints, came to this barren country and met with the pioneers, he looked upon the desolation and barrenness and tried with all the power he had to persuade President Young not to stop here, but to go on to California. I heard President Young give his answer to Samuel Brannan in the following language, striking his cane into the soil: "No sir, I am going to stop right here. I am going to build a city here. I am going to build a temple here, and I am going to build a country here." And by the help of God he lived to see all this fulfilled.

Diary of Wilford Woodruff, pp. 322-23. Office of the Church Historian, Salt Lake City, Utah.

BRIGHAM YOUNG

"Go, Said President Young; We Will Remain Here"

The following was told by President Joseph F. Smith.

I am happy to express to this audience my knowledge of the successors of Joseph Smith. They raised me, in part, so to speak. In other words, with them I journeyed across the deserts, by the side of my ox-team, following President Brigham Young and his associates to these barren wastes, barren as they were when we first entered this valley. I believed in him then, and I know him now! I believed in his associates, and I know them now; for I lived with them. I slept with them, I traveled with them, I heard them preach and teach and exhort, and I saw their wisdom of Almighty God.

When President Young set his foot down here, upon this desert spot, it was in the midst of persuasion, prayers and petitions on the part of some Latter-day Saints who had gone forward and landed upon the coast of California, that beautiful, rich country, semi-tropical, abounding in resources that no inland country could possess, inviting and appealing for settlers at that time. And just such settlers as President Brigham Young could have taken there—honest people, people who were firm in their faith, who were established in the knowledge of truth and righteousness and in the testimony of Jesus Christ—which is the spirit of prophecy—and in the testimony of Joseph Smith which was a confirmation of the spirit of Christ and His mission—these people pleaded with President Young. "Come with us," they said, "and let us go to the coast. Go where roses bloom all the year 'round, where the fragrance of flowers scents the air from May until May, where beauty reigns; where the elements of wealth are to be found and only need to be developed. Come with us."

"Go," said President Young; "we will remain here, and we will make the desert blossom like the rose. We will fulfill the scriptures by remaining here." . . . Why, bless your soul, what did President Young know about Utah, at that early day? We did not know that there was even a lump of coal in existence in the land. I myself passed the first fall and winter after our entrance into this valley hauling wood out of Mill Creek Canyon and Parley's Canyon; and during that fall and winter I hauled forty loads of wood with my oxen and wagon out of these canyons. Every load I cut and hauled diminished the supply of wood for fuel for the future; and I said to myself: What will we do when the wood is all gone? How will we live here when we can't get any more fuel, for it was going rapidly. I followed that pursuit until it took me three days in the mountains with my ox-team and wagon, to get a load of wood for winter fuel; and what were we to do? Yet President Young said, "This is the place." Well, ordinarily, our judgment and our faith would have been tried, in the decision of the President, if we had not had implicit confidence in him. If we had not known that he was the mouthpiece of God, that he was the real and legitimate successor of the Prophet Joseph Smith in the presidency of The Church of Jesus Christ of Latter-day Saints, we could have doubted his wisdom, and we could have faltered in our faith in his promise and word. But no, we believed him; and we stayed; and so far as I am concerned I am here yet. And I propose to remain here as long as the Lord wants me to stay.

And what has developed? Well, before the wood gave out entirely in the mountains we discovered coal up in Summit County, and then we began to discover it all along the mountains here, and we kept on discovering it. . . . We have discovered that this country was really the gold-mine country of the world; that here abounded silver as well as gold. . . . We have discovered now that some of our mountains here are practically made of copper, and men are hewing copper out of the mountains by millions of tons. . . .

. . . I was a farmer. I had to plow my land and farm it, but I did not have a spear of grass or hay to feed my team, and how was I going to do my spring work? This valley produced very little hay at that time. I hitched up my team, my brother and I, and we drove sixty miles to the south and bought a couple of loads of wild grass hay, and carted that hay down sixty miles to feed our teams in order to plow our land. I used to think, how in the world are we going to live in Utah without feed for our teams? Just then the Lord sent a handful of alfalfa seed into the valley, and Christopher Layton planted it, watered it, and it matured; and from that little beginning, Utah can now produce a richer crop of hay than Illinois or Missouri can do. So the hay question was settled, and the coal question was settled, then the question of producing food from the land. Why, it was a marvel . . . the soil is rich, and everything is favorable for Zion here

61

where President Young determined that he would stay. If we had not stayed here it is clear we would have been overwhelmed and swallowed up by the multitudes who rushed to California [Gold Rush in 1849].

. . . Now, my brethren and sisters, I know whereof I speak with reference to these matters. . . . I have seen it and experienced it all the way through; and I am satisfied with my experience.

Preston Nibley, *Faith Promoting Stories* (Salt Lake City: Deseret Book Co., 1943), pp. 78-84.

BRIGHAM YOUNG

"Some You Will Find with Their Feet Frozen"

November 30 was a Sunday. The faithful Saints were assembled in the Tabernacle, with President Young presiding. Having been appraised of the imminent arrival of the belated handcart emigrants, he spoke to the congregation:

When those persons arrive I do not want to see them put into homes by themselves; I want to have them distributed in the city among the families that have good and comfortable houses; and I wish all the sisters now before me, and all who know how and can, to nurse and wait upon the newcomers and prudently administer medicine and food to them. To speak upon those things is a part of my religion, for it pertains to taking care of the Saints.

As soon as this meeting is dismissed I want the brethren and sisters to repair to their homes, where their bishops will call on them to take in some of this company; the bishops will distribute them as the people can receive them.

The afternoon meeting will be omitted, for I wish the sisters to go home and prepare to give those who have just arrived a mouthful of something to eat, and to wash them and nurse them up. You know that I would give more for a dish of pudding and milk, or a baked potato and salt, were I in the situation of those persons who have just come in, than I would for all your prayers, though you were to stay here all the afternoon and pray. Prayer is good, but when baked potatoes and pudding and milk are needed, prayer will not supply their place on this occasion; give every duty its proper time and place.

Some you will find with their feet frozen to their ankles; some are frozen to their knees and some have their hands frosted . . . we want you to receive them as your own children, and to have the same feeling for them. We are their temporal saviors, for we have saved them from death.

Salt Lake *Deseret News*, December 10, 1856, p. 320.

Biographical Sketch

The bodies of Joseph and Hyrum were in wagons shielded from the burning sun by brush. John Taylor had been placed on a sled because the pain caused by the movement of a wagon was to much to bear. At intervals loyal friends would bathe his wounds with ice water to lessen the pain. The procession neared Nauvoo, and it was met by a mournful host.

John Taylor survived Carthage Jail. The Lord had chosen this young apostle to lead this church one day. Even before his demonstration of courage at Carthage, the stalwart John Taylor had been given the title "Defender of the Faith" by his fellow Saints. John Taylor, like Brigham Young, never wavered.

Parley P. Pratt was called by Heber C. Kimball to undertake a mission to Canada in 1836, and the Lord carefully directed Elder Pratt to John Taylor. The following was written by Parley P. Pratt:

> My place of destination was Toronto, around on the north side of the lake. If I went by land I would have a circuitous route, muddy and tedious to go on foot. The lake had just opened, and steamers had commenced plying between the two places; two dollars would convey me to Toronto in a few hours, and save some days of laborious walking; but I was an entire stranger

in Hamilton, and also in the province; and money I had none. Under these circumstances I pondered what I should do. I had many times received answers to prayers in such matters; but now it seemed hard to exercise faith, because I was among strangers and entirely unknown. The Spirit seemed to whisper to me to try the Lord, and see if anything was too hard for him, that I might know and trust Him under all circumstances. I retired to a secret place in a forest and prayed to the Lord for money to enable me to cross the lake. I then entered Hamilton and commenced to chat with some of the people. I had not tarried many minutes before I was accosted by a stranger, who inquired my name and where I was going. He also asked me if I did not want some money. I said yes. He then gave me ten dollars and a letter of introduction to John Taylor of Toronto. . . . (*Autobiography of Parley P. Pratt*, pp. 134-35.)

The means to pursue his journey and the name of John Taylor came to Parley P. Pratt as a direct answer to prayer. John Taylor was converted to the Church and journeyed to Kirtland to meet Joseph Smith.

John Taylor was born in Milnthrope, Westmoreland County, England, on November 1, 1808. In 1830 he emigrated with his family to Canada. He was ordained an apostle on December 19, 1838, under the hands of Brigham Young and Heber C. Kimball. Elder Taylor was a courageous missionary, writer, and newspaper editor.

In the summer of 1857, Elder Taylor spoke of the approach of Johnson's Army during the Utah War. His remarks exemplify the courage and determination that were so characteristic of his life:

So far as I am concerned, I say let everything come as God has ordained it. I do not desire trials; I do not desire affliction; I would pray to God to leave me not in temptation; . . . but if the earthquake bellows, the lightnings flash, the thunders roll and the powers of darkness are let loose, and the spirit of evil is permitted to rage and an evil influence is brought to bear on the Saints, and my life with theirs, is put to the test—let it come. . . . I know that President Young and those associated with him are full of the spirit of revelation, and they know what they are doing; I feel to acquiesce and put my shoulder to the work, whatever it is. If it is for peace, let it be peace; if it is for war, let it be to the hilt.[1]

President Brigham Young said of John Taylor:

With regard to brother John Taylor, I will say that he has one of the

---

[1]B. H. Roberts, *The Life of John Taylor* (Salt Lake City: Bookcraft, 1963), p. 273.

strongest intellects of any man that can be found; he is a powerful man, he is a mighty man, and we may say that he is a powerful editor, but I will use a term to suit myself, and say that he is one of the strongest editors that ever wrote. . . .

After the death of Brigham Young, the Quorum of the Twelve, with John Taylor as the quorum president, presided over the Church until October, 1880, at which time John Taylor became the President of the Church.

His administration lasted until July 25, 1887. On that day he died at Kaysville, Utah. The day after his death the following appropriate tribute appeared in the *Deseret News:*

Once more the Latter-day Saints are called upon to mourn the death of their leader—the man who has held the keys of the Kingdom of God upon earth. President John Taylor departed this life at five minutes to eight o'clock on the evening of Monday, July 25th, 1887, aged 78, 8 months and 25 days.

In communicating this sad intelligence to the Church, over which he has so worthily presided for nearly ten years past, we are filled with emotion too deep for utterance. A faithful, devoted and fearless servant of God, the Church in his death has lost its most conspicuous and experienced leader. Steadfast to and immovable in the truth, few men have ever lived who have manifested such integrity and such unflinching moral and physical courage as our beloved President who has just gone from us. He never knew the feeling of fear connected with the work of God. But in the face of angry mobs, and at other times when in imminent danger of personal violence from those who threatened his life, and upon occasions when the people were menaced with public peril, he never blanched—his knees never trembled, his hand never shook. Every Latter-day Saint always knew beforehand, on occasions when firmness and courage were needed, where President John Taylor would be found and what his tone would be. He met every issue squarely, boldly and in a way to call forth the admiration of all who saw and heard him. Undaunted courage, unyielding firmness were among his most prominent characteristics, giving him distinction among men who were distinguished for the same qualities. With these were combined an intense love of freedom and hatred of oppression. He was a man whom all could trust, and throughout his life he enjoyed, to an extent surpassed by none, the implicit confidence of the Prophets Joseph, Hyrum and Brigham and all the leading men and members of the Church. The title of "Champion of Liberty," which he received at Nauvoo, was always felt to be most appropriate for him to bear. But it was not only in the possession of these qualities that President Taylor was great. His judgment was remarkably sound and clear, and through life he has been noted for the wisdom of his counsels and teachings.

His great experience made his suggestions exceedingly valuable; for there has scarcely been a public movement of any kind commenced, carried on, or completed since he joined the Church, in which he has not taken part. (Nibley, *The Presidents of the Church,* pp. 118-20.)

John Taylor was a powerful man, well built—six feet tall —a brilliant orator, debator and writer, an unwavering servant of the Lord Jesus Christ. He was an intimate friend of the Prophet Joseph Smith and has taken his unique place in Church history.

JOHN TAYLOR

"When I Was a Little Boy"

I am reminded of my boyhood. At
that early period of my life I learned to approach God. Many
a time I have gone into the fields and concealing myself behind
some bush, would bow before the Lord and call upon him to
guide and direct me. And he heard my prayer. At times I would
get other boys to accompany me. It would not hurt you, boys
and girls, to call upon the Lord in your secret places, as I did.
That was the spirit which I had when a little boy. And God
has led me from one thing to another. But I did not have the
privilege that you have. There was nobody to teach me, while
you have access to good men at any time who can direct you in
the way of life and salvation. But my spirit was drawn out after
God then; and I feel the same yet.

John Taylor in *Journal of Discourses*, 22:313-15.

JOHN TAYLOR

"He May Be a Man of God"

Elder Parley P. Pratt was called on a mission to Toronto, Canada, in 1836.

Elder Pratt applied to all the ministers of Toronto, and the city officials having charge of public buildings, for a place in which to deliver his message, without avail. Disheartened at his unpropitious reception, he was about to leave a city where he could see no prospect of making an opening. In this spirit he called on Mr. Taylor to say farewell.

Mr. Taylor's turning shop adjoined his house, and it was here that Elder Pratt found him. While talking to him, valise in hand ready to depart, a Mrs. Walton called on Mrs. Taylor in the adjoining room. The latter told Mrs. Walton about Elder Pratt and his strange mission, and how, failing to get an opportunity to preach, he was on the eve of departing. "He may be a man of God," said Leonora, "I am sorry to have him depart."

At this Mrs. Walton expressed her willingness to open her house for Elder Pratt to preach in and proposed to lodge and feed him. Here at last was an opening. He began holding meetings at Mrs. Walton's, and was soon afterwards introduced to the investigation meetings held by Mr. Taylor and his religious friends.

They were delighted with his preaching. He taught them faith in God, and in Jesus Christ; called upon them to repent of their sins and to be baptized in the likeness of Christ's burial, for the remission of them; and promised them the Holy Ghost through the laying on of hands, together with a full enjoyment of all its gifts and blessings. All this, and much more that he taught, was in strict harmony with what they themselves believed; but what he had to say about Joseph Smith and the Book of Mormon perplexed a great many, and some of their members even refused to investigate the Book of Mormon, or examine the claims of Apostle Pratt to having divine authority to preach the gospel and administer in the ordinances thereof.

It was at this juncture that the noble independence and boldness of spirit, so conspicuous in John Taylor throughout his life, asserted itself. He addressed the assembly to the following effect:

"We are here, ostensibly in search of truth. Hitherto we have fully investigated other creeds and doctrines and proven them false. Why should we fear to investigate Mormonism? This gentleman, Mr. Pratt, has brought to us many doctrines that correspond with our own views. We have endured a great deal and made many sacrifices for our religious convictions. We have prayed to God to send us a messenger, if he has a true church on earth. Mr. Pratt has come to us under circumstances that are peculiar; and there is one thing that commends him to our consideration; he has come amongst us without purse or scrip, as the ancient apostles traveled; and none of us are able to refute his doctrine by scripture or logic. I desire to investigate his doctrines and claims to authority, and shall be very glad if some of my friends will unite with me in this investigation. But if no one will unite with me, be assured I shall make the investigation alone. If I find his religion true, I shall accept it, no matter what the consequences may be; and if false, then I shall expose it."

After this, John Taylor began the investigation of Mormonism in earnest. He wrote down eight sermons which Apostle Pratt preached and compared them with the scripture. He also investigated the evidences of the divine authenticity of the Book of Mormon and the Doctrine and Covenants. "I made a regular business of it for three weeks," he says, "and followed Brother Parley from place to place." The result of his thorough investigation was conviction; and on the 9th of May, 1836, himself and wife were baptized. "I have never doubted any principle of Mormonism since," was the comment he made in relating, when well advanced in life, how he came to accept the gospel.

Roberts, *Life of John Taylor*, pp. 36-38.

JOHN   TAYLOR

"I Have a Dollar I Will Give You"

It was the 8th of August 1839 that John Taylor left Montrose to fill his mission to England. He dedicated his wife and family to the care of the Lord, and blessed them in his name. "The thought of the hardships they had just endured," he remarks, "the uncertainty of their continuing in the house they then occupied—and that only a solitary room—the prevalence of disease, the poverty of the brethren, their insecurity from mobs, together with the uncertainty of what might take place during my absence, produced feelings of no ordinary character. . . . But the thought of going forth at the command of the God of Israel to revisit my native land, to unfold the principles of eternal truth and make known the things that God had revealed for the salvation of the world, overcame every other feeling."

In Nauvoo Elder Taylor joined Wilford Woodruff, who was scarcely able to drag himself along. . . . After taking leave of the Prophet and his counselors, Sidney Rigdon and Hyrum Smith, Elder Taylor and his sick companion left Nauvoo.

On the outskirts of the settlement they passed Parley P. Pratt and Heber C. Kimball, who were building a log house. Parley, who, it will be remembered, had carried the gospel to Elder Taylor, was stripped—bare headed and bare footed. He hailed the brethren as they were passing and gave them a purse; it was all he had. Elder Heber C. Kimball, who was but a short distance away, stripped as Elder Pratt was, came up and said, "As Brother Parley has given you a purse, I have a dollar I will give you to put in it." Then mutually blessing each other, they said farewell. Elders Taylor and Woodruff were the first of their quorum to start on their mission.

Roberts, *Life of John Taylor,* pp. 67-68.

"I Shut Up the Book and Rushed Back to the President"

The following is by President Heber J. Grant:

I shall tell you one incident in my life.

A man was cut off from the Church for adultery and asked to be restored. President John Taylor wrote a letter to the brethren that had taken action against the man, in which he said: "I want every man to vote his own convictions, and not to vote to make it unanimous unless it is unanimous."

When the matter was presented and voted upon, the vote stood half for and half against restoration.

Later he came up again, and a majority were in favor of his being baptized.

Finally, all of the men that were at the trial, except one, voted to let him be baptized. President John Taylor sent for me and told me I was the only man that stood in the way of this man's being baptized, and he said: "How will you feel when you meet the Lord, if this man is permitted to come up and say he repented although his sins were as scarlet, and you refused to let him be baptized?"

I said: "I will look the Lord squarely in the eye, and I will tell Him that any man that can destroy the virtue of a girl and then lie and claim that she was maligning him and blackmailing him, will never get back into this Church with my vote. You said in your letter to vote our convictions, and I will vote them and stay with them unless you want me to change."

He said: "Stay with your convictions, my boy."

I walked to my home, only one block away. I picked up the Doctrine and Covenants. I was reading it prayerfully and humbly, and marking passages. Instead of its opening at the bookmark, it opened at the passage:

Wherefore, I say unto you, that ye ought to forgive one another; for he that forgiveth not his brother his trespasses standeth condemned before the Lord; for there remaineth in him the greater sin.

I, the Lord, will forgive whom I will forgive, but of you it is required to forgive all men. (D&C 64:9-10.)

I shut up the book and rushed back to the President, and I said, "I give my consent."

Brother Taylor had a habit, when something pleased him, of shaking himself and laughing, and he said: "My gracious, Heber, this is remarkable; what has happened?" And I told him. He said: "Heber, when you left here a few minutes ago did you not think: what if he had defiled my wife or daughter? And when you thought that, did you not feel as if you would like to just knock the life out of that man?"

I said, "I certainly did."

"How do you feel now?"

"Well, really and truly Brother Taylor, I hope the poor old sinner can be forgiven."

"You feel a whole lot better, don't you?"

I said, "I certainly do."

He added: "I put that clause in that letter for you and my son. You have learned a lesson as a young man. You have learned a good lesson, that this gospel is one of forgiveness of sin, of awful sin, if there is true repentance; and it brings peace into your heart when you forgive the sinner. It brings peace when you love the man that you hated, provided the man turns to doing right. You have learned a lesson in your youth. Never forget it." And I never have.

Heber J. Grant in *Conference Report*, October 5, 1941, pp. 148-49.

"Under a Dark Cloud"

Shortly after his baptism, John Taylor was ordained an elder in the Church, and began his labors in the ministry. He was now preaching the gospel in America in fulfillment of the revelation he received in his youth.

So rapidly did the work spread in Canada, that apostles Orson Hyde and Orson Pratt were sent to assist Parley. The country was excited on the subject of "Mormonism," and the ministers alarmed. Public discussions were frequent, and the truth everywhere triumphed. All through the summer of 1836, Elder Taylor was actively engaged in the ministry, and when in the autumn the apostles departed for Kirtland, he was appointed to preside over the churches they had founded.

In March of the following year, Elder Taylor visited Kirtland and there met the Prophet Joseph Smith, who entertained him at his house and gave him many items of information pertaining to the work of the Lord in this dispensation. At that time there was a bitter spirit of apostasy rife in Kirtland. A number in the Quorum of the Twelve were disaffected towards the Prophet, and the Church seemed on the point of disintegration. Among others, Parley P. Pratt was floundering in darkness and, coming to Elder Taylor, told him of some things wherein he considered the Prophet Joseph in error. To his remarks Elder Taylor replied:

"I am surprised to hear you speak so, Brother Parley. Before you left Canada you bore a strong testimony to Joseph Smith being a prophet of God, and to the truth of the work he has inaugurated; and you said you knew these things by revelation, and the gift of the Holy Ghost. You gave to me a strict charge to the effect that though you or an angel from heaven was to declare anything else I was not to believe it. Now Brother

Parley, it is not man that I am following, but the Lord. The principles you taught me led me to him, and I now have the same testimony that you then rejoiced in. If the work was true six months ago, it is true today; if Joseph Smith was then a prophet, he is now a prophet."

To the honor of Parley, be it said, he sought no further to lead Elder Taylor astray; nor did he use much argument in the first place. "He with many others," says Elder Taylor, "was passing under a dark cloud; he soon made all right with the Prophet Joseph, and was restored to full fellowship."

Roberts, *Life of John Taylor*, pp. 39-40.

<hr>

JOHN TAYLOR

"Walk on a Higher Plane"

I will tell you a circumstance that took place with me upwards of forty years ago. I was living in Canada at the time, and was a traveling elder. I presided over a number of the churches in that district of country. A difficulty existed in a branch of the Church, and steps were taken to have the matter brought before me for settlement. I thought very seriously about it, and thought it a very insignificant affair. Because we ought to soar above such things, and walk on a higher plane, for we are the children of God and should be willing to suffer wrong rather than do wrong; to yield a good deal to our brethren for the sake of peace and quietness, and to secure and promote good feelings among the Saints. At that time I did not have the experience I now have, and yet I do not know that I could do anything better than I did then. Before going to the trial I bowed before the Lord, and sought wisdom from him to conduct the affair aright, for I had the welfare of the people at heart. When we had assembled I opened the meeting with prayer, and then called upon a number of those present to pray; they did so, and the Spirit of God rested upon us. I could perceive that a good feeling existed in the hearts of those who had come to present their grievances, and I told them to bring forward their case. But they said they had not anything to bring forward. The feelings and spirit they had been in possession of had left them, the Spirit of God had obliterated these feelings out of their hearts, and they knew it was right for them to forgive one another.

John Taylor in *Journal of Discourses*, 21:366-67.

JOHN TAYLOR

"Is Not That Plenty?"

When Elder Taylor arrived in New York, Elder Woodruff had been there some time, and was all impatience to embark for England, but as yet the former had no means with which to pay for his ocean passage. Although supplied with all the means necessary on his journey thus far, after paying his cab-fare to the house of Brother Pratt he had but one cent left. Still he was the last man on earth to plead poverty, and in answer to inquiries of some of the brethren as to his financial circumstances, he replied that he had plenty of money.

This was reported to Brother Pratt, who the next day approached Elder Taylor on the subject:

Elder Pratt: "Brother Taylor, I hear you have plenty of money?"

Elder Taylor: "Yes, Brother Pratt, that's true."

Elder Pratt: "Well, I am about to publish my 'Voice of Warning' and 'Millennial Poems.' I am very much in need of money, and if you could furnish me two or three hundred dollars I should be very much obliged."

Elder Taylor: "Well, Brother Parley, you are welcome to anything I have, if it will be of service to you."

Elder Pratt: "I never saw the time when means would be more acceptable."

Elder Taylor: "Then you are welcome to all I have."

And putting his hand into his pocket Elder Taylor gave him his copper cent. A laugh followed.

"But I thought you gave it out that you had plenty of money," said Parley.

"Yes, and so I have," replied Elder Taylor. "I am well clothed, you furnish me plenty to eat and drink and good lodging; with all these things and a penny over, as I owe nothing, is not that plenty?"

That evening at a council meeting Elder Pratt proposed that the brethren assist Elder Taylor with means to pay his passage to England as Brother Woodruff was prepared and desired to go. To this Elder Taylor objected and told the brethren if they had anything to give to let Parley have it, as he had a family to support and needed means for publishing. At the close of the meeting Elder Woodruff expressed his regret at the course taken by Elder Taylor, as he had been waiting for him, and at last had engaged his passage.

Elder Taylor: "Well, Brother Woodruff, if you think it best for me to go, I will accompany you."

Elder Woodruff: "But where will you get the money?"

Elder Taylor: "Oh, there will be no difficulty about that. Go and take a passage for me on your vessel, and I will furnish you the means."

A Brother Theodore Turley, hearing the above conversation, and thinking that Elder Taylor had resources unknown to himself or Brother Woodruff, said: "I wish I could go with you, I would do your cooking and wait on you."

The passage to be secured was in the steerage—these

missionaries were not going on flowery beds of ease—hence the necessity of such service as Brother Turley proposed rendering. In answer to this appeal, Elder Taylor told Brother Woodruff to take a passage for Brother Turley also.

At the time of making these arrangements Elder Taylor had no money, but the Spirit had whispered him that means would be forthcoming, and when had that still, small voice failed him! In that he trusted, and he did not trust in vain. Although he did not ask for a penny of anyone, from various persons in voluntary donations he received money enough to meet his engagements for the passage of himself and Brother Turley, but no more.

Elder Taylor and his two companions embarked on the 10th of December, 1839.

Roberts, *Life of John Taylor*, pp. 72-74.

JOHN TAYLOR

"Your Victim Is Ready"

Near Columbus, the capital of Ohio, they [John Taylor and his companions] stayed at a town where a number of brethren resided, and all were anxious to hear Elder Taylor preach. As they had no hall, it was arranged that he should speak in the open air.

A little before meeting time a number of the brethren came running to the house where he was stopping with the information that the whole town was gathering and that a number of men had proposed tar and feathers, and boasted they would dress him with them if he undertook to preach. The brethren advised him not to attempt it as they were not strong enough to protect him. After a moment's reflection, however, he decided to go and preach. The brethren remonstrated; they knew the tar and feathers were prepared and that he could not escape. He replied that he had made up his mind to go; they could go with him if they chose, if not, he would go alone.

A very large concourse of people had assembled to listen to him. He began his remarks by informing them that he had lately come from Canada—a land under monarchical rule; that standing as he then did on free soil, among free men, he experienced peculiar sensations.

"Gentlemen, I now stand among men whose fathers fought for and obtained one of the greatest blessings ever conferred upon the human family—the right to think, to speak, to write; the right to say who shall govern them, and the right to worship God according to the dictates of their own consciences—all of them sacred, human rights, and now guaranteed by the American Constitution. I see around me the sons of those noble sires, who, rather than bow to the behests of a tyrant, pledged their lives, fortunes and sacred honors to burst those fetters, enjoy freedom themselves, bequeath it to their posterity, or die in the attempt.

"They nobly fought and nobly conquered; and now the cap of liberty is elevated on the tops of your liberty poles throughout the land, and the flag of freedom waves from Wisconsin to Louisiana—from Maine to Missouri. Not only so, but your vessels—foremost in the world—sail over oceans, seas and bays, visiting every nation; and wherever those vessels go your flag flutters in the breeze, a hope is inspired among the down-trodden millions, that they, perchance, if they cannot find liberty in their own land, may find it with you. . . . Gentlemen, with you liberty is more than a name; it is incorporated in your system; it is proclaimed by your senators, thundered by your cannon, lisped by your infants, taught to your school-boys; it echoes from mountain to mountain, reverberates through your valleys, and is whispered by every breeze. Is it any wonder, gentlemen, under these circumstances—having lately emerged from a monarchical government—that I should experience peculiar sensations in rising to address you?

"But, by the by, I have been informed that you purpose to tar and feather me, for my religious opinions. Is this the boon you have inherited from your fathers? Is this the blessing they purchased with their dearest hearts' blood—this your liberty? If so, you now have a victim, and we will have an offering to the goddess of liberty." Here he tore open his vest and said: "Gentlemen come on with your tar and feathers, your victim is ready; and ye shades of the venerable patriots, gaze upon the deeds of your degenerate sons! Come on, gentlemen! Come on, I say, I am ready!"

No one moved, no one spoke. He stood there drawn to his full height, calm but defiant—the master of the situation.

After a pause of some moments he continued his remarks and preached with great boldness and power for some three hours.

At the conclusion of his discourse, he was waited upon by some of the leading citizens of the place who expressed their pleasure at what they had heard, and disclaimed, in behalf of the people, any intention of tarring and feathering him; but the brethren still insisted that such was the intention of the crowd, and that the tar and feathers had been provided; but they had been awed into silence by the boldness of Elder Taylor.

Roberts, *Life of John Taylor*, pp. 53-55.

JOHN TAYLOR

"I Have Had a Singular Dream"

The Prophet Joseph told us just before we left for England (1839) that we must not preach the gathering to the people, because at that time there was no place to gather to. "Preach the first principles of the gospel," said he, "but do not say anything about the gathering." We did as he directed us. The principle of gathering was not preached; but a great many came into the Church—a great many thousands were baptized. Myself and an uncle of Brother Joseph F. Smith—that is, his mother's brother—ministered in Liverpool; we raised up a church there. I remember on one occasion a certain sister came to me and said: "Elder Taylor, I have had a singular dream, and I do not know what it means." We had not preached, as I have said, the principle of gathering, because Joseph told us not to preach it. "What is the nature of the dream?" I inquired. "I thought," she said, "there were a number of Saints standing on the pier head (the place where the vessels start from), and they seemed as if they were bound for somewhere. They said they were going to Zion, and they sang the songs of Zion; and you were with them. Now, can you interpret the dream for me? "I guess I could," said I, "but let it alone for the present." We could not prevent people from being impressed in this way. We could not help the Lord giving them dreams, neither could Joseph Smith. It was the privilege of the Saints to have revelation for themselves. . . . Joseph Smith might tell us it was not wisdom to preach the principle of gathering; but we could not help the Lord revealing that principle through the medium of the Holy Ghost, which was to teach us all things. The Holy Ghost had operated upon this woman—and upon many others at the same time—in this way. Afterwards we received a letter from Brother Joseph stating that we might teach the principle and instruct the people to gather to Nauvoo. Now I could interpret the dream. I could have done so before had I not been prohibited.

John Taylor in *Journal of Discourses*, 24:199-200.

JOHN TAYLOR

"He Heard My Prayer"

When I was in Paris, France, about thirty years ago, I had a dream that troubled me very much, in which I saw my first wife . . . lying sick at the point of death. And it so affected me that I awoke, being troubled in my feelings. I fell asleep again, and again the same scene presented itself to me when I again awoke and experienced the same feeling of sorrow, and after some time slept again, and it was repeated a third time. I knew then that my wife was very sick, lying at the point of death.

I got up and fervently prayed the Lord to spare her life until, at least, I should have another opportunity of meeting her in the flesh. *He heard my prayer.* I took a note of the circumstance at the time, and learned afterward that such had been the case exactly as it had been shown to me. On the following morning I remember meeting a gentleman who was a Protestant minister, and he observed that my countenance looked sorrowful, and then inquired the cause. I told him that my wife was lying at the point of death, and he asked me if I had received a letter. I told him how it had been shown to me. But, I said, I got up and prayed the Lord to spare her life, and I feel consoled in *knowing* that she will be healed.

John Taylor in *Journal of Discourses*, 22:354; italics added.

JOHN TAYLOR

"The Lord Raised Her Up"

The object for which the apostles had visited Great Britain was accomplished. They had established the Church there on a sound basis. The Book of Mormon and the Hymn Book had been published; a periodical to advocate and defend the faith delivered to the Saints was established; a permanent shipping agency founded to aid the Saints in gathering to Zion; branches had been organized in nearly all the principal towns of the kingdom, and some eight thousand souls had been baptized. In all this labor Elder Taylor had taken an active, prominent part; and now, in company with his fellow apostles, Brigham Young, Heber C. Kimball, Orson Pratt, Wilford Woodruff, George A. Smith and Willard Richards, he sailed on the ship *Rochester* for America.

Elder Taylor arrived in Nauvoo on the first of July, 1841. Here a great sorrow was awaiting him—his faithful, patient Leonora was sick nigh unto death. The hardships in Missouri, the separation from her husband—on whose strong arm and steadfast courage she was wont to lean—and the consequent increase of care in watching over her family, had at last broken down her strength; and hence he found her pale and wan, and death clutching at her precious life. He called in twenty Elders, who prayed for her; she was anointed with oil, hands were laid upon her, and, in fulfillment of God's promise, the prayer of faith healed the sick—the Lord raised her up.

Roberts, *Life of John Taylor*, pp. 97-98.

JOHN TAYLOR

"Well, Mr. Taylor, I Can Say Nothing"

John Taylor was called in 1849 to take the gospel to France.

Shortly after the discussion Elder Taylor left Boulogne for Paris, where he began studying the French language and teaching the gospel. Among the interesting people whom he met there was M. Krolokoski, a disciple of M. Fourier, the distinguished French socialist.

M. Krolokoski was a gentleman of some standing, being the editor of a paper published in Paris in support of Fourier's views. Another thing which makes the visit of this gentleman to Elder Taylor interesting is the fact that it was the society to which he belonged that sent M. Cabet to Nauvoo with the French Icarians, to establish a community on Fourier's principles. At his request Elder Taylor explained to him the leading principles of the gospel. At the conclusion of that explanation the following conversation occurred:

M. Krolokoski: "Mr. Taylor, do you propose no other plan to ameliorate the condition of mankind than that of baptism for the remission of sins?"

Elder Taylor: "This is all I propose about the matter."

M. Krolokoski: "Well, I wish you every success; but I am afraid you will not succeed."

Elder Taylor: "Monsieur Krolokoski, you sent Monsieur Cabet to Nauvoo, some time ago. He was considered your leader —the most talented man you had. He went to Nauvoo shortly after we had deserted it. Houses and lands could be obtained at a mere nominal sum. Rich farms were deserted, and thousands of us had left our houses and furniture in them, and almost everything calculated to promote the happiness of man was there. Never could a person go to a place under more happy circumstances. Besides all the advantages of having everything made ready to his hand, M. Cabet had a select company of colonists. He and his company went to Nauvoo—what is the result? I read in all your reports from there—published in your own paper here, in Paris—a continued cry for help. The cry is money, money! We want money to help us carry out our designs. While your colony in Nauvoo with all the advantages of our deserted fields and homes—that they had only to move into—have been dragging out a miserable existence, the Latter-day Saints, though stripped of their all and banished from civilized society into the valleys of the Rocky Mountains, to seek that protection among savages—among the *peau rouges* as you call our Indians —which Christian civilization denied us—there our people have built houses, enclosed lands, cultivated gardens, built school-houses, and have organized a government and are prospering in all the blessings of civilized life. Not only this, but they have sent thousands and thousands of dollars over to Europe to assist the suffering poor to go to America, where they might find an asylum.

"The society I represent, M. Krolokoski," he continued, "comes with the fear of God—the worship of the great Elo-heim; we offer the simple plan ordained of God, viz: repentance, baptism for the remission of sins, and the laying on of hands for the gift of the Holy Ghost. Our people have not been seeking the influence of the world, nor the power of government, but they have obtained both. Whilst you, with your philosophy, independent of God, have been seeking to build up a system of communism and a government which is, according to your own accounts, the way to introduce the Millennial reign. Now, which is the best, our religion, or your philosophy?"

M. Krolokoski: "Well, Mr. Taylor, I can say nothing."

Roberts, *Life of John Taylor,* pp. 225-27.

"The Brethren Were Melted to Tears"

The following is by President Heber J. Grant.

I recall one incident showing how song has the power to soothe irritated feelings and bring harmony to the hearts of men who are filled with a contentious spirit. It occurred many years ago and involved a quarrel between two old and faithful brethren whose membership dated back to the days of Nauvoo. These men had been full of integrity and devotion to the work of the Lord. They had been through many of the hardships of Nauvoo and had suffered the drivings and persecutions of the Saints, as well as the hardships of pioneering incident to the early settlement of the west. These men had quarreled over some business affairs, and finally concluded that they would try to get President John Taylor to help them adjust their difficulties.

John Taylor was then the president of the Council of the Twelve Apostles. These brethren pledged their word of honor that they would faithfully abide by whatever decision Brother Taylor might render. Like many others, even in these days, they were not willing to accept the conclusions and counsels of their teachers, or bishops, or presidents of stakes, who would have been the authorized persons, in their order, to consult, and which would have been the proper course to pursue. But they must have some higher authority. Having been personally acquainted with President Brigham Young, in the days of Nauvoo, and feeling their importance in their own devotion to the work of the Lord, nothing short of an apostle's advice would seem to satisfy them.

Accordingly they called on President Taylor. They did not immediately tell him what their trouble was, but explained that they had seriously quarreled and asked him if he would listen to their story and render his decision. President Taylor willingly consented. But he said: "Brethren, before I hear your case, I would like very much to sing one of the songs of Zion for you."

Now President Taylor was a very capable singer, and interpreted sweetly and with spirit, our sacred hymns.

He sang one of our hymns to the two brethren.

Seeing its effect, he remarked that he never heard one of the songs of Zion but that he wanted to listen to one more, and so asked them to listen while he sang another. Of course, they consented. They both seemed to enjoy it; and, having sung the second song, he remarked that he had heard there is luck in odd numbers and so with their consent he would sing still another, which he did. Then in his jocular way, he remarked: "Now, brethren, I do not want to wear you out, but if you will forgive me, and listen to one more hymn, I promise to stop singing, and will hear your case."

The story goes that when President Taylor had finished the fourth song, the brethren were melted to tears, got up, shook hands, and asked President Taylor to excuse them for having called upon him, and for taking up his time. They then departed without his even knowing what their difficulties were.

President Taylor's singing had reconciled their feelings toward each other. The spirit of the Lord had entered their hearts, and the hills of difference that rose between them had been leveled and become as nothing. Love and brotherhood had developed in their souls. The trifles over which they had quarreled had become of no consequence in their sight. The songs of the heart had filled them with the spirit of reconciliation.

Heber J. Grant, "The Editor's Page," *Improvement Era*, 43 (Sept. 1940): 522.

"Richard, He Did Not Give Any Reasons."

As told by President Heber J. Grant.

As a young man Richard W. Young graduated as a cadet at West Point, and before going to the school he was set apart by his grandfather, President Brigham Young, to serve as a missionary while in the school, and then, after graduation, to continue as a missionary in the army.

After his graduation there was a surplus, so he assured me, of graduates from West Point, and more second lieutenants than the army needed, and it was considered no disgrace whatever for the graduates to resign. On the contrary, the government was pleased to receive their resignations with the understanding that they would volunteer should our country ever be engaged in war.

Richard consulted his uncle, Colonel Willard Young, and other friends including myself, stating that he would like to resign, as he was the only living child of his widowed mother. He hated to be separated from her, and an army career would not permit him to be near her.

Some of us agreed to lend him money to secure a legal education, which would cost, he thought, from four to six thousand dollars. We had no doubt he would make a success as a lawyer and would repay the loan.

After he had partially arranged for the money to pay his expenses for his education as a lawyer, he said to me:

"Heber, inasmuch as grandfather blessed me and set me apart as an army missionary, do you think it is proper for me to resign that missionary labor without consulting his successor, President John Taylor?"

I told him it would not be right. He consulted President Taylor, and was told to remain in the army. It was a great disappointment to Richard.

When he secured his appointment in the army after his graduation, he was assigned to Governor's Island, a few minutes' ride from New York City. He entered Columbia Law School in New York, was graduated with honors, and during the time of securing his education he received a salary as second lieutenant and had quarters for himself and his family on Governor's Island, then counted by many as the finest army post in the entire United States. He not only escaped being in debt several thousand dollars for his legal education, but in addition received a salary while securing his education.

After he had been graduated from Columbia Law School, General Winfield Scott Hancock, who was in command at Governor's Island, commended him on the industry he had exhibited in preparing himself for the battle of life. . . .

General Hancock also said he wished he could promote Richard W. Young. But as that was out of the question, he was pleased that he could do one thing for him, and that was to choose him as one of his own staff officers. He remarked: "Lieutenant Young, you are chosen on my staff with the rank of major."

I was in New York City at the funeral of ex-President U. S. Grant. As I recall it, the procession was over five miles long. I was watching the procession from one of the insurance offices on Broadway, and it filled my heart with pride and gratitude to see a grandson of Brigham Young riding with the commanding general on the first line of that great five mile funeral procession.

After graduation as a lawyer, Richard still kept in mind his wish to return to Salt Lake City, to be at home with his mother and to help take care of her, but feared that with the limited salary he was getting after graduation from West Point he could do little or nothing for her.

Subsequently, when the permanent judge advocate-general had been given a special assignment at Washington, General Hancock appointed Richard temporary judge advocate-general of the eastern department of the army, and . . . was working to have him permanently appointed judge advocate-general of the Missouri department at the time General Hancock died.

Richard then fell back to the rank of lieutenant, as another "Pharoah," figuratively speaking, had arisen who did not know "Joseph." Richard came home on a vacation, and in the meantime I had become one of the apostles. He then asked me, also his uncle, Brigham Young, Jr., to plead with President Taylor to permit him to resign, as he had secured his education as a lawyer and wanted to come home and get behind him the starvation period of a young legal graduate.

Brother Brigham Young, Jr., and I argued to the best of our ability at a meeting in the old Endowment House for Richard to be released from the army. Some others spoke in favor of his resignation, and when we had finished our talks, President Taylor said: "The time has not yet arrived for that young man to resign from the army."

This was a very great disappointment to Richard. He wanted to know what the reasons were. I told him there were no reasons given, only that President Taylor said he ought not to resign.

He said: "I would like to have some reasons."

I smiled and said: "Richard, he did not give any reasons when he told you to stay in the army, and you secured your education free of debt and were paid a salary by the government while you were doing so, and upon graduation you were honored by being chosen on the staff of General Hancock. I think you can now well afford to take the advice of President Taylor." He said: "Oh, I wouldn't think of doing anything else, but I wish there were some reasons."

I assured him that when Brother Taylor said, "Your young friend ought to stay in the army," I had an impression that that was exactly the right thing.

Richard was on his way to his new assignment—I have forgotten to what place he was assigned—when he met one of his fellow students who had graduated in the same class, and he was bewailing his fate because he had to come way out to Utah. He thought Richard—as I remember the expression—was a lucky dog, in having the appointment which had been assigned to him, having previously had the best place in the army, namely, Governor's Island, and then getting another fine appointment.

Richard suggested to his fellow graduate that they apply to the secretary of war for an exchange of assignments. They did so. The exchange was made, and Richard was stationed at Fort Douglas for four years and was able to be in the law office of his relative, the late LeGrand Young, and get through what is known as the starvation period of four years as a young lawyer, drawing a good salary from the government and having a fine residence at Fort Douglas without expense.

The day that the announcement was made that Richard's assignment at Fort Douglas had expired I called at President John Taylor's office—I have forgotten for what purpose—and he said, "I see by the morning paper that your dear friend Richard W. Young's term has expired at Fort Douglas and he is about to go East. You may tell him that the time has now arrived for his missionary labors in the army to end, and he is at liberty to resign."

Faith, we are told, is a gift of God, and Richard had the faith to accept the counsel and advice of President Taylor. And it is little less than wonderful that he should have secured the finest post, so considered, in the army, secured his education without running into debt, and received a salary from the government while securing it.

Certainly God moves in a mysterious way his wonders to perform.

My experience is that men who have sufficient faith to trust in God come out of difficulties, financial and otherwise, in a most miraculous and wonderful way.

Heber J. Grant, "On Following Counsel," *Improvement Era*, 39 (March 1936): 131-32.

"I Do Not Feel Like Singing"

The Prophet Joseph, his brother Hyrum, John Taylor, and Willard Richards were imprisoned in the Carthage Jail. Elder Taylor to cheer the Prophet sang the following sacred song, which had recently been introduced into Nauvoo.

> Once when my scanty meal was spread
> He entered—not a word he spake!
> Just perishing for want of bread;
> I gave him all; he blessed it, brake.
>
> In prison I saw him next,—condemned
> To meet a traitor's doom at morn;
> The tide of lying tongues I stemmed,
> And honored him 'mid shame and scorn.
>
> My friendship's utmost zeal to try,
> He asked if I for him would die;
> The flesh was weak, my blood ran chill,
> But the free spirit cried, 'I will.'
>
> Then in a moment to my view,
> The stranger started from disguise;
> The tokens in his hands I knew;
> The Savior stood before mine eyes.
>
> He spake, and my poor name he named—
> "Of me thou hast not been ashamed;
> These deeds shall thy memorial be;
> Fear not, thou didst them unto me."

The afternoon was sultry and hot. The four brethren sat listlessly about the room with their coats off, and the windows of the prison were open to receive such air as might be stirring. Late in the afternoon Mr. Stigall, the jailor, came in and suggested that they would be safer in the cells. Joseph told him that they would go in after supper.

Hyrum Smith asked Elder Taylor to sing again "A Poor Wayfaring Man of Grief."

Elder Taylor: "Brother Hyrum, I do not feel like singing."

Hyrum: "Oh, never mind; commence singing and you will get the spirit of it."

Soon after finishing the song the second time, as he was sitting at one of the front windows, Elder Taylor saw a number of men, with painted faces, rushing round the corner of the jail towards the stairs. They were halted at the entrance but a moment. "The guards were hustled away from the door, good naturedly resisting until they were carefully disarmed."

The brethren must have seen this mob simultaneously, for they all leaped to the door to secure it, as the lock and latch were of little use. The mob reaching the landing in front of the door fired a shot into the lock. Hyrum and Doctor Richards sprang back, when instantly another ball crashed through the panel of the door and struck Hyrum in the face; at the same instant a ball, evidently from the window facing the public square where the main body of the Carthage Greys were stationed, entered his back, and he fell, calmly exlaiming: "I am a dead man!"

With an expression of deep sympathy in his face, Joseph bent over the prostrate body of the murdered man and exclaimed: "Oh, my poor, dear brother Hyrum!"

While Joseph was firing the pistol Elder Taylor stood close behind him.

Elder Taylor beat down the muzzles of those murderous guns.

"That's right, Brother Taylor, parry them off as well as you can," said the Prophet, as he stood behind him.

Meantime the crowd on the landing grew more dense and were forced to the door by the pressure of those below crowding their way up stairs. The guns of the assailants were pushed further and further into the room—the firing was more rapid and accompanied yells and horrid oaths. Certain that they would be overpowered in a moment, Elder Taylor sprang for the open window directly in front of the prison door, and also exposed to the fire of the Carthage Greys from the public square. As he was in the act of leaping from the window, a ball fired from the doorway struck him about midway of his left thigh. He fell helplessly forward towards the open window, and would have dropped on the outside of the jail, but that another ball from the outside, striking the watch in his vest pocket, threw him back into the room.

As Elder Taylor was thrown back from the window Joseph Smith attempted to leap out, but in doing so was instantly shot and fell to the ground with the martyr-cry upon his lips: "O Lord, my God!"

B. H. Roberts, *A Comprehensive History of the Church* (Provo: Brigham Young University Press, 1965), 2:283-86.

JOHN TAYLOR

"Nerves Like the Devil"

While I lay there a number of persons came around, among whom was a physician. The doctor, on seeing a ball lodged in my left hand, took a pen-knife from his pocket and made an incision in it for the purpose of extracting the ball therefrom, and having obtained a pair of carpenter's compasses, made use of them to draw or pry out the ball, alternately using the penknife and compasses. After sawing for some time with a dull penknife, and prying and pulling with the compasses, he ultimately succeeded in extracting the ball, which weighed about half an ounce. Some time afterwards he remarked to a friend of mine that "I had nerves like the devil," to stand what I did in its extraction. I really thought I had need of nerves to stand such surgical butchery, and that, whatever my nerves may be, his practice was devilish.

Roberts, *History of the Church,* 7:107.

———◄—•—►———

JOHN TAYLOR

"Applying Ice Water to My Wounds"

I do not remember the time that I stayed at Carthage, but I think three or four days after the murder, when Brother Marks with a carriage, Brother James Allred with a wagon, Dr. Ellis, and a number of others on horseback, came for the purpose of taking me to Nauvoo. I was very weak at the time, occasioned by the loss of blood and the great discharge of my wounds, so when my wife asked me if I could talk I could barely whisper no. Quite a discussion arose as to the propriety of my removal, the physicians and people of Carthage protesting that it would be my death.

It was finally agreed, however, that I should go; but as it was thought that I could not stand riding in a wagon or carriage, they prepared a litter for me. I was carried downstairs and put upon it. A number of men assisted to carry me, some of whom had been engaged in the mob. As soon as I got downstairs, I felt much better and strengthened, so that I could talk; I suppose the effect of the fresh air.

I found that the tramping of those carrying me produced violent pain, and a sleigh was produced and attached to the end of Brother James Allred's wagon, a bed placed upon it, and I propped up on the bed. Mrs. Taylor rode with me, applying ice water to my wounds. As the sleigh was dragged over the prairie,

which was quite tall, it moved very easily and gave me very little pain.

When I got within five or six miles of Nauvoo the brethren
commenced to meet me from the city, and they increased in
number as we drew nearer until there was a very large company
of people of all ages and both sexes, principally, however, men.

For some time there had been almost incessant rain, so
that in many low places on the prairie it was from one to three
feet deep in water, and at such places the brethren whom we
met took hold of the sleigh, lifted it, and carried it over the
water; and when we arrived in the neighborhood of the city;
where the roads were excessively muddy and bad, the brethren
tore down the fences, and we passed through the fields.

Never shall I forget the differences of feeling that I experienced between the place that I had left and the one that I
had now arrived at. I found myself very much better after my
arrival at Nauvoo than I was when I started on my journey, although I had traveled eighteen miles.

Roberts, *History of the Church*, 7:117-19.

Biographical Sketch

WILFORD WOODRUFF

Wilford Woodruff spent New Year's Day, 1847 in his log cabin at Winter Quarters, reading and working with his journals which he had been faithfully keeping for thirteen years.

Following is the report recorded that day, as he totaled up the record of his accomplishments during the time he had been a member of the Church:

I looked over my journals commencing with 1834 and ending with 1846, making thirteen years, during which time I have traveled 61,692 miles; crossed the Atlantic four times; traveled through England, Scotland, Wales and on six islands of the sea; through twenty of the United States and parts of Canada; held 1,069 meetings; held 86 conferences, 123 councils; baptized 634 persons and assisted in baptizing hundreds of others; was baptized for 36 dead; confirmed 813; ordained 2 patriarchs, 9 bishops, 3 high priests, 3 seventies, 156 elders, 142 priests, 63 teachers, and 13 deacons. I have administered by annointing and laying on hands unto 364 sick persons, many of whom were healed. I blessed 194 children. I married 7 couples. I planted 51 churches (branches); had 10 mobs rise against me. I recorded 30 of the Prophet Joseph's sermons and 25 of the quorum of Twelve Apostles. I wrote 1,040 letters; received 699. I collected for the building of the Temples of the Lord in Kirtland and Nauvoo, $1,674; also $5,000 for assisting in the printing of the works of the Latter-day Saints. I procured

205 subscribers for the periodicals published by the Saints; printed the Times and Seasons and Neighbor in company with Elder Taylor two years; printed 2,500 copies of the Millennial Star at Liverpool and published 3,000 copies of the Book of Mormon, Doctrine and Covenants and secured the copyright at Stationer's Hall, London. I printed 3,000 Hymn Books and 20,000 of the proclamation called the "Proclamation of the Twelve Apostles." During the above period I was ordained to the office of Teacher, Priest, Elder, member of the second quorum of Seventies, the first quorum of Seventies, and one of the Twelve Apostles.[1]

He was ordained as an apostle at Far West, Missouri, in 1839. He literally had to take his life into his hands to go to Far West for that meeting because it was held in the midst of bitter enemies of the Church. A year previous to that the Prophet Joseph Smith had said that there would be such a meeting, and there was no question in the mind of the faithful and the loyal that the meeting would be held. Wilford Woodruff was thirty-two years of age when he became a member of the Twelve.

President Woodruff was born at Farmington, Connecticut, on March 1, 1807. He was baptized in December, 1833. He served as a missionary in the Southern States and also labored on the Fox Islands. His most famous mission was to England, beginning in 1839. Many Church members think of Wilford Woodruff as a great missionary. Heber J. Grant said of him, "Perhaps he [Wilford Woodruff] was the greatest converter of men we have ever had in the Church." (*Conference Report,* April, 1942.)

After half a century among the Twelve—half a century of astonishing Church service—the venerable Wilford Woodruff became the President of the Church on April 7, 1889. He was the epitomy of faithfulness, integrity, and spirituality, a pillar of strength. On the day he became the President of the Church, Wilford Woodruff recorded this statement in his journal:

This 7th day of April, 1889, is one of the most important days in my life, for I was made President of the Church of Jesus Christ of Latter-day Saints by the unanimous vote of ten thousand of them. The vote was first taken by quorums and then by the entire congregation as in the case of

---

[1]Preston Nibley, *Exodus to Greatness* (Salt Lake City: Deseret News Press, 1947), pp. 301-2.

President John Taylor. This is the highest office ever conferred upon any man in the flesh. It came to me in the eighty-third year of my life. I pray God to protect me and give me power to magnify my calling to the end of my days. The Lord has watched over me until the present time.[2]

Wilford Woodruff presided over the Church for nine years as its President. He died on September 2, 1898.

During his entire life he never wavered. His sensitivity to the Spirit of the Lord and his capacity for work in the Kingdom of God are almost unparalleled. The example of his life continues to inspire each new generation of Latter-day Saints. His memory will never be dimmed.

---

[2]Matthias F. Cowley, *Wilford Woodruff* (Salt Lake City: Bookcraft, Inc., 1964), pp. 564-65.

WILFORD WOODRUFF

"I, Indeed, Thought of the Old Prophet"

When I was a boy, there was an old man who used to visit at my father's house. His name was Robert Mason, and I heard teachings from him from the time that I was eight years old and upwards, and they were teachings that I shall ever remember. And he taught my father's household many important truths concerning the church and kingdom of God, and told them many things in relation to the prophets and the things that were coming upon the earth. But his teachings were received by but few. They were unpopular with the Christian world, but nearly all who did receive his teachings have joined the Latter-day Saints.

Prophets were not popular in that day any more than now, and I have often thought of many things which the old man taught me in the days of my youth since I received the fulness of the Gospel and became a member of the Church of Christ.

He said, "When you read the Bible, do you ever think that what you read there is going to be fulfilled? The teachers of the day," said he, "spiritualize the Bible, but when you read in the Bible about the dreams, visions, revelations and predictions of Ezekiel, Isaiah, Jeremiah, or any other of the prophets or apostles, relative to the gathering of Israel and the building up of Zion, . . . you may understand that it means just what it says, and that it will be fulfilled upon the earth in the last days. And when you read of men laying hands upon the sick and healing them, and casting out devils and working miracles in the name of Jesus Christ, it means what it says." And he further said, "The church of Christ and Kingdom of God is not upon the earth, but it has been taken from the children of men through unbelief, and because they have taken away from the gospel some of its most sacred ordinances, and have instituted in their stead forms and ceremonies without the power of God, and have turned from the truth unto fables, but," said he, "it will soon be restored again unto the children of men upon the earth, with its ancient gifts and powers, for the scriptures cannot be fulfilled without it. I shall not live to see it, but," said he to me, "you will live to see that day, and you will become a conspicuous actor in that kingdom, and when you see that day, then that which the prophets have spoken will be fulfilled."

I did not join any church, believing that the church of Christ in its true organization did not exist upon the earth. But when the principles of the everlasting gospel were first proclaimed unto me, I believed it with all my heart, and was baptized the first sermon I heard, for the Spirit of God bore testimony to me in power that it was true.

And I believe that I should never have joined any church had I not heard the fulness of the gospel. I was greatly blessed in receiving it, and was filled with joy unspeakable, and I have never been sorry but I have rejoiced all the day long. . . . I thought of the teaching and words of the old prophet Mason, for he came the nearest to being a true prophet of God in his predictions and works of any man I ever saw, until I saw men administering in the Holy Priesthood.

. . . "But," said he, "I have no right to administer in the ordinances of the gospel, neither has any man unless he receives it by revelation from God out of heaven, as did the ancients. But if my family or friends are sick, I have the right to lay hands upon them, and pray for them in the name of Jesus Christ. And if we can get faith to be healed, it is our privilege." And I will here say that many were healed through his faith and prayers.

Journal of Discourses, 4:99-100.

WILFORD WOODRUFF

"In About Twenty Days I Began To Walk"

On the fifteenth day of October, 1846, while with the Camp of Israel building up Winter Quarters, on the west side of the Missouri River (then Indian Country), I passed through one of the most painful and serious misfortunes of my life. I took my ax and went two and one-half miles upon the bluff to cut some shingle timbers to cover my cabin. I was accompanied by two men. While felling the third tree, I stepped back of it some eight feet, where I thought I was entirely out of danger. There was, however, a crook in the tree, which, when the tree fell, struck a knoll and caused the tree to bound endwise back of the stump. As it bounded backwards, the butt end of the tree hit me in the breast, and knocked me back and above the ground several feet, against a standing oak. The falling tree followed me in its bounds and severely crushed me against the standing tree. I fell to the ground, alighting upon my feet. My left thigh and hip were badly bruised, also my left arm; my breastbone and three ribs on my left side were broken. I was bruised about my lungs, vitals, and left side in a serious manner. After the accident I sat upon a log while Mr. John Garrison went a quarter of a mile and got my horse. Notwithstanding I was so badly hurt, I had to mount my horse and ride two and one-half miles over an exceedingly rough road. On account of severe pain I had to dismount twice on my way home. My breast and vitals were so badly injured that at each step of the horse pain went through me like an arrow. I continued on horseback until I arrived at Turkey Creek, on the north side of Winter Quarters. I was then exhausted, and was taken off the horse and carried in a chair to my wagon. I was met in the street by Presidents Brigham Young, Heber C. Kimball, Willard Richards, and others, who assisted in carrying me to the wagon. Before placing me upon my bed they laid hands upon me, and in the name of the Lord rebuked the pain and distress, and said that I should live, and not die. I was then laid upon my bed in the wagon, as my cabin was not yet done. As the apostles prophesied upon my head, so it came to pass; I did not die. I . . . was administered to by the elders of Israel, and nursed by my wife. I lay upon my bed, unable to move, until my breastbone began to knit together on the ninth day. In about twenty days I began to walk, and in thirty days from the time I was hurt, I returned to my laborious employment.

I have not now a lame limb about me, notwithstanding it all. I have been able to endure the hardest kind of manual labor, exposures, hardships, and journeys. I have walked forty, fifty, and, on one occasion, sixty miles in a single day.

Nibley, *Faith Promoting Stories*, pp. 20-22.

> ◆————◆

WILFORD WOODRUFF

"Instantly I Found Myself Upon My Feet"

In the winter of 1833, and on the twenty-ninth day of December, there came to his home two humble elders of The Church of Jesus Christ of Latter-day

Saints. They were Zera Pulsipher and Elijah Cheney. At the time of their appearance, he and his brother Azmon were away from the house engaged in their daily labors; but Azmon's wife knew very well the frame of mind, both of her husband and his brother Wilford. Their hopes and expectations had been the subject of conversation in their humble home. She therefore received the elders kindly and gave them to understand that her husband and his brother would be anxious to hear them preach.

According to the custom of the Mormon elders then . . . a meeting was appointed at the schoolhouse and notices were circulated throughout the village. The story of this new experience is told by Wilford Woodruff in a simple and beautiful manner: "Upon my arrival home my sister-in-law informed me of the meeting. I immediately turned out my horses and started for the schoolhouse without waiting for supper. On my way I prayed most sincerely that the Lord would give me his spirit, and that if these men were the servants of God I might know it, and that my heart might be prepared to receive the divine message they had to deliver.

"When I reached the place of meeting, I found the house already packed. My brother Azmon was there before I arrived. He was equally eager to hear what these men had to say. I crowded my way through the assembly and seated myself upon one of the writing desks where I could see and hear everything that took place.

"Elder Pulsipher opened with prayer. He knelt down and asked the Lord in the name of Jesus Christ for what he wanted. His manner of prayer and the influence which went with it impressed me greatly. The spirit of the Lord rested upon me and bore witness that he was a servant of God. After singing, he preached to the people for an hour and a half. The spirit of God rested mightily upon him, and he bore a strong testimony of the divine authenticity of the Book of Mormon and of the mission of the Prophet Joseph Smith. I believed all that he said. The spirit bore witness of its truth. Elder Cheney then arose and added his testimony to the truth of the words of Elder Pulsipher.

"Liberty was then given by the elders to any one in the congregation to arise and speak for or against what they had heard as they might choose. Almost instantly I found myself upon my feet. The spirit of the Lord urged me to bear testimony of the truth of the message delivered by these elders. I exhorted my neighbors and friends not to oppose these men, for they were the true servants of God. They had preached to us that night the pure gospel of Jesus Christ. When I sat down, my brother Azmon arose and bore a similar testimony. He was followed by several others."

Cowley, *Wilford Woodruff*, pp. 32-33.

WILFORD WOODRUFF

"That Spirit of Revelation"

My missions have been by that Spirit of revelation. I was told to go to Fox Islands by that same still small voice. In the time of the great apostasy in Kirtland the Spirit of the Lord said to me, "Get you a partner and go to Fox Islands." I knew no more what was in Fox Islands than what was in Kolob. I went there, however, baptized a hundred, and brought them up to Zion with me. It was upon that island where I received a letter from Joseph Smith, telling me that I was called by revelation to fill the place of one of the Twelve who had fallen. You will see it in the Doctrine and Covenants. That thing was revealed to me before I received the letter from Joseph Smith, but I did not feel disposed to tell it to any mortal man, for I knew it was my duty to keep such things to myself.

Nibley, *Faith Promoting Stories*, pp. 25-26.

WILFORD WOODRUFF

"Get up, and Move Your Carriage"

President Wilford Woodruff, who was specially susceptible to spiritual impressions and guidance, has related many instances of the Spirit prompting him to do or refrain from doing certain things, with the results of his action in the premises, from which the following are culled as samples:

"In 1848, after my return to Winter Quarters from our pioneer journey, I was appointed by the Presidency of the Church to take my family and go to Boston, to gather up the remnant of the Saints and lead them to the valleys of the mountains.

"While on my way east I put my carriage into the yard of one of the brethren in Indiana, and Brother Orson Hyde set his wagon by the side of mine, and not more than two feet from it.

"Dominicus Carter, of Provo, and my wife and four children were with me. My wife, one child and I went to bed in the carriage, the rest sleeping in the house.

"I had been in bed but a short time, when a voice said to me, 'Get up, and move your carriage.'

"It was not thunder, lightning nor an earthquake, but the still, small voice of the Spirit of God—the Holy Ghost.

"I told my wife I must get up and move my carriage. She asked, 'What for?'

"I told her I did not know, only the Spirit told me to do it.

"I got up and moved my carriage several rods, and set it by the side of the house.

"As I was returning to bed, the same Spirit said to me. 'Go and move your mules from that oak tree,' which was about one hundred yards north of our carriage.

"I moved them to a young hickory grove and tied them up. I then went to bed.

"In thirty minutes a whirlwind caught the tree to which my mules had been fastened, broke it off near the ground and carried it one hundred yards, sweeping away two fences in its course, and laid it prostrate through that yard where my carriage stood; and the top limbs hit my carriage as it was.

"In the morning I measured the trunk of the tree which fell where my carriage had stood, and I found it to be five feet in circumference. It came within a foot of Brother Hyde's wagon, but did not touch it.

"Thus, by obeying the revelation of the Spirit of God to me, I saved my life, the lives of my wife and child, as well as my animals.

"In the morning I went on my way rejoicing."

George C. Lambert, *Gems of Reminiscence* (Salt Lake City, 1915), pp. 92-93.

WILFORD WOODRUFF

"Mr. Woodruff Has Told Me the Truth"

This puts me in mind of a circumstance that happened when I was preaching in Kentucky. I preached upon the first principles of the gospel, and at the close of my discourse I gave the privilege for anyone to ask questions or to make remarks, if they felt so disposed. A gentle man arose, and I noticed that a great many of the congregation began to laugh; and I afterwards learned that the gentleman was an infidel, and hence the congregation were disposed to make fun of him. He said, "I will not detain you long, but I wish to state to this large congregation that Mr. Woodruff has taught me more this evening than I ever learned in my whole life before. From my boyhood I have been searching into religion; and when I have asked a minister in relation to the way of life, he would point me to the way he was walking himself; then I would ask another and he would point out a different way; and I might have asked a hundred, and they would all have pointed out a different road, and they would tell me that I must be born again. I observed men who were said to be born again, and one class of men who were said to be born again would take one way, and another would take quite a different road; and I always marveled at this, for I did not see any sense in men taking different roads to lead to the kingdom of heaven. But now this man, Mr. Woodruff, has told me the truth, and shown me the reason they took so many different roads after they were born again; and the reason is, because they were all born *blind*."

This in reality is the case, for many of us have been born again according to the traditions of our fathers; but those that keep the celestial law and obey the principles of the gospel of Christ—you never find them taking different roads. There is but one right road, and it is a straight-forward one; and the principles and rules that govern you in that path are simple and easy to be understood. This is the path for us to walk in, and I consider that we are greatly blessed in having learned the true way and in being delivered from that yoke of bondage that has chained us down with error, false doctrine, and false teachers.

This I count one of the greatest blessings that God has given to the children of men, to have the plain truth pointed out to them.

Wilford Woodruff in *Journal of Discourses*, 6:140.

WILFORD WOODRUFF

"The Light Continued with Us"

On the sixteenth of November, I preached at Brother Camp's, and baptized three. On the day following, it being Sunday, I preached again at Brother Clapp's, and baptized five. At the close of the meeting I mounted my horse to ride to Clark's River, in company with Seth Utley, four other brethren, and two sisters. The distance was twenty miles.

We came to a stream which was so swollen by rains that we could not cross without swimming our horses. To swim would not be safe for the females, so we went up the stream to find a ford. In the attempt we were overtaken by a severe storm of wind and rain, and lost our way in the darkness and wandered through creeks and mud. But the Lord does not forsake his Saints in any of their troubles. While we were in the woods suffering under the blast of the storm, groping like the blind for the wall, a bright light suddenly shone around us, and revealed to us our dangerous situation of the edge of a gulf. The light continued with us until we found the road. We then went on our way rejoicing, though the darkness returned and the rain continued.

Wilford Woodruff, "Autobiography of Wilford Woodruff," *Tullidge's Quarterly Magazine,* 3 (Oct. 1883):9.

"Yes, I Will Do It"

My wife Phoebe was attacked on the twenty-third of November by a severe headache, which terminated in brain fever. She grew more and more distressed daily as we continued our journey. It was a terrible ordeal for a woman to travel in a wagon over such rough roads, afflicted as she was. At the same time our child was also very sick.

The first of December was a trying day to my soul. My wife continued to fail, and about four o'clock in the afternoon appeared to be stricken with death. I stopped my team, and it seemed as if she then would breathe her last, lying there in the wagon. Two of the sisters sat beside her, to see if they could do anything for her in her last moments. I stood upon the ground, in deep affliction, and meditated. Then I cried to the Lord, praying that she might live and not be taken from me, and claiming the promises the Lord had made to me through the Prophet and Patriarch. Her spirit revived, and I drove a short distance to a tavern, got her into a room and worked over her and her babe all night, praying to the Lord to preserve their lives.

In the morning, circumstances were such that I was under the necessity of removing them from the inn, as there was so much noise and confusion there that my wife could not endure it. I carried her out to her bed in the wagon and drove two miles, when I alighted at a house and carried my wife and her bed into it, with a determination to tarry there until she recovered her health or passed away. This was on Sunday morning, December second. After getting my wife and things into the house and providing wood to keep up a fire, I employed my time in taking care of her. It looked as if she had but a short time to live. She called me to her bedside in the evening, and said she felt as if a few moments more would end her existence in this life. She manifested great confidence in the cause we had embraced, and exhorted me to have confidence in God and to keep His commandments. To all appearances she was dying. I laid hands upon her and prayed for her, and she soon revived and slept some during the night.

December 3 found my wife very low. I spent the day in taking care of her, and the day following I returned to Eaton to get some things for her. She seemed to be sinking gradually, and in the evening the spirit apparently left her body, and she was dead. The sisters gathered around, weeping, while I stood looking at her in sorrow. The spirit and power of God began to rest upon me until, for the first time during her sickness, faith filled my soul, although she lay before me as one dead.

I had some oil that was consecrated for my anointing while in Kirtland. I took it and consecrated it again before the Lord, for anointing the sick. I then bowed down before the Lord, prayed for the life of my companion, and in the name of the Lord anointed her body with the oil. I then laid my hands upon her, and in the name of Jesus Christ I rebuked the power of death and of the destroyer, and commanded the same to depart from her and the spirit of life to enter her body. Her spirit returned to her body, and from that hour she was made whole; and we all felt to praise the name of God, and to trust in him and keep his commandments.

While I was undergoing this ordeal (as my wife related afterwards) her spirit left her body, and she saw it lying upon the bed and the sisters there weeping. She looked at them and at me, and upon her babe. While gazing upon this scene, two persons came into the room, carrying a coffin, and told her they had come for her body. One of these messengers said to her that she might have her choice. She might go to rest in the spirit world, or, upon one condition, she could have the privilege of returning to her tabernacle and of continuing her labors upon the earth. The condition was that if she felt she could stand by her husband, and with him pass through all the cares, trials, tribulations, and afflictions of life which he would be called upon to pass through for the gospel's sake unto the end, she might return. When she looked at the situation of her husband and child she said, "Yes, I will do it." At the moment that decision was made the power of faith rested upon me, and when I administered to her, her spirit re-entered her tabernacle.

Cowley, *Wilford Woodruff*, pp. 96-98.

———◆———

WILFORD WOODRUFF

"The Result of Not Obeying the Voice of the Spirit"

I will now give an example from my own experience of the result of not obeying the voice of the Spirit.

Some years since I had part of my family living in Randolph, Rich County. I was there on a visit, with my team, in the month of December.

One Monday morning my monitor, the Spirit watching over me, said: "Take your team and go home to Salt Lake City."

When I named it to my family who were at Randolph they urged me strongly to stop longer.

Through their persuasion I stayed until Saturday morning, with the Spirit continually prompting me to go home. I then began to feel ashamed to think that I had not obeyed the whisperings of the Spirit to me before.

I took my team and started early on Saturday morning. When I arrived at Woodruff, the Bishop urged me to stop until Monday and he would go with me.

I told him, "No, I have tarried too long already."

I drove on sprightly, and when within fifteen miles of

Wasatch, a furious storm overtook me, the wind blowing heavily in my face.

In fifteen minutes I could not see any road whatever, and knew not how or where to guide my horses.

I left my lines loosely on my animals, went inside my wagon, tied down my cover, and committed my life and guidance into the hands of the Lord, trusting to my horses to find the way, as they had twice before passed over that road.

I prayed to the Lord to forgive my sin in not obeying the voice of the Spirit to me, and implored him to preserve my life.

My horses brought me into the Wasatch station at 9 o'clock in the evening, with the hubs of my wagon dragging in the snow.

I got my horses under cover and had to remain there until next Monday night, with the snow six feet deep on the level and still snowing.

It was with great difficulty at last that I saved the lives of my horses by getting them into a box car and taking them to Ogden; while, if I had obeyed the revelation of the Spirit of God to me, I should have traveled to Salt Lake City over a good road without any storm.

As I have received the good and the evil, the fruits of obedience and disobedience, I think I am justified in exhorting all my young friends to always obey the whisperings of the Spirit of God, and they will always be safe.

Nibley, *Three Mormon Classics*, pp. 100-1.

WILFORD WOODRUFF

"Don't Go Aboard That Steamer"

After spending two years and one-half in New England and Canada, getting the Saints out, I started back with the last lot, about a hundred, from Boston. We landed in Pittsburg at dusk. We were anxious not to stay there, but to go on to St. Louis. I saw a steamer making steam ready to go out. I went to the captain and asked him how many passengers he had. "Three hundred and fifty." "Could you take another hundred?" "Yes." The Spirit said to me, "Don't go aboard that steamer; you nor your company." All right, said I. I had learned something about that still, small voice. I did not go aboard that steamer, but waited till the next morning.

In thirty minutes after that steamer left, it took fire. It had ropes instead of wheel chains, and they could not go ashore. It was a dark night, and not a soul was saved. If I had not obeyed the influence of that monitor within me, I would have been there myself, with the rest of the company.

The Thirteenth ward would not have had an Atwood for a bishop; the Church would not have had a Leonard W. Hardy as bishop. They were both with me, and their families, including Brother Samuel Hardy, who is in St. George now, upwards of ninety years old.

I never disobeyed that Spirit but once in my life; I did it then through the urgency of other persons, and it nearly cost me my life. I have been acquainted with this spirit. It was not the blow of trumpets, nor thunder and lightning; it was the still small voice to me. All the way from my boyhood I have been governed and controlled by that Spirit.

Nibley, *Faith Promoting Stories*, pp. 24-25.

WILFORD WOODRUFF

"I Feel Like a Subject for a Dissecting Room"

The whole of that mission to England, from the beginning to the end, placed the apostles in such a position that they had to walk by faith from first to last. . . . As soon as we prepared ourselves to go on our mission to England . . . the devil undertook to kill us. I have myself been in Tennessee and Kentucky for two or three years, where, in the fall, there were not enough well persons to take care of the sick during the ague months, and yet I never had the ague in my life until called to go upon that mission to England. There was not one solitary soul in the Quorum of the Twelve but what the devil undertook to destroy; and, as we said yesterday, when Brother Taylor and myself, the two first of the quorum ready for the trip, were on hand to start, I was shaking with the ague. And I had it every other day. And on my well day, when I did not have it, my wife had it. I got up and laid my hands upon her and blessed her, and blessed my child, having only one at the time, and I started across the river. And that man who sits behind me today, Brigham Young the President of the Church and kingdom of God upon the earth, paddled me across the Missouri river in a canoe, and that is the way I landed in Nauvoo. I lay down on a side of sole leather by the post office, and I did not know where to go. . . . I was not able to stand on my feet, and I lay down there. By and by the Prophet came along, and, said he: "Brother Woodruff, you are going on a mission?"

"Yes," I said, "but I feel more like a subject for the dissecting room than for a mission."

He reproved me for what I said and told me to get up and go. Brother Taylor, the only member of the Quorum of the Twelve who was well, and I traveled together, and on the way he fell to the ground. . . . Brother Taylor fell twice in that way, taken with the bilous fever, and no man in that quorum could boast that he went on that mission without feeling the hand of the destroyer, for it was laid upon us all. I had the shaking ague and lay on my back in a wagon, and was rolled over stumps and stones until it seemed as if my life would be shaken out of me. I left Brother Taylor behind, by his advice, for said he, "We are both sick, and if you stay you can't do anything here." . . . I got to Buffalo, New York.

From there I traveled along to Farmington, Connecticut, my native place, and I stayed there fifteen days at my father's house, coughing and shaking every day. My father never expected that I should leave my bed, and my stepmother did not expect that I should ever get better. A message came from an uncle of mine, who had just died, and his last words were: "I want you to send for friend Wilford. I want him to come and preach my funeral sermon."

My father said: "You can't go and preach that sermon, for you can't sit up in your bed."

Said I: "Never mind, get . . . your horse and wagon." And he did so, and I got into it, and rode over that morning in a chilly wind. And the hour that my ague was coming on I got before a big blazing fire and preached the funeral sermon of my friend. And the ague left me from that day, and I went back and went on my way rejoicing.

In process of time Brother Taylor came along, and he and I crossed the ocean together and arrived in England. And here I want to make a little statement of my experience in those days concerning circumstances that took place with me. When Brother Brigham left home he told me that all his family had was one barrel of rotten flour. Two hundred cents would have bought every pound of provision I left with my family when I left home. But we left our wives, for we had the commandment of God upon us; and we were either going to obey it, or die trying. That was the spirit of the elders of Israel; and I blessed my wife and child and left them in the hands of God, and to the tender mercies of our noble bishops. . . . We traveled without purse and scrip, and we preached without money and without price. Why? Because the God of heaven had called upon us to go forth and warn the world.

Journal of Discourses, 18:122-25.

—◆—▶—

WILFORD WOODRUFF

"Many Souls Were Waiting for the Word of God"

March 1, 1840, was my birthday, when I was thirty-three years of age. It being Sunday, I preached twice through the day to a large assembly in the city hall, in the town of Hanley [England], and administered the sacrament unto the Saints.

In the evening I again met with a large assembly of the Saints and strangers, and while singing the first hymn the Spirit of the Lord rested upon me. And the voice of God said to me, "This is the last meeting that you will hold with this people for many days."

I was astonished at this, as I had many appointments out in that district.

When I arose to speak to the people, I told them that it was the last meeting I should hold with them for many days. They were as much astonished as I was.

At the close of the meeting four persons came forward for baptism, and we went down into the water and baptized them.

In the morning I went in secret before the Lord and asked him what his will was concerning me.

The answer I got was that I should go to the south, for the Lord had a great work for me to perform there, as many souls were waiting for the word of the Lord.

On the third of March, 1840, in fulfillment of the word of the Lord to me, I took coach and rode to Wolverhampton, twenty-six miles, and spent the night there.

On the morning of the fourth I again took coach and rode through Dudley, Stourbridge, Stourport and Worcester, and then walked a number of miles to Mr. John Benbow's, Hill Farm, Castle Frome, Ledbury, Herefordshire. This was a farming country in the south of England, a region where no elder of the Latter-day Saints had visited.

I found Mr. Benbow to be a wealthy farmer, cultivating three hundred acres of land, occupying a good mansion, and having plenty of means. His wife, Jane, had no children.

I presented myself to him as a missionary from America, an elder of The Church of Jesus Christ of Latter-day Saints who had been sent to him by the commandment of God as a messenger of salvation, to preach the gospel of life unto him and his household, and the inhabitants of the land.

Mr. Benbow and his wife received me with glad hearts and thanksgiving. It was in the evening when I arrived, having traveled forty-eight miles by coach and on foot during the day; but after receiving refreshments we sat down together, and conversed until two o'clock in the morning.

Mr. Benbow and his wife rejoiced greatly at the glad tidings which I brought unto them of the fulness of the everlasting gospel, which God had revealed through the mouth of his prophet, Joseph Smith, in these last days.

I rejoiced greatly at the news that Mr. Benbow gave me, that there was a company of men and women—over six hundred in number—who had broken off from the Wesleyan Methodists and taken the name of United Brethren. They had forty-five preachers among them, and had chapels and many houses that were licensed according to the law of the land for preaching in.

This body of United Brethren were searching for light and truth, but had gone as far as they could and were continually calling upon the Lord to open the way before them and send them light and knowledge that they might know the true way to be saved.

When I heard these things I could clearly see why the Lord had commanded me, while in the town of Hanley, to leave that place of labor and go to the south, for in Herefordshire there was a great harvest-field for gathering many Saints into the kingdom of God.

I retired to my bed with joy after offering my prayers and thanksgiving to God, and slept sweetly until the rising of the sun.

I arose on the morning of the fifth, took breakfast, and told Mr. Benbow I would like to commence my Master's business by preaching the gospel to the people.

He had a large hall in his mansion which was licensed for preaching, and he sent word through the neighborhood that an American missionary would preach at his house that evening.

As the time drew nigh, many of the neighbors came in, and I preached my first gospel sermon in the house. I also preached on the following evening at the same place and baptized six persons, including Mr. John Benbow and his wife, and four preachers of the United Brethren.

I spent most of the following day in clearing out a pool of water and preparing it for baptizing in, as I saw many to be baptized there. I afterwards baptized six hundred in that pool of water.

Nibley, *Three Mormon Classics*, pp. 88-91.

◄────◆────►

WILFORD WOODRUFF

"Mr. Woodruff, I Would Like to Be Baptized"

On Sunday, the eighth, I preached at Frome's Hill in the morning, at Standley Hill in the afternoon, and at John Benbow's Hill Farm in the evening.

The parish church that stood in the neighborhood of Brother Benbow's, presided over by the rector of the parish, was attended during the day by only fifteen persons, while I had a large congregation, estimated to number a thousand, attend my meeting through the day and evening.

When I arose in the evening to speak at Brother Benbow's house, a man entered the door and informed me that he was a constable and had been sent by the rector of the parish with a warrant to arrest me.

I asked him, "For what crime?"

He said, "For preaching to the people."

I told him that I, as well as the rector, had a license for preaching the gospel to the people, and that if he would take a chair I would wait upon him after meeting.

He took my chair and sat beside me. I preached the first principles of the everlasting gospel for an hour and a quarter. The power of God rested upon me, the Spirit filled the house, and the people were convinced.

At the close of the meeting I opened a door for baptism, and seven offered themselves. Among the number were four preachers and the constable.

The latter arose and said, "Mr. Woodruff, I would like to be baptized."

I told him I would like to baptize him. I went down to the pool and baptized the seven. We then met together and I confirmed thirteen and broke bread unto the Saints. And we all rejoiced together.

The constable went to the rector and told him if he wanted Mr. Woodruff taken up for preaching the gospel, he must go himself and serve the writ, for he had heard him preach the only true gospel sermon he had ever listened to in his life.

The rector did not know what to make of it, so he sent two clerks of the Church of England as spies, to attend our meeting and find out what we did preach.

But they were both pricked in their hearts, and received the word of the Lord gladly, and were baptized and confirmed members of The Church of Jesus Christ of Latter-day Saints.

The rector became alarmed and did not dare to send anybody else.

123

The ministers and rectors of the South of England called a convention and sent a petition to the archbishop of Canterbury to request Parliament to pass a law prohibiting the Mormons from preaching in the British dominion.

In this petition the rector stated that one Mormon missionary had baptized fifteen hundred persons, mostly members of the English church, during the last seven months.

But the archbishop and council, knowing well that the laws of England gave free toleration to all religions under the British flag, sent word to the petitioners that if they had the worth of souls at heart as much as they had the ground where hares, foxes and hounds ran, they would not lose so many of their flock.

I continued to preach and baptize daily.

Nibley, *Three Mormon Classics*, pp. 91-93.

WILFORD WOODRUFF

"Three Men Dressed in White"

The prospect in London at that time was the darkest it had ever been in since entering the vineyard; but the Lord was with us, and we were not discouraged. On Sunday we met with the Saints three times at Brother Corner's, read the Book of Mormon, gave instruction, and broke bread unto them. We had a good time, although there were only about half a dozen present. I felt the Spirit bear testimony that there would be a work done in London.

Having retired to rest in good season, I fell asleep and slept until midnight, when I awoke and meditated upon the things of God until three o'clock in the morning. And, while forming a determination to warn the people in London, and by the assistance and inspiration of God to overcome the power of darkness, a person appeared to me whom I consider as the prince of darkness. He made war upon me and attempted to take my life. As he was about to overcome me I prayed to the Father, in the name of Jesus Christ, for help. I then had power over him and he left me, though I was much wounded. Afterwards three men dressed in white came to me and prayed with me, and I was healed immediately of all my wounds, and delivered of my troubles.

Cowley, *Wilford Woodruff*, p. 130.

WILFORD WOODRUFF

"Take Your Team and Go to the Farm"

In another instance, after attending a large annual conference in Salt Lake City, and, having a good deal of business to attend to, I was somewhat weary. And at the close of the conference I thought I would repair to my home and have a rest.

As I went into the yard the Spirit said to me, "Take your team and go to the farm," which is some three miles south of the Tabernacle.

As I was hitching the horse to the wagon, Mrs. Woodruff asked where I was going.

I said, "To the farm."

"What for?" she asked.

"I do not know," I replied; but when I arrived there I found out.

The creek had overflowed, broken through my ditch, surrounded my home, and filled my barnyard and pig pen . . .

Through my own exertions I soon turned it and prevented much damage that might have occurred had I not obeyed the voice of the Spirit.

This same Spirit of revelation has been manifested to many of my brethren in their labors in the kingdom of God. . . .

Lambert, *Gems of Reminiscense,* p. 94.

———◆——◆———

WILFORD WOODRUFF

"The Signers of the Declaration of Independence"

I feel to say little else to the Latter-day Saints wherever and whenever I have the opportunity of speaking to them, than to call upon them to build these temples now under way, to hurry them up to completion. The dead will be after you; they will seek after you as they have after us in St. George. They called upon us, knowing that we held the keys and power to redeem them.

I will here say, before closing, that two weeks before I left St. George, the spirits of the dead gathered around me, wanting to know why we did not redeem them. Said they, "You have had the use of the Endowment House for a number of years, and yet nothing has ever been done for us. We laid the foundation of the government you now enjoy, and we never apostatized from it; but we remained true to it and were faithful to God." These were the signers of the Declaration of Independence, and they waited on me for two days and two nights.

I thought it very singular that notwithstanding so much work had been done, and yet nothing had been done for them. The thought never entered my heart—from the fact, I suppose, that heretofore our minds were reaching after our more immediate friends and relatives. I straightway went into the baptismal font and called upon Brother McAllister to baptize me for the signers of the Declaration of Independence and fifty other eminent men, making one hundred in all, including John Wesley, Columbus, and others. I then baptized him for every president of the United States except three; and when their cause is just, somebody will do the work for them.

Wilford Woodruff in *Journal of Discourses*, 19:229.

Biographical Sketch

LORENZO SNOW

Many came to visit the Prophet Lorenzo Snow in his later years. That which they wrote reveals the kind of man he was. A Mr. Prentis of South Carolina wrote:

> . . . I had expected to find intellect, intellectuality, benevolence, dignity, composure, and strength depicted upon the face of the President of The Church of Jesus Christ of Latter-day Saints; but when I was introduced to President Lorenzo Snow, for a second I was startled to see the holiest face but one I had ever been privileged to look upon. His face was a poem of peace, his presence a benediction of peace. In the tranquil depths of his eyes were the 'home of silent prayer' and the abode of spiritual strength. As he talked of the more sure word of prophecy and the certainty of the hope which was his, and the abiding faith which had conquered the trials and difficulties of a tragic life. . . I watched the play of emotions and studied with fascinated attention, the subtle shades of expression which spoke so plainly the workings of his soul; and the strangest feeling stole over me, that I stood on holy ground . . .[1]

The Reverend W. D. Cornell wrote of Elder Snow:

> I . . . found myself shaking hands with one of the most congenial and lovable men I ever met . . . a master in the art of conversation, with a rare

---

[1]Thomas C. Romney, *The Life of Lorenzo Snow* (Salt Lake City: S.U.P. Foundation, 1955), pp. 14-15.

genius, enabling him to make you feel a restful welcome in his society.

President Snow is a cultured man, in mind and soul and body. His language is choice, diplomatic, friendly, scholarly. . . . The tenor of his spirit is as gentle as a child. You are introduced to him. You are pleased with him. You converse with him, you like him. You visit with him long, you love him.[2]

The great and impressive prophet of God, Lorenzo Snow, was the last of the first generation prophets. He was born at Mantua, Portage County, Ohio, on April 3, 1814.

Lorenzo Snow, at the time he first heard of the restored Church, was a very capable college student interested in a military career. Eliza R. Snow, his sister, was converted to the Church and attempted to convert her brother. President Snow was impressed with Joseph Smith's father and writes of his great influence upon him:

He surprised me when he said, "Don't worry, take it calmly and the Lord will show you the truth of this great latter-day work, and you will want to be baptized." . . . I studied the principles . . . I heard the Prophet discourse upon the grandest of subjects. At times he was filled with the Holy Ghost, speaking as with the voice of an archangel and filled with the power of God; his whole person shone and his face was lightened until it appeared as the whiteness of the driven snow. . . . Finally my prayers were answered and I was convinced of the truth sufficiently to want to be baptized to get a knowledge for myself of the testimony that Joseph Smith had seen God. . . .

I was at that time a young man full of worldly aspirations, with bright prospects and means to gratify my ambition in acquiring a liberal, collegiate education. Besides I had many wealthy, proud . . . friends and relatives who watched eagerly for me to achieve high honors in life. It will therefore be easily understood that no small effort was needed to form the resolution to abandon those prospects, disappoint those expectations, and join the poor, ignorant, despised 'Mormons,' as they at that early day, were regarded . . .

However, through the help of the Lord—for I feel certain he must have helped me—I laid my pride, worldly ambition and aspirations upon the altar, and, humble as a child, went to the waters of baptism, and received the ordinances of the gospel, administered by one who claimed to be an Apostle.[3]

Elder Snow continued to investigate the Church and was baptized in June, 1836, at Kirtland, Ohio. At age thirty-five he

---

[2]*Millennial Star*, 61 (Sept. 1899): 579.

[3]*Juvenile Instructor*, Jan. 1886, p. 22.

was ordained an apostle in February of 1849. President Snow was a great missionary. He served in the British Mission from 1840-1843. During the mission, he presented a copy of the Book of Mormon to Queen Victoria. In 1849 he was called to a mission in Italy. He was always a leader in educational, cultural, and civic affairs.

President Snow became the President of the Council of Twelve in 1889 and at age eighty-four was sustained as President of the Church. He died on October 10, 1901.

Because of his excellent preparation and greatness of soul, in just three years as prophet, seer, and revelator, he was able to make great contributions that have been of continuing benefit to the Church and its members.

Brigham Young, Junior, paid this tribute to Lorenzo Snow:

I have looked upon President Lorenzo Snow as a second father. I have loved him as a father, and I mourn his departure; but I feel thankful that he was surrounded with every comfort, that peace prevailed in his home and with the people, and that he passed to his rest in the midst of his loving family and friends. About two hours before his death I laid my hand upon his brow and said, "President Snow, do you recognize me?" He looked at me with his sweet smile and eyes full of intelligence, and said, "I rather think I do." He was intelligent nearly to the last, and he knew that his time had come, for he spoke of it. If the prayers and faith of the people could have saved him, President Snow would be alive today; but God has willed it otherwise, and we are deprived of a man who has been one of the most valiant of those who were raised up by the Almighty to assist in laying the foundations of the great cause which he instituted for the salvation of his sons and daughters.

I have known President Snow since before the death of the Prophet Joseph Smith. I knew him well before the Prophet was martyred, and I knew he was a friend of the Prophet, a friend of the leaders of the Church, and a friend of God. Though but a boy, I recognized in this man a power that was born of the Holy Spirit. I have known his works since 1843, and no man that has lived among us has been more thorough, more diligent, wiser in all positions where he has been placed, and shown more integrity to the work, than the late President Lorenzo Snow. I loved that man, as I loved his predecessors; and the grand work that he has accomplished in the last three years will live in the history of the Church, showing forth the greatness and the executive and financial ability of the man. He will stand among the foremost of those who have inaugurated this great and glorious work of the latter days. Thank God that I was acquainted with him! Though I mourn the loss of his society, I know that he has gone to a reward that is great and glorious; for him there is a crown laid up that shall never fade. I know his family will miss him, and his brethren will miss him; but Lorenzo Snow has done a magnificent work, and his example is worthy of emulation.[4]

President Snow was laid to rest in Brigham City on Sunday, October 13, 1901.

---

[4]Nibley, *Presidents of the Church*, pp. 219-221.

LORENZO SNOW

"I Heard a Sound Just Above My Head"

Some two or three weeks after I was
baptized, one day while engaged in my studies, I began to reflect
upon the fact that I had not obtained a *knowledge* of the truth
of the work—that I had not realized the fulfillment of the promise that "he that doeth my will shall know of the doctrine," and
I began to feel very uneasy. I laid aside my books, left the house,
and wandered around through the fields under the oppressive
influence of a gloomy, disconsolate spirit, while an indescribable
cloud of darkness seemed to envelop me. I had been accustomed,
at the close of the day, to retire for secret prayer to a grove a
short distance from my lodgings, but at this time I felt no in-
clination to do so. The spirit of prayer had departed, and the
heavens seemed like brass over my head. At length, realizing
that the time had come for secret prayer, I concluded I would
not forego my evening service, and, as a matter of formality,
knelt as I was in the habit of doing, and in my accustomed retired place, but not feeling as I was wont to feel.

I had no sooner opened my lips in an effort to pray, than
I heard a sound, just above my head, like the rustling of silken
robes, and immediately the Spirit of God descended upon me,

from the crown of my head to the soles of my feet. And oh, the joy and happiness I felt! No language can describe the almost instantaneous transition from a dense cloud of mental and spiritual darkness into a refulgence of light and knowledge that God lives, that Jesus Christ is the Son of God, and of the restoration of the holy priesthood, and the fulness of the gospel. It was a complete baptism—a tangible immersion in the heavenly principle or element, the Holy Ghost; and even more real and physical in its effects upon every part of my system than the immersion by water; dispelling forever, so long as reason and memory last, all possibility of doubt or fear in relation to the fact handed down to us historically, that the "Babe of Bethlehem" is truly the Son of God; also the fact that he is now being revealed to the children of men and communicating knowledge, the same as in the apostolic times. I was perfectly satisfied, as well I might be, for my expectations were more than realized, I think I may say in an infinite degree.

I cannot tell how long I remained in the full flow of the blissful enjoyment and divine enlightenment, but it was several minutes before the celestial element which filled and surrounded me began gradually to withdraw. On arising from my kneeling posture, with my heart swelling with gratitude to God, beyond the power of expression, I felt—I *knew*—that he had conferred upon me what only an omnipotent being can confer—that which is of greater value than all the wealth and honors worlds can bestow. That night, as I retired to rest, the same wonderful manifestations were repeated, and continued to be for several successive nights. The sweet remembrance of those glorious experiences, from that time to the present, bring them fresh before me, imparting an inspiring influence which pervades my whole being, and I trust will to the close of my earthly existence.

Eliza R. Snow Smith, *Biography and Family Record of Lorenzo Snow* (Salt Lake City: Deseret News Press, 1884), pp. 7-9.

LORENZO SNOW

"My Pocket Bible"

On another occasion, one evening, I was preaching in a large room of a private house, and afterwards learned that a portion of my audience had gathered for the purpose of mobbing me. They had arranged with a party that lay concealed at a little distance, and within call, to join them immediately on my leaving the house to return to my lodgings, and all proceed together to execute their schemes of vengeance. It was a very cold night, and after the close of the services I stood with my back to the chimney fire, with a number of others—some of whom belonged to the mob party. One of the latter persons amid the jostling of the crowd, accidentally brought his hand in contact with one of the pockets in the skirt of my coat, which struck him with sudden alarm on his feeling what he supposed to be a large pistol. He immediately communicated the discovery to his affrightened coadjutors, all of whom directly withdrew and, to their fellow outside, imported the astounding news that the "Mormon" Elder was armed with deadly weapons. That was sufficient the would-be outlaws abandoned their evil designs for fear of signal punishment; but the supposed pistol which caused their alarm and my protection, was my pocket Bible, a precious gift to me from the dearly beloved Patriarch, father Joseph Smith.

Eliza Smith, *Biography and Family Record of Lorenzo Snow*, p. 37-38.

LORENZO SNOW

"Weapons for Protection"

A spirit of mobocracy, which has previously manifested itself, was continually on the increase all around us, and very naturally suggested to our minds the thought of preparation for defense.

. . . Amid the threatenings of mobocrats to either drive or destroy us, a circumstance occurred, which, though seriously exciting at the time, afterwards afforded us much amusement. One night at about eleven o'clock, we all were suddenly aroused from sleep by the discharge of firearms, accompanied with loud shouts, apparently about a mile distant. We supposed that our enemies had commenced their depredations by putting their threats into execution and were making an attack on our people; and the probability was that they would visit us in turn. We immediately began to prepare for defense by barricading the doors and windows and distributing among all the members of the family such weapons for protection as were available; viz: one sword, two or three guns, pitchforks, axes, shovels and tongs, etc. We proposed that mother take her choice, and she thought that she could do the best execution with a shovel. With no small degree of anxiety, not only for ourselves, but also in behalf of our friends situated at the point from which the exciting sounds proceeded, we kept a sleepless watch until morning, when intelligence was brought, explaining the cause of the night alarm as follows: A company of our brethren had been to a distant settlement to accomplish some business requisite in consequence of threatened mob violence, and on their return, having peacefully and successfully accomplished their object, discharged their firearms, accompanied with a shout expressive of their happy success—resulting in our false alarm and subsequent amusement.

Eliza Smith, *Biography and Family Record of Lorenzo Snow*, pp. 28-29.

LORENZO SNOW

"Mr. Snow, It Is Too Late"

The following incident took place as Lorenzo Snow returned from a mission to England aboard the ship *Swanton.*

The steward, a German by birth, was a young man, very affable in manner and gentlemanly in deportment—a general favorite and respected by all. During the latter part of the voyage he took sick and continued growing worse and worse, until death seemed inevitable. All means proved unavailing, and the captain, by whom he was much beloved, gave up all hope of his recovery and requested the officers and crew to go in, one by one, and take a farewell look of their dying friend, which they did silently and solemnly, as he lay unconscious and almost breathless on his dying couch.

Immediately after this sad ceremony closed, one of our sisters, by the name of Martin, without my brother's knowledge went to the captain and requested him to allow my brother to lay hands on the steward, according to our faith and practice under such circumstances, saying that she believed that the steward would be restored. The captain shook his head and told her that the steward was now breathing his last, and it would be useless to trouble Mr. Snow. But Sister Martin was not to be defeated; she not only importuned, but earnestly declared her faith in the result of the proposed administration, and he finally yielded and gave consent.

As soon as the foregoing circumstance was communicated to my brother, he started toward the cabin where the steward lay, and in passing through the door met the captain, who was in tears. He said, "Mr. Snow, it is too late; he is expiring; he is breathing his last!" My brother made no reply, but took a seat beside the dying man. After devoting a few moments to secret prayer, he laid his hands on the head of the young man, prayed, and in the name of Jesus Christ rebuked the disease and commanded him to be made whole. Very soon after, to the joy and astonishment of all, he was seen walking the deck, praising and glorifying God for his restoration. The officers and sailors acknowledged the miraculous power of God, and on landing at New Orleans several of them were baptized, also the first mate, February 26, 1843.

Eliza Smith, *Biography and Family Record of Lorenzo Snow*, pp. 65-66.

LORENZO SNOW

"The Dream Flashed Across My Mind"

When at the house of Brother Smith, in Stark County, Ohio, I dreamed one night that arrangements were in progress to mob me. The following evening after I had the dream, as I sat conversing with friends who had called on me, a loud rap at the door preceded the entrance of two well-dressed young men, who politely invited me to accompany them to a school house about one mile distant and to address an audience already assembled. After a little hesitation on my part, they began to urgently request my acceptance of their invitation, when the dream of the preceding night instantaneously flashed across my mind, and I told them I could not comply with their wishes. They still persisted to urge and insist on my accompanying them. When they were convinced that I was immovable in my determination of non-compliance, they not only manifested disappointment, but were exceedingly angry.

The next day I learned that they told the truth so far as a congregated audience waiting my appearance at the schoolhouse was concerned, but the object was entirely different from that reported by the young men—it corresponded precisely with my dream.

Eliza Smith, *Biography and Family Record of Lorenzo Snow*, p. 17.

LORENZO SNOW

"You Have Been Drowned"

The following occurred in Hawaii.

As we were moving along, probably more than a quarter of a mile from where we expected to land, my attention was suddenly arrested by Captain Fisher calling to the oarsmen in a voice which denoted some alarm, "Hurry up, hurry up!" I immediately discovered the cause of the alarm. A short distance behind us I saw an immense surf, thirty or forty feet high, rushing towards us swifter than a race horse. We had scarcely a moment for reflection before the huge mass was upon us. In an instant our boat, with its contents, as though it were a feather, was hurled into a gulf of briny waters, and all was under this rolling, seething mountain wave. It took me by surprise. I think, however, that I comprehended the situation—in the midst of turbulent waves—a quarter of a mile from the shore, without much probability of human aid.

I felt confident, however, there would be some way of escape—that the Lord would provide the means—for it was not possible that my life and mission were thus to terminate. This reliance on the Lord banished fear and inspired me up to the last moment of consciousness. In such extreme cases of excitement, we seem to live hours in a minute, and volume of thoughts crowd themselves into one single moment. It was so with me in that perilous scene.

Having been somewhat subject to faint, I think that after a few moments in the water I must have fainted, as I did not suffer that pain common in the experience of drowning persons. I had been in the water only a few moments until I lost consciousness. The first I knew afterwards, I was on shore, receiving the kind and tender attention of my brethren.

The first recollection I had of returning consciousness was that of a small light—the smallest imaginable. This soon disappeared, and I was again in total darkness. Again it appeared much larger than before, then sank away and left me, as before, in forgetfulness. Thus it continued to come and go, until, finally, I recognized, as I thought, persons whispering, and soon after I asked in a feeble whisper, "What is the matter?" I immediately recognized the voice of Elder Cluff as he replied, "You have been drowned; the boat upset in the surf." Quick as lightning the scene of our disaster flashed upon my mind. I immediately asked, "Are you brethren all safe?" The emotion that was awakened in my bosom by the answer of Elder Cluff, will remain with me as long as life continues: "Brother Snow, we are all safe." I rapidly recovered, and very soon was able to walk and accompany the brethren to our lodgings."

LeRoi C. Snow, "Thou Shalt Have Long Life," *Improvement Era*, 44 (Oct. 1941): 630.

"The Gentleman Seemed Struck with Amazement"

On one occasion (having been joined by Brother A. Butterfield) I called at a hotel for our night's lodging. . . . As we approached the house, we saw the landlord standing upon the porch. Accosting him, I told him we were Mormon preachers, traveling as the elders in former times, and asked him if he would be so kind as to accommodate us with supper and a night's lodging. He very gruffly refused, saying that he kept travelers for their money—not for gospel pay, and advised us to go home, get employment, earn money, then give him a call, and he would be happy to entertain us. I replied that inasmuch as he had met our request with a decided refusal, we would bid him a good evening. But as I was turning to go, it forcibly occurred to me to say something further. Therefore, I said to him, "My friend, it is not our wish to crowd ourselves upon you, but we think it might be well for you to know the fact that two servants of God have called upon you for a supper and a night's lodging, which you have thought proper to refuse. The future results of what you have done you do not *now* know; but we know, and a time will come when you also will know. When that scripture is fulfilled which says, 'When the Son of Man shall come in his glory, and all the holy angels with him, then shall he sit upon the throne of his glory: and before him shall be gathered all nations: and he shall separate them as a shepherd divideth his sheep from the goats. Then shall the King say unto them on his right hand, Come ye blessed of my Father, inherit the kingdom prepared for you from the foundation of the world, for I was hungry, and ye fed me; I was thirsty, and ye gave me drink; I was a stranger, and ye took me in; naked, and ye clothed me. Then shall the righteous say, Lord, when saw we hungry and fed Thee? Or when saw we

Thee a stranger and took Thee in? Then shall the King say to them, Inasmuch as ye have done it unto the least of these my brethren, ye have done it unto me.' When this event takes place, you will then know that we were servants of God commissioned to preach his Gospel; and when engaged in this work, we asked you to administer to our necessities, and you turned us away. This is all I wish to say; we will now go. Good night."

The gentleman seemed struck with amazement and at a loss what to say or do. We had not proceeded far, however, before our ears were saluted with, "Stop, gentlemen, hold on. Turn back, gentlemen, walk in, walk in." Of course, we turned back and walked in, and were invited to sit down to a good supper, after which the neighbors were called in, who, with the landlord and family, listened attentively with apparent interest to our preaching. We had excellent lodging and a good breakfast in the morning, and left without a question whether we had money or not.

Eliza Smith, *Biography and Family Record of Lorenzo Snow*, pp. 17-19.

LORENZO SNOW

"Brother Snow, That Is True Gospel Doctrine"

In the spring of 1840, just before leaving on his first mission to England, Lorenzo Snow spent an evening in the home of his friend Elder H. G. Sherwood, in Nauvoo. Elder Sherwood was endeavoring to explain the parable of the Savior about the husbandman who sent forth servants at different hours of the day to labor in the vineyard. While thus engaged in thought this most important event occurred, as told by President Snow himself.

"While attentively listening to his (Elder Sherwood's) explanation, the Spirit of the Lord rested mightily upon me; the eyes of my understanding were opened, and I saw as clear as the sun at noon-day, with wonder and astonishment, the pathway of God and man. I formed the following couplet which expresses the revelation as it was shown to me, and explains Father Smith's dark saying to me at a blessing meeting in the Kirtland temple, prior to my baptism, as previously mentioned in my first interview with the Patriarch:

> As man now is, God once was:
> As God now is, man may be.

"I felt this to be a sacred communication which I related to no one except my sister Eliza, until I reached England, when in a confidential, private conversation with President Brigham Young in Manchester, I related to him this extraordinary manifestation."

Soon after his return from England, in January, 1843, Lorenzo Snow related to the Prophet Joseph Smith his experience in Elder Sherwood's home. This was in a confidential interview in Nauvoo. The Prophet's reply was: "Brother Snow, that is true gospel doctrine, and it is a revelation from God to you."

Let us understand clearly that while Lorenzo Snow, through a revelation from God, was the author of the above couplet expression, the Lord had revealed this great truth to the Prophet and to Father Smith long before it was made known to Lorenzo Snow. In fact, it was the remarkable promise given to him in the Kirtland Temple, in 1836, by the Patriarch that first awakened the thought in his mind, and its expression in the frequently quoted couplet was not revealed to President Snow until the spring of 1840. We cannot emphasize the fact too strongly that this revealed truth impressed Lorenzo Snow more than perhaps all else; it sank so deeply into his soul that it became the inspiration of his life and gave him his broad vision of his own great future and the mighty mission and work of the Church.

LeRoi C. Snow, "Devotion to a Divine Inspiration," *Improvement Era*, 22 (June 1919): 656.

LORENZO SNOW

"President Snow Said I Would Not Die"

As told by Andrew May of Rockland, Idaho (1939).

I was born February 22, 1871, at Call's Fort, north of Brigham City, in Box Elder County, Utah, and I was living there in 1894. I was twenty-three years of age. During June of this year, I was stacking hay for Thad Wight. It was about eleven a.m. in the forenoon, and Conrad Nelson was running the Jackson fork. The hay was green. A load came up, and I called for Nelson to trip it. And I thought the fork had gone over me. As I raised up the long fork tine struck me in the back and went right through my body. The tine broke my ribs and pushed the bones through my breast.

Hyrum G. Smith (late Patriarch of the Church) was working across the fence and was one of the first to reach me. He helped carry me on a sheet into Brother Wight's house. They sent to Brigham City for Dr. Carrington, who arrived about five p.m. He just looked over me, probed the wound, took some blood out of my lungs through my breast and said, "Tom Yates, there is no use doing anything for a dead man . . . He will not need anything more. I cannot do anything for him."

They carried me over to my own home, then my mother-in-law came; she put her hand on my breast. I became semiconscious and everything seemed like a dream. I could not remember anything during the night. Dr. Carrington said, "If he should live he will not amount to anything because he will never get well and will be subject to all kinds of diseases and will have a weak lung and system." He said he could do nothing for me and then went back to Brigham City.

President Lorenzo Snow was in Brigham City, and the next morning he heard of my accident . . . and came to our house to see me. He and my father were very close friends. He came in, looked me over, and my wife asked him to administer to me. Instead of doing so he stood by the bedside and asked if I had been anointed. He was told that I had. He then put his hands on my head and gave me a wonderful blessing. The doctor said I was going to die, but President Snow said to me I would not die, but that I would live just as long as life was desirable unto me.

Romney, *The Life of Lorenzo Snow*, pp. 395-97.

LORENZO SNOW

"He Called Me Back"

As told by Lorenzo Snow's son LeRoi C. Snow.

For several long weeks Ella Jensen had lingered, almost between life and death, with scarlet fever. In order to relieve the tired parents from their weary hours of loving care, the kind neighbors took turns in staying at the Jensen home overnight to help look after the sick girl.

[After being visited at about four o'clock in the morning by her dead uncle, who informed her that messengers would come at ten o'clock to conduct her into the spirit world, Ella continued to grow weaker.]

Towards ten o'clock, Uncle Jake, the father, who was holding his daughter's hand, felt the pulse become very weak. A few moments later he turned to his wife saying: "Althea, she is dead; her pulse has stopped." The heartbroken parents wept and grieved at the loss of their beautiful daughter.

"We talked the matter over and wondered what we should

do. I told my wife that I would go to town, more than a mile from home, and see President Snow, tell him about her death and have him arrange for the funeral.

"I went out to the barn, hitched up, and drove to the tabernacle where your father, President Lorenzo Snow, whom we all loved so much, was in meeting. I went into the vestry, behind the main hall, wrote a note and had it sent to your father, who was speaking to the congregation. When the note was placed upon the pulpit, President Snow stopped his talking, read the note, and then explained to the Saints that it was a call to visit some people who were in deep sorrow and asked to be excused.

"President Snow came into the vestry, and after I told him what had happened he meditated a moment or two and then said: 'I will go down with you.' Just as we were about to leave, President Snow stopped me, saying: 'Wait a moment, I wish you would go into the meeting and get Brother Clawson. I want him to go also.' President Clawson was then the president of the Box Elder Stake."

President Rudger Clawson . . . being invited by President Snow to go along, says:

"As we entered the home we met Sister Jensen, who was very much agitated and alarmed. We came to Ella's bedside and were impressed by the thought that her spirit had passed out of the body and gone beyond.

"Turning to me President Snow said: 'Brother Clawson, will you anoint her.' Which I did. We then laid our hands upon her head and the anointing was confirmed by President Snow, who blessed her and among other things, used this very extraordinary expression, in a commanding tone of voice, 'Come back, Ella, come back. Your work upon the earth is not yet completed, come back.' Shortly afterward we left the home."

Uncle Jake, Ella's father, continues his account: "After President Snow had finished the blessing, he turned to my wife and me and said, 'Now do not mourn or grieve any more. It will be all right.' "

As already stated, it was ten o'clock in the morning when Ella died. It was towards noon when Jacob Jensen reported to

President Snow at the tabernacle service, and not long after twelve o'clock, noon, when President Snow and President Clawson left the home after the administration.

Uncle Jake says that he and his wife remained at the bedside. The news of the death spread about the city. Friends continued to call at the home, express their sympathy to the sorrowing parents, and leave. Continuing in Uncle Jake's words:

"Ella remained in this condition for more than an hour after President Snow administered to her, or more than three hours in all after she died. We were sitting there watching by the bedside, her mother and myself, when all at once she opened her eyes. She looked about the room, saw us sitting there, but still looked for someone else. And the first thing she said was: 'Where is he? Where is he?' We asked, 'Who? Where is who?' 'Why, Brother Snow,' she replied. 'He called me back.'"

LeRoi C. Snow, "Raised from the Dead," *Improvement Era*, 22 (Sept. 1929): 881-86, 972-80.

LORENZO SNOW

"The Lord Jesus Christ Appeared"

For some time President Woodruff's health had been failing. Nearly every evening President Lorenzo Snow visited him at his home. This particular evening the doctors said that President Woodruff could not live much longer, that he was becoming weaker every day. President Snow was greatly worried.

My father went to his room in the Salt Lake Temple,

dressed in his robes of the priesthood, knelt at the sacred altar in the Holy of Holies in the House of the Lord, and there plead to the Lord to spare President Woodruff's life, that President Woodruff might outlive him, and that the great responsibility of Church leadership would not fall upon his shoulders. Yet he promised the Lord that he would devotedly perform any duty required at his hands. At this time he was in his eighty-sixth year.

Soon after this President Woodruff was taken to California, where he died Friday morning at 6:40 o'clock, September 2, 1898. President George Q. Cannon at once wired the information to the President's office in Salt Lake City. The telegram was delivered to him on the street in Brigham. He read it to President Rudger Clawson, then president of Box Elder Stake, who was with him, went to the telegraph office, and replied that he would leave on the train about 5:30 that evening. He reached Salt Lake City about 7:15, proceeded to the President's office, gave some instructions, and then went to his private room in the Salt Lake Temple.

President Snow put on his holy temple robes, repaired again to the same sacred altar, offered up the signs of the Priesthood, and poured out his heart to the Lord. He reminded the Lord how he plead for President Woodruff's life to be spared, that President Woodruff's days would be lengthened beyond his own, that he might never be called upon to bear the heavy burdens and responsibilities of the Church. "Nevertheless," he said, "Thy will be done. I have not sought this responsibility, but if it be Thy will, I now present myself before Thee for Thy guidance and instruction. I ask that Thou show me what Thou wouldst have me do."

After finishing his prayer he expected a reply, some special manifestation from the Lord. So he waited—and waited—and waited. There was no reply, no voice, no visitation, no manifestation. He left the altar and the room in great disappointment. Passing through the Celestial room and out into the large corridor, a glorious manifestation was given President Snow which I relate in the words of his granddaughter, Allie Young Pond:

One evening while I was visiting Grandpa Snow in his room in the Salt Lake Temple, I remained until the door keepers had gone and the night-watchmen had not yet come in, so grandpa said he would take me to the main front entrance and let me out that way. He got his bunch of keys from his dresser. After we left his room, and while we were still in the large corridor leading into the celestial room, I was walking several steps ahead of grandpa when he stopped and said: "Wait a moment, Allie, I want to tell you something. It was right here that the Lord Jesus Christ appeared to me at the time of the death of President Woodruff. He instructed me to go right ahead and reorganize the First Presidency of the Church at once and not wait as had been done after the death of the previous presidents, and that I was to succeed President Woodruff."

Then grandpa came a step nearer and held out his left hand and said: "He stood right here, about three feet above the floor. It looked as though he stood on a plate of solid gold."

Grandpa told me what a glorious personage the Savior is and described his hands, feet, countenance and beautiful white robes, all of which were of such a glory of whiteness and brightness that he could hardly gaze upon him.

Then he came another step nearer and put his right hand on my head and said: "Now granddaughter, I want you to remember that this is the testimony of your grandfather, that he told you with his own lips that he actually saw the Savior, here in the temple, and talked with him face to face."

LeRoi C. Snow, "An Experience of My Father's," *Improvement Era*, 36 (Sept. 1933): 677.

LORENZO SNOW

"Now I Know Why I Came to St. George"

President Snow, after his call to the presidency, humbly admitted that he did not know just what he would do; but he was confident that the Lord would show him, and he placed such dependence upon the promptings of God's spirit, and was so sure that he would follow those instructions that he said: "My administration will not be known as mine, but as God's administration through me."

The day after President John Taylor's funeral, proceedings for the confiscation of Church property were begun in the United States Court (because of plural marriage in the Church). All the property of the Church was seized, and for nearly ten years tedious and expensive litigation continued. Then, too, for several years the General Authorities had been compelled by prosecution under the Edmunds-Tucker Law, to remain from home. Therefore, during this period, the business interests of the Church suffered greatly.

These are but two of the several contributing causes which brought about serious financial distress. . . . I well remember my father's approaching his personal clerk, James Jack, with the warning, "Brother Jack, we must raise some money. Go through all the securities we have and see if you can find something we can sell to make some money."

One prominent business man presented a plan to solicit contributions from the entire Church membership. He suggested a "one thousand dollar club" to include all who would contribute one thousand dollars each, a "five hundred dollar club," etc., but President Snow shook his head and said: "No, that is not the Lord's plan." The Lord had not yet shown his servant just how the problem was to be solved, but he revealed the plan a little later.

One morning my father said he was going to St. George in Southern Utah. I was much surprised at the thought of his making this long and hard trip. Mother expressed considerable surprise, but asked no questions.

Upon entering the President's office, father informed Secretary George F. Gibbs of the contemplated trip to St. Goerge. Brother Gibbs at once asked how soon President Snow expected to leave and who would be in the party. The reply was that he would leave just as soon as arrangements could be made, and that he would take as many of the General Authorities as could be spared from the important work at home.

President Snow stood the trip exceptionally well, but was very tired on reaching St. George. . . .

He had the most painful and anxious expression on his face that I had ever seen, and he must have been going through intense mental suffering. After pacing up and down the floor several times, he commenced talking aloud as follows: "Why have I come to St. George, and why have I brought so many of the Church authorities, when we are so much needed at home to look after the important affairs of the Church? Haven't I made a mistake? Why have I come here?"

When the Lord instructed his servant to go to St. George, the purpose of the journey was withheld. President Snow answered the call promptly, and then wondered and worried until further light was given.

He finally went to bed and rested very well during the night, appearing to feel very much better the following morning. It was Wednesday, May 17, the day on which the general conference opened in the tabernacle in St. George. It was during one of these meetings that President Snow received the revelation on tithing. I was sitting at a table on the stand, recording the proceedings, when all at once father paused in his discourse.

Complete stillness filled the room. I shall never forget the thrill as long as I live. When he commenced to speak again his voice strengthened, and the inspiration of God seemed to come over him, as well as over the entire assembly. His eyes seemed to brighten and his countenance to radiate. He was filled with unusual power. Then he revealed to the Latter-day Saints the vision that was before him.

God manifested to him there and then not only the purpose of the call to visit the Saints in the South, but also Lorenzo Snow's special mission, the great work for which God had prepared and preserved him. And he revealed the vision to the people. He told them that he could see, as he had never realized before, how the law of tithing had been neglected by the people; also that the Saints themselves were heavily in debt, as well as the Church. And now through strict obedience to this law—the paying of a full and honest tithing—not only would the Church be relieved of its great indebtedness, but through the blessings of the Lord this would also be the means of freeing the Latter-day Saints from their individual obligations. And they would become a prosperous people.

Directly on tithing President Snow said:

"The word of the Lord is: The time has now come for every Latter-day Saint, who calculates to be prepared for the future and to hold his feet strong upon a proper foundation, to do the will of the Lord and to pay his tithing in full. That is the word of the Lord to you, and it will be the word of the Lord to every settlement throughout the land of Zion."

President Snow then referred to the terrible drought which had continued so severely for three years in the South. The Virgin River and all its tributaries were virtually dry.

President Snow said:

"All through Dixie we found everything dying out. The stock were dying by hundreds; we could see them as we traveled along, many of them being nothing but skin and bones, and many lying down never I suppose to get up again."

In speaking of these serious drought conditions President Snow told the people that if they would observe the law of tithing from then on, and pay a full and honest tithing, that they might go ahead, plough their land and plant the seed. And he promised them, in the name of the Lord, that the clouds would gather, the rains from heaven descend, their lands would be drenched and the rivers and ditches filled, and they would reap a bounteous harvest that very season.

Many of the people had become so discouraged that they were not willing to risk the seeds of another planting, and many had not even ploughed their fields. Cattle everywhere were dying, and the country was parched. It was now getting very late in the planting season in that southern country, and here the prophet of the Lord made this wonderful prediction. Everyone present in that vast congregation knew that he was speaking under the inspiration of the Holy Spirit.

That evening, father, mother, and I were again in the room together and father walked up and down the floor as he had done the previous night, but there was a sweet expression of happiness and joy on his face. He talked aloud again, as he did the night before, and this is what he said:

"Now I know why I came to St. George. The Lord sent me here, and he has a great work for me to perform. There is no mistake about it. I can see the great future for the Church, and I can hardly wait to get back to Salt Lake City to commence the great work."

When the returning party reached Nephi, where we were to take train for home, President Snow called the members all together in a meeting which will never be forgotten by those who were present. He commissioned every one present to be his special witness to the fact that the Lord had given this revelation to him. He put all the party under covenant and promise not only to obey the law of tithing themselves, but also that each would bear witness to this special manifestation and would spread the tithing message at every opportunity. He made wonderful promises to those who would be faithful to these admonitions. He was filled with great power and inspiration and spoke with such feeling that Elder Francis M. Lyman says in his journal: "I was almost overcome, could hardly control my feelings. . . ."

President Snow, with his party, returned to Salt Lake City, Saturday, May 27, 1899. During his absence of eleven days, he visited sixteen settlements, held twenty-four meetings, delivered twenty-six addresses.

President Snow gathered and compiled data regarding the tithes being paid by the people, but kept especially in mind the Saints in the south. He called for a daily report showing the exact amount of tithing received from those settlements. I well remember handing him one of these reports. After looking it over carefully he said, "Wonderful, wonderful. The good people in Dixie are not only paying one-tenth of their income, but they must be giving all they have to the Lord's work!"

But the rains did not come, and the drought was not broken. President Snow had the daily weather report placed on his desk, which he carefully looked over; but there was no indication of any storms moving in the direction of the south. Week after week passed, and the only word was that southern Utah was burning up under the hot weather, and there seemed to be no prospect of any change.

One morning, as I was going up the stairway leading to father's bedroom, I was surprised to hear him talking to someone. I did not know that anyone had preceded me to the room that morning, but not wanting to disturb him, I walked quietly down the heavily carpeted stairway leading to his room. The door was open as I reached it. There I saw an aged, gray-haired prophet, down on his knees before his bedside in the manner of praying, but seemingly talking to the Lord as if he might have been right in his very presence. He was pouring out his heart and pleading for the Saints in the south. I stood at the open door for a few moments and heard him say:

"Oh Lord, why didst thou make those promises to the good people in St. George if they are not to be fulfilled? Thou didst promise them, if they would accept the command to obey the law of tithing thou wouldst send the rains from heaven and bless them with a bounteous harvest. These good people accepted Thy word and are not only paying a tenth of their income, but they are offering all they have to thee. Do keep thy promise and vindicate the words of thy servant through whom thou didst speak."

I could not bear to hear any more. I turned from the door with my heart bleeding and went down the stairs.

When father came into his office that morning, I noticed that he looked discouraged and seemed to have little interest in his work. There was no report of rain in St. George. Several days passed. One day there was a knock at the door. Brother Gibbs the secretary, being near, answered the call. It was a messenger boy with a telegram. I signed for it, opened the telegram and as I was approaching father's desk I could see on the face of the telegram: "Rain in St. George." I was so happy I could not wait, but cried out: "Father, they have had rain in St. George."

"Read it, my boy, read it," he said, and I read the telegram telling of a great rain that had come to the people there, filling the river and its tributaries and the canals and reaching the entire country.

Father took the telegram from my hand, read it very slowly, and after a few moments, got up from his desk and left the office. A little while afterwards I followed him into the house and asked mother where he was. When she told me she had not seen him, I knew he must have gone to his room. I walked quietly up the stairway and before reaching the top I heard him talking, as I had on the other occasion. I went to his room and there he was again, down on his knees pouring out his heart in gratitude and thanksgiving to the Lord. He said:

"Father, what can I do to show my appreciation for the blessing which thou hast given to the good people in St. George? Thou hast fulfilled thy promise to them and vindicated the words spoken through thy servant. Do show me some special thing I can do to prove my love for thee."

This faithful servant of the Lord, who had devoted all his long life in beautiful and unwavering service to God, felt that he had not done enough and wanted to do more. There he was in the presence of his Heavenly Father, overcome with joy and happiness. The last words I heard, as I was returning down the stairs, were: "Thou canst not ask anything of me that I am not willing to do, even though it be the offering of my life, to prove my love for thee."

When father returned to his office, his face was filled with happiness, and I am very sure that his heart was lightened and his difficult task made much easier.

During the MIA conference in 1899, at one of the officers' meetings, President Snow spoke on tithing. At the conclusion of his address the following resolution was presented by Elder B. H. Roberts:

"Resolved: That we accept the doctrine of tithing, as now presented by President Snow, as the present word and will of the Lord unto us, and we do accept it with all our hearts; we will ourselves observe it, and we will do all in our power to get the Latter-day Saints to do likewise."

LeRoi C. Snow, "The Lord's Way out of Bondage," *Improvement Era*, 41 (July 1938): 400-1, 439-42.

Biographical Sketch

JOSEPH F. SMITH

The year was 1844. Hyrum Smith was riding at the side of his Brother, the Prophet Joseph Smith. They stopped by a little six-year-old boy, Hyrum's son, Joseph F. Smith. His father didn't dismount. He reached down and swept him up in his strong arms, held him close, kissed him, and lowered him back to the street, and then they rode on to carthage.

Joseph F. also remembered being awakened in the night by a rapping on the window. As he awoke, he heard someone say, "Sister Smith, your husband has been killed." He never forgot coming into the mansion house so he could see the faces of his father and the Prophet Joseph as they lay in their coffins.[1]

Joseph Fielding Smith (known throughout his life as Joseph F. Smith) was born in Far West in 1838. While he was an infant his mother, Mary Fielding Smith, herself very weak and ill, went to visit his father, Hyrum Smith, in the Liberty Jail where he was confined for nearly six months.

Although Joseph Fielding was only six when his father, assistant President and Presiding Patriarch of the Church was

---

[1]Preston Nibley, *Presidents of the Church*, pp. 28-29.

martyred, he remembered him well and throughout his life. His favorite Church hymns were the ones his father had taught him.

And what a noble father he had. He stood next to the Prophet Joseph Smith in the kingdom of God and in life. The prophet said of his devoted brother on one occasion:

> There was Brother Hyrum who next took me by the hand—a natural brother. Thought I to myself, Brother Hyrum what a faithful heart you have got! O may the Eternal Jehovah crown eternal blessings upon your heart, as a reward for the care you have had for my soul! O how many are sorrows we have shared together; and again we find ourselves shackled with the unrelenting hand of oppression. Hyrum, thy name shall be written in the book of the law of the Lord, for those who come after thee to look upon, that they may pattern after thy works.[2]

The last words of Joseph on this occasion are prophetic and interesting in that Hyrum's own Son, who grew to love and honor the name "Joseph" would be one to pattern his own life after the life and works of his father.

When just nine years old, he assumed the role of a man and assisted his mother in moving to Salt Lake City from Winter Quarters by driving two yoke of oxen with a heavy loaded wagon the entire distance.[3]

Before Joseph F. turned fourteen, his mother died. No finer woman has ever lived in this Church; her courage is legend. At fifteen, he was ordained an elder, received his temple endowments, and departed for a mission in the Hawaiian Islands.

He prayed fervently that the Lord would bless him that he might be able to speak the language. In just over three months, he could speak the language fluently.

After nearly four years, he was called by President Young to return to Utah because of the threat of the approaching United States Army.

After more than a year's service defending the Saints during the Utah War, young Joseph F. was given a job in the

---

[2]*History of the Church,* 5:107-108.
[3]Joseph Fielding Smith, *Gospel Doctrine* (Salt Lake City: Deseret Book Co., 1968), p. 529.

Church Historian's office. When he was twenty-seven, he was ordained an apostle by President Brigham Young and was called to also serve as a counselor to the First Presidency.

When John Taylor became the President of the Church, he selected Joseph F. Smith as his second counselor, and Lorenzo Snow also chose him for the same position. Upon the death of President Snow, Joseph F. Smith became the Prophet, Seer, and Revelator. How remarkable that the young son of Hyrum would grow up to be a counselor to four great presidents, all of whom had been closely associated with Hyrum Smith in the leading counsels of the Church, and then became the President of the Church himself.

President Wilford Woodruff during his life observed the son of Hyrum carefully and in 1866 wrote the following in his journal:

> Joseph F. Smith spoke an hour and fifteen minutes, and the power of God was upon him. He manifested the same spirit that was upon his uncle Joseph Smith, the Prophet, and upon his father, Hyrum Smith.[4]

Wilford Woodruff prophesied twenty years before Joseph F. Smith became President of the Church that he would be called to occupy that position. Following is an account of that prophecy:

> Elder Woodruff interested the children by speaking of incidents in the life of the Prophet Joseph Smith and of his labors. He then turned to Elder Joseph F. Smith and asked him to arise to his feet. Elder Smith complied. "Look at him, children," Wilford Woodruff said, "for he resembles the Prophet Joseph more than any man living. He will become the President of The Church of Jesus Christ of Latter-day Saints. I want you, everyone of you, to remember what I have told you this morning."[5]

As President Smith stood to give his opening address in April conference in 1916, he said:

> . . . I feel sure that the Prophet Joseph Smith and his associates, who, under the guidance and inspiration of the almighty, and by his power began this latter-day work, would rejoice and do rejoice. I was going to say if they were permitted to look down upon the scene that I beheld in this tabernacle, but I believe they do have the privilege of looking down upon

---

[4]Cowley, *Wilford Woodruff*, p. 445.
[5]*Ibid.*, pp. 535-36.

us as the all-seeing eye of God beholds every part of his handiwork. For I believe that those who have been chosen in this dispensation and in former dispensations, to lay the foundation of God's work in the midst of the children of men for their salvation and exaltation, will not be deprived in the spirit world from looking down upon the results of their own labors. . . .

I have a feeling in my heart that I stand in the presence not only of the Father and of the Son, but in the presence of those whom God commissioned, raised up, and inspired to lay the foundations of the work in which we are engaged.

I thank God for the feeling that I possess and enjoy and for the realization that I have, that I stand, not only in the presence of Almighty God, my Maker and Father, but in the presence of His Only Begotten Son in the flesh, the Savior of the world; and I stand in the presence of Peter and James (and perhaps the eyes of John are also upon us and we know it not), *and that I stand in the presence of Joseph and Hyrum and Brigham and John,* and those who have been valiant in the testimony of Jesus Christ and faithful to their mission in the world, who have gone before. When I go, I want to have the privilege of meeting them with the consciousness that I have followed their example, that I have carried out the mission in which they were engaged as they would have it carried out; that I have been as faithful in the discharge of duty committed to me and required at my hand as they were faithful in their time, and that when I meet them I shall meet them as I met them here, in love, in harmony, in unison, and in perfect confidence that I have done theirs.

I hope you will forgive me for my emotion. You would have peculiar emotions, would you not, if you felt that you stood in the presence of your Father, in the very presence of Almighty God, in the very presence of the Son of God and of holy angels? You would feel rather emotional, rather sensitive; I feel it to the very depths of my soul this moment. So I hope you will forgive me, if I exhibit some of my real feelings."[6]

What a beautiful, touching and dramatic moment as the son of Hyrum, who saw his father last when he was just six years old, stands filled with emotions in the presence of heavenly beings including his own great father, whom he has not seen for more than seventy years; and what honor he had brought to his father, Hyrum, and his uncle, the Prophet Joseph Smith.

Joseph F. Smith, one who served as an apostle and a counselor to four great presidents, then stood at the head of the Church himself for seventeen years.

President Joseph F. Smith died on November 19, 1918,

---

[6]*Conference Report*, April, 1916, pp. 1-4; italics added.

just eleven days after the close of World War I. He was eighty years of age.

At this time an influenza epidemic was sweeping the country. Consequently, no public funeral was held, yet many saints echoed in their hearts the words uttered at the graveside by President Heber J. Grant: "I loved Joseph F. Smith as I never loved any other man that I have ever known. May God bless his memory."[7]

Shortly after President Joseph F. Smith died, Charles W. Nibley, a life-long friend and associate, among other things said the following about him:

As a preacher of righteousness, who could compare with him? He was the greatest that I ever heard—strong, powerful, clear, appealing. It was marvelous how the words of living light and fire flowed from him.[8]

I have visited at his home when one of his children was down sick. I have seen him come home from his work at night tired, as he naturally would be, and yet he would walk the floor for hours with that little one in his arms . . . loving it, encouraging it in every way. . . .[9]

Never was man more moral and chaste and virtuous to the last fiber of his being than he. Against all forms or thoughts of licentiousness, he was set, and as immovable as a mountain.[10]

How fitting that his son, his namesake, should bring additional honor to his great name.

Joseph F. Smith lived as he taught. He did not ask anything of the Latter-day Saints that he was not practicing himself.

He stressed love, kindness, and a personal testimony, but these things could never be a substitute for diligence, study, and knowledge. He asked for excellence in all areas, and he himself stood as an example of excellence.

He was a noble man and an exceptional prophet-leader.

---

[7]*Church History as Viewed Through the Lives of the Presidents of the Church,* student supplement, Seminaries and Institutes of Religion, 1969, p. 59.

[8]Joseph F. Smith, *Gospel Doctrine,* p. 522.

[9]*Ibid.,* p. 523.

[10]*Ibid.,* p. 524.

JOSEPH F. SMITH

"The Lord's Hand Was in It"

I can remember the time when I was quite a little boy, when we were hurried very unceremoniously across the river Mississippi from the city of Nauvoo just previous to the bombardment of the town by the mob. I had a great anxiety then—that is for a child—to know where on earth we were going to. I knew we had left home. We had left it willingly—because we were obliged to—we left it in a hurry, and we were not far away when we heard the cannonade on the other side of the river; but I felt just as certain in my mind then—as certain as a child could feel—that all was right, that the Lord's hand was in it, as I do today. My feelings have been the same from that day to this.

Joseph F. Smith in *Journal of Discourses*, 24:151.

JOSEPH F. SMITH

"Well, Mary, the Cattle Are Gone"

We camped one evening in an open prairie on the Missouri River bottoms, by the side of a small spring creek which emptied into the river about three quarters of a mile from us. We were in plain sight of the river and could apparently see over every foot of the little open prairie where we were camped, to the river on the southwest, to the bluffs on the northwest, and to the timber which skirted the prairie on the right and left. Camping nearby, on the other side of the creek, were some men with a herd of beef cattle. . . . We usually unyoked our oxen and turned them loose to feed during our encampments at night, but this time, on account of the proximity of this herd of cattle, fearing that they might get mixed up and driven off with them, we turned our oxen out to feed in their yokes. Next morning when we came to look them up, to our great disappointment our best yoke of oxen was not to be found. Uncle Fielding [Joseph Fielding] and I spent all the morning, well nigh until noon, hunting for them, but to no avail. The grass was tall, and in the morning was wet with heavy dew. Tramping through this grass and through the woods and over the bluff, we were soaked to the skin, fatigued, disheartened, and almost exhausted. In this pitiable plight I was the first to return to our wagons, and as I approached I saw my mother kneeling down to prayer. I halted for a moment and then drew gently near enough to hear her pleading with the Lord not to suffer us to be left in this helpless condition, but to lead us to recover our lost team, that we might continue our travels in safety. When she arose from her knees I was standing nearby. The first expression I caught upon her precious face was a lovely smile which, discouraged as I was, gave me renewed hope and an assurance I had not felt before. A few moments later Uncle Joseph Fielding came to the camp, wet with the dews, faint, fatigued, and thoroughly disheartened. His first words were: "Well, Mary, the cattle are gone!"

Mother replied in a voice which fairly rang with cheerfulness, "Never mind; your breakfast has been waiting for hours, and now, while you and Joseph are eating, I will just take a walk out and see if I can find the cattle."

My uncle held up his hands in blank astonishment, and if the Missouri River had suddenly turned to run upstream, neither of us could have been much more surprised. "Why, Mary," he exclaimed, "what do you mean? We have been all over this country, all through the timber and through the herd of cattle, and our oxen are gone—they are not to be found. I believe they have been driven off, and it is useless for you to attempt to do such a thing as to hunt for them."

"Never mind me," said mother; "get your breakfast and I will see," and she started towards the river, following down spring creek. Before she was out of speaking distance the man in charge of the herd of beef cattle rode up from the opposite side of the creek and called out: "Madam, I saw your oxen over in that direction about daybreak," pointing in the opposite direction from that in which mother was going. We heard plainly what he said, but mother went right on and did not even turn her head to look at him. A moment later the man rode off rapidly toward his herd, which had been gathered in the opening near the edge of the woods, and they were soon under full drive for the road leading toward Savannah and soon disappeared from view. My mother continued straight down the little stream of water, until she stood almost on the bank of the river. And then she beckoned to us. I was watching her every moment and was determined that she should not get out of my sight. Instantly we rose from the "mess-chest" on which our breakfast had been spread and started toward her. And like John, who outran the other disciple to the sepulchre, I outran my uncle and came first to the spot where my mother stood. There I saw our oxen fastened to a clump of willows growing in the bottom of a deep gulch which had been washed out of the sandy bank of the river by the little spring creek, perfectly concealed from view. We were not long in releasing them from bondage and getting back to our camp, where the other cattle had been fastened to the wagon wheels all the morning. And we were soon on our way home rejoicing.

Joseph Fielding Smith, *Life of Joseph F. Smith* (Salt Lake City: Deseret Book Co., 1938), pp. 131-33.

→→→

JOSEPH F. SMITH

"The Indians Overtook Me"

One bright morning in company with my companions—namely, Alden Burdick, almost a young man grown and a very sober, steady boy; Thomas Burdick, about my own age, but a little older; and Isaac Blocksome, a little younger than myself—I started out with my cattle, comprising the cows, and young stock, and several yoke of oxen which were unemployed that day, to go to the herd grounds about one and a half or two miles from the town (Winter Quarters). We had two horses, both belonging to the Burdicks, and a young pet jack belonging to me. Alden proposed to take it afoot through the hazel and some small woods by a side road and gather some hazel nuts for the crowd while we took out the cattle, and we would meet at the spring on the herd ground. This arrangement just suited us, for we felt when Alden was away we were free from all restraint; his presence, he being the oldest, restrained us, for he was very sedate and operated as an extinguisher upon our exuberance of youthful feelings. I was riding Alden's bay mare, Thomas, his father's black pony, and Isaac, my jack. On the way we had some sport with "Ike" and the jack, which plagued "Ike" so badly that he left us with disgust, turning the jack loose with the bridle on. And he went home. When Thomas and I arrived at the spring we set down our dinner pails, mounted our horses, and amused ourselves by running short races and jumping the horses across ditches, Alden not having arrived as yet. While we were thus amusing ourselves, our cattle were feeding along down the little spring creek towards a rolling point about half a mile distant. The leaders of the herd had stretched out about half-way to this point, when all of a sudden a gang of Indians, stripped to the breechclout, painted and daubed and on horseback, came charging at full speed from behind this point, towards us.

Thomas Burdick immediately started for home, crying "Indians!" "Indians!" Before he reached the top of the hill, however, for some cause he abandoned his pony, turning it loose with bridle and rope, or lariat, attached. My first impression, or impulse, was to save the cattle from being driven off, for in a most incredibly short time I thought of going to the valley; of our dependence upon our cattle, and the sorrow of being compelled to remain at Winter Quarters. I suited the action to the thought and at full speed dashed out to head the cattle and, if possible, turn them toward home. I reached the van of the herd just as the greater number of Indians did. Two Indians had passed me, in pursuit of Thomas. I wheeled my horse in almost one bound and shouted at the cattle which, mingled with the whoops of the Indians and the sudden rush of a dozen horses, frightened the cattle and started them on the keen run towards the head of the spring, in the direction of home. As I wheeled I saw the first Indian I met, whom I shall never forget. He was a tall, thin man, riding a light roan horse, very fleet; he had his hair daubed up with stiff white clay. He leaped from his horse and caught Thomas Burdick's, then he jumped on his horse again and started back in the direction he had come. While this was going on the whole gang surrounded me, trying to head me off, but they did not succeed until I reached the head of the spring, with the whole herd under full stampede ahead of me, taking the lower road to town, the road that Alden had taken in the morning. Here my horse was turned around at the head of the spring, and down the stream I went at full speed till I reached a point opposite the hill, where other Indians had concentrated and I was met at this point by this number of Indians who had crossed the stream to head me off. This turned my horse, and once more I got the lead in the direction of home. I could outrun them, but my horse was getting tired or out of wind and the Indians kept doubling on me, coming in ahead of me and checking my speed, till finally, reaching the head of the spring again, I met, or overtook, a platoon which kept their horses so close together and veering to right and left as I endeavored to dodge them, that I could not force my horse through. I was thus compelled to slacken speed and the Indians behind overtook me. One Indian rode upon the left side and one on the right side of me, and each took me by an arm and leg and lifted me from my horse; they then slackened their speed until my horse ran from under me, then they chucked me down with great violence to the ground. Several horses from behind jumped over me, but did not hurt me. My horse was secured by the Indians, and without slacking speed they rode on in the direction from whence they had come. About this moment a number of men appeared on the hill with pitchforks in hand, whom Thomas had alarmed with the cry of "Indians!" These men were on their way to the hay field, and at this juncture, as the men appeared on the hill, an Indian who had been trying to catch the jack with corn, made a desperate lunge to catch the animal and was kicked over, spilling his corn, which in his great haste to get away before the men could catch him, he left on the ground. The jack cooly turned and ate the corn, to the amusement of the men on the hill as well as my own.

At this point I thought I better start after Thomas, and as I reached the top of the hill I saw him just going down into the town. The Indians having departed, the men returned with the pitchforks to their wagons and I continued on to the town. When I arrived a large assembly was counseling in the bowery, Thomas having told them of our trouble. My folks were glad to see me, you may be sure. A company was formed and on horses started in pursuit of the Indians, and a second company on foot with Thomas and myself to pilot them, went in pursuit of the cattle. We took the road we had traveled in the morning and went to the spring. In the meantime Alden had arrived at the spring, found nobody there, dinner pails standing as we had left them, became alarmed, took the herd by the lower road and drove them home. We who did not know this hunted most of the day, and, not finding our cattle, we returned home disheartened. And I was filled with fears that we would not now be able to journey to the valley. When we returned home we learned that Alden had found the cattle and they were all home, safely cared for, and so this trouble was soon forgotten. Thomas's horse was recovered, but the one I was riding was not found. It cost the Indians too much for them ever to part with it. I was at this time about nine years of age.

Joseph Fielding Smith, *Life of Joseph F. Smith,* pp. 134-37.

JOSEPH F. SMITH

"Leaving the Company Behind"

After leaving Winter Quarters, we coupled two of our wagons together and hitched one team on the two wagons. Then we started out to cross the plains in that way—by uncoupling the wagons at the bottom of each hill, and pulling one wagon at a time up the hill, then coupling them together again and driving on to the next hill, and so on, till we reached Elk Horn River. This was the place where the Camp of Israel had assembled to fit out for the journey.

The widow, my mother, went to the supervisor, the man in charge of public cattle of the Company, and tried to obtain assistance to go on with the company. But after diagnosing our case, considering the number of wagons we had and the helplessness of the whole company, he very sternly informed the widow that there was no use for her to attempt to cross the plains that year, and advised her to go back to the river, to Winter Quarters, and wait another year, when perhaps she could be helped out.

I am happy to say, the widow had a little mettle in her, and she straightened up and informed the gentleman that she would beat him to the Valley, and would ask no help from him, either, and turned away.

Returning to camp, we unloaded the wagon, took the best two yoke of oxen we had, and the widow and her brothers started back to the Missouri River. Here they succeeded in borrowing and hiring enough cattle to suffice for the journey. Then they returned to the Elk Horn. Strange to say, the widow and her family were assigned to the company of fifty over which the good captain to whom she had applied for help presided, and we journeyed in that way, having a good many troubles and difficulties on the road. . . .

But we finally struck the east side of East Mountains on the Pioneer trail. . . . Our worn-out cattle wearily dragged our heavy wagons up the eastern side of the mountain, and when we reached the summit we obtained a glimpse over the tops of the mountains of the valley and the Great Salt Lake. It was a most delightful sight to some of us! . . .

Early next morning, the captain gave notice to the company to arise, hitch up, and roll over the mountain into the valley.

To our consternation, when we gathered up our cattle, the essential part of our means of transportation for some reason had strayed away and were not to be found with the herd. A brother of mine, who was also a boy scout at that time, then obtained a horse and rode back over the road in search of the lost cattle. The captain ordered the march to begin, and, regardless of our predicament, the company started out up the mountain. The morning sun was then shining . . . without a cloud appearing anywhere.

I had happened to hear the promise of my dear mother

that we would beat the captain into the Valley, and wouldn't ask any help from him, either. I sat in front of the wagon with the teams we had in hand hitched to the wheels, while my brother was absent hunting the others. I saw the company winding its slow way up the hill, the animals struggling to pull their heavy loads. The forward teams now had almost reached the summit of the hill, and I said to myself, "True enough, we come thus far, and we have been blessed, and not the slightest help from anyone has been asked by us." But the last promise seemed to be now impossible, and the last chance of getting into the valley before the rest of our company was vanishing, in my opinion.

You have doubtless heard the descriptions of the terrific thunder storms that sometimes visit the mountains. The pure crystal streams a few moments before flow gently down their channels; but often after one of these rains, in a few minutes they become raging torrents, muddy, and sometimes bringing down fallen trees and roots and rocks.

All of a sudden, and in less time than I am taking now to tell you, a big, dark, heavy cloud arose up from the northwest going directly southeast. In a few minutes it burst in such terrific fury that the cattle could not face the storm, and the captain seemed forced to direct the company to unhitch the teams, turn them loose, and block the wheels to keep the wagons from running back down the hill! The cattle fled before the storm down into the entrance into Parley's Canyon, from the park, into and through the brush.

Luckily, the storm lasted only a short time. As it ceased to rain, and the wind ceased to blow, my brother drove up with our lost cattle. We then hitched them to the wagon, and the question was asked by uncle of my mother:

"Mother, what shall we do? go on, or wait for the company to gather up their teams?" She said: "Joseph (that was her brother's name), they have not waited for us, and I see no necessity for us to wait for them."

So, we hitched up and rolled up the mountain, leaving the company behind. And this was on the twenty-third day of September, 1848.

We reached the Old Fort about 10 o'clock that Saturday

night. The next morning, in the Old Bowery, we had the privilege of listening to President Brigham Young and President Kimball, Erastus Snow, and some others, give some very excellent instructions. Then on the afternoon of that Sunday, we went out and met our friends coming in, very dusty, and very sorefooted and tired.

The prediction of the widow was actually fulfilled; we beat them into the valley, and we asked no help from them, either!"

Joseph F. Smith, "A Plucky Pioneer Mother," *Improvement Era*, 21 (July 1918): 755-58.

◆——◆

JOSEPH F. SMITH

"He Chided My Mother for Paying Her Tithing"

I recollect very vividly a circumstance that occurred in the days of my childhood. My mother was a widow with a large family to provide for. One spring when we opened our potato pits she had her boys get a load of the best potatoes, and she took them to the tithing office; potatoes were scarce that season. I was a little boy at the time and drove the team. When we drove up to the steps of the tithing office, ready to unload the potatoes, one of the clerks came out and said to my mother: "Widow Smith, it's a shame that you should have to pay tithing."

He said a number of other things that I remember well, but they are not necessary for me to repeat here. The first two letters of the name of that tithing clerk were William Thompson, and he chided my mother for paying her tithing, called her anything but wise and prudent, and said there were others able to work that were supported from the tithing office.

My mother turned upon him and said: "William, you ought to be ashamed of yourself. Would you deny me a blessing? If I did not pay my tithing I should expect the Lord to withhold his blessings from me. I pay my tithing, not only because it is a law of God but because I expect a blessing by doing it. By keeping this and other laws, I expect to prosper and to be able to provide for my family." Though she was a widow, you may turn to the records of the Church from the beginning unto the day of her death, and you will find that she never received a farthing from the Church to help her support herself and her family. But she paid in thousands of dollars in wheat, potatoes, corn, vegetables, meat, etc. The tithes of her sheep and cattle, the tenth pound of her butter, her tenth chicken, the tenth of her eggs, the tenth pig, the tenth calf, the tenth colt a tenth of everything she raised was paid. Here sits my brother, who can bear testimony to the truth of what I say, as can others who knew her. She prospered because she obeyed the laws of God. She had abundance to sustain her family. We never lacked so much as many others did; for while we found nettle greens most acceptable when we first came to the valley, and while we enjoyed thistle roots, segoes, and all that kind of thing, we were no worse off than thousands of others, and not so bad off as many, for we were never without cornmeal and milk and butter, to my knowledge. Then that widow had her name recorded in the book of the law of the Lord. That widow was entitled to the privileges of the House of God. No ordinance of the gospel could be denied her, for she was obedient to the laws of God, and she would not fail in her duty or become discouraged when observing one in an official position failing to keep the commandments of God. This may be said to be personal. By some it may be considered egotistical. But I do not speak of it in this light. When William Thompson told my mother that she ought not to pay tithing, I thought he was one of the finest fellows in the world. I believed every word he said. I had to work and dig and toil myself. I had to help plow the ground, plant the potatoes, hoe the potatoes, dig the potatoes, and all that sort of thing, and then to load up a big wagonbox full of the very best we had, leaving out the poor ones, and bring the load to the tithing office. I thought in my childish way that it looked a little hard, especially when I saw certain of my play-mates and early associates of childhood playing, riding horses, and having good times, and who scarcely ever did a lick of work in their lives, and yet were being fed from the public crib. Where are those boys today? Are they known in the Church? are they prominent among the people of God? Are they or were they ever valiant in the testimony of Jesus? Have they a clear testimony of the truth in their hearts? Are they diligent members of the Church? No, and never have been—as a rule—and most of them are dead or vanished out of sight.

Well, after I got a few years experience, I was converted, I found that my mother was right and that William Thompson was wrong. He denied the faith, apostatized, left the country, and led away as many of his family as would go with him. I do not want you to deny me the privilege of being numbered with those who have the interests of Zion at heart and who de-sire to contribute their proportion to the upbuilding of Zion and for the maintenance of the work of the Lord in the earth. It is a blessing that I enjoy, and I do not propose that anybody shall deprive me of that pleasure.

Joseph Fielding Smith, *Life of Joseph F. Smith*, pp. 158-60.

JOSEPH F. SMITH

"One Respectable Suit Between Them"

On the third of June, 1846, this storehouse and the meeting house were burned through an accident on the part of young Charles Clement Hurst (young, new missionary to Hawaiian mission), and the elders who had placed their trunks and other belongings in this place lost all that they had, including clothing and journals. As it was with other elders, most of the belongings of Elder Joseph F. Smith were stored in this building and through the fire were almost totally lost. Among his effects were clothing, copies of the Book of Mormon, the Doctrine and Covenants, which had been given as a present to the Patriarch Hyrum Smith. In one of these books Elder Joseph F. Smith had placed his elder's certificate. When the house was destroyed with its contents, Elder Smith's trunk, and every article in it, was reduced to ashes except his missionary certificate. In some remarkable manner it was preserved intact, except that it was scorched around the edges. But not one word was obliterated, even though the book in which it was contained was entirely consumed. Not only were the books destroyed but also Elder Smith's journals which he had faithfully kept. Out of all of this came another amusing incident, but serious at the time, nevertheless. The clothing of the missionaries being destroyed, Joseph F. Smith and his companion had to share, for a season, one respectable suit between them. One was under the necessity of remaining in bed while the other wore the suit and went to meetings.

Joseph Fielding Smith, *Life of Joseph F. Smith*, p. 184.

———◄—•—►———

JOSEPH F. SMITH

"True Blue, Through and Through"

It was while on [his] homeward journey [from his mission] that he was forced to pass through a very trying scene. It should be understood that the feeling existing towards the Latter-day Saints was running very high. The terrible scene at Mountain Meadows was fresh in the minds of the people, and of course they erroneously blamed President Brigham Young, in particular, and all of the Mormon people of being guilty of that horrible deed. Then, also, the army of the United States was on its way to Utah by orders from the President of the United States, their coming being based upon false charges that had been made by government officials from Utah who were extremely antagonistic against the Latter-day Saints. There were many men scattered abroad who had murder in their hearts, who said they would not hesitate to kill Mormons wherever they were found. Under these circumstances the members of the Church were forced to travel in small companies on their journey homeward bound. One day after the little company of wagons had traveled a short distance and made their camp, a company of drunken men rode into the camp on horseback, cursing and swearing and threatening to kill any Mormons that came within their path. It was the lot of Joseph F. Smith to meet these marauders first. Some of the brethren, when they heard them coming, had cautiously gone into the brush down the creek, out of sight, where they waited for this band to pass. Joseph F. was a little distance from the camp, gathering wood for the fire when these men rode up. When he saw them, he said his first thought was to do what the other brethren had done and seek shelter in the trees and in flight. Then the thought came to him, "Why should I run from these fellows?" With that thought in mind he boldly marched up with his arms full of wood to the campfire. As he was about to deposit his wood, one of the ruffians, still with his pistols in his hands and pointing at the youthful elder, and cursing as only a drunken rascal can, declaring that it was his duty to exterminate every Mormon he should meet, demanded in a loud, angry voice, "Are you a Mormon?"

Without a moment of hesitation and looking the ruffian in the eye, Joseph F. Smith boldly answered, "Yes, siree; dyed in the wool; true blue through and through."

The answer was given boldly and without any sign of fear,

which completely disarmed the belligerent man. And in his bewilderment, he grasped the missionary by the hand and said:

"Well, you are the _____ _____ pleasantest man I ever met! Shake, young fellow. I am glad to see a man that stands up for his convictions."

Joseph F. said in later years that he fully expected to receive the charge from this man's pistols, but he could take no other course, even though it seemed that his death was to be the result. This man, evidently the leader of the band, then rode off, the others following him, and the Mormon company was not molested further. It was a tense moment, nevertheless, and the company thanked the Lord for their safe deliverance.

Joseph F. arrived in Salt Lake City, February 24, 1858, having been absent from his home since May 8, 1854, nearly four years.

Joseph Fielding Smith, *Life of Joseph F. Smith*, pp. 188-89.

JOSEPH F. SMITH

"Iosepa, Iosepa"

One touching little incident I recall which occurred on our first trip to the Sandwich Islands. As we landed at the wharf in Honolulu, the native Saints were out in great numbers with their wreaths of leis, beautiful flowers of every variety and hue. We were loaded with them, he, of course, more than anyone else. The noted Hawaiian band was there playing welcome, as it often does to incoming steamship companies. But on this occasion the band had been instructed by the mayor to go up to the Mormon meetinghouse and there play selections during the festivities which the natives had arranged for. It was a beautiful sight to see the deep-seated love, the even tearful affection, that these people had for him. In the midst of it all I noticed a poor, old blind woman, tottering under the weight of about ninety years, being led in. She had a few choice bananas in her hand. It was her all—her offering. She was calling, "Iosepa, Iosepa." Instantly, when he saw her, he ran to her and clasped her in his arms, hugged her, and kissed her over and over again, patting her on the head saying, "Mama, mama, my dear old mama."

And then with tears streaming down his cheeks he turned to me and said, "Charlie, she nursed me when I was a boy, sick and without anyone to care for me. She took me in and was a mother to me."

Charles W. Nibley, "Reminiscences of President Joseph F. Smith," *Improvement Era*, 22 (Jan. 1919): 193-94.

JOSEPH F. SMITH

"I Would Rather a Thousand Times Die"

It is a very difficult matter to say anything at a time of sorrow and bereavement like the present that will give immediate relief to the sorrowing hearts of those who mourn. Such griefs can only be fully relieved by the lapse of time and the influence of the good Spirit upon the hearts of those that mourn, by which they can obtain comfort and satisfaction in their hopes of the future. For the loss of a father or mother in the family there is no adequate reparation, no remedy in this world which will supply such a loss; and about the only consolation we have is in the hope that we may so live that we may be permitted to meet again with our beloved, faithful, and true friends who go before, or who come after us, and enjoy their society once more in another sphere or state, which will be immortal. if we can only be satisfied in our minds of the witness of the good Spirit, to know that the course we pursue in this life is such as will secure to us this privilege, then in this reflection there is a degree of comfort and satisfaction, if not of joy, notwithstanding our separation, in time, from those that we have loved and cherished. For although they are gone from us, we know we shall meet them again in a better and more enduring sphere. I remember my feelings when first called upon to part with one of my children—my first born. It seemed to me to be an irreparable loss, a calamity, and if I had not restrained my feelings, I should have felt that it was cruel for the Lord to suffer one so bright, so pure and innocent, to be taken away by the hand of death, after remaining with us just long enough to become the joy of our hearts and the light of our home. Indeed it was a severe trial of our feelings to part with one who seemed so indispensable to our happiness, and for a time it seemed that the substance of our joy and hope had fled forever. But I have learned that there are a great many things which are far worse than death. With my present feelings and views and the understanding that I have of life and death, I would far rather follow every child I have to the grave in their innocence and purity, than to see them grow up to man and womanhood and degrade themselves by the pernicious practices of the world, forget the gospel, forget God and the plan of life and salvation, and turn away from the only hope of eternal reward and exaltation in the world to come.

Far better, in my judgment, to follow them to their graves before they have commenced such fearful acts, or fall into such fearful errors. I would rather a thousand times die while I have the faith of the gospel in my heart and the hope of eternal life within me, with the prospect of becoming worthy of inheriting a crown of eternal life which is the greatest gift of God unto man, than to live in possession of all the world affords and lose that gift.

It would be far better for me and my whole family to die in the faith than to live and deny it and bring shame, disgrace, and ruin upon us forever.

Joseph F. Smith in *Journal of Discourses*, 4:75-76.

JOSEPH F. SMITH

"John Roothoff by Name"

It was on the seventh day of August, 1906, that President Smith and party arrived in Rotterdam, having come from the boat at Antwerp two days before. There was living in that city a boy of eleven years of age, John Roothoff by name, who had suffered greatly for a number of years with his eyes. His mother was a faithful member of the Church, as also was the boy, who was slowly losing his sight and was unable to attend school The boy said to his mother: "The Prophet has the most power of any missionary on earth. If you will take me with you to the meeting and he will look into my eyes, I believe they will be healed."

According to his desire he was permitted to accompany his mother to the meeting. At the close of the meeting, as was the custom, President Smith moved towards the door and began to shake hands and speak encouragingly to the people as they passed from the hall. As John Roothoff approached him, led by his mother and his eyes bandaged, President Smith took him by the hand and spoke to him kindly. He then raised the bandage slightly and looked sympathetically into the inflamed eyes, at the same time saying something in English which the boy did not understand. However he was satisfied. President Smith had acted according to the boy's faith, and according to his faith it came to pass. When he arrived home, he cried out with great joy: "Mama, my eyes are well; I cannot feel any more pain. I can see fine now, and far too."

Joseph Fielding Smith, *Life of Joseph F. Smith*, p. 397.

JOSEPH F. SMITH

"Administering Comfort and Encouragement"

His [Joseph F. Smith's] kind thoughtfulness for the aged and his tender care for little children were among his most pronounced characteristics. While enjoining reverence for parents and a due regard from youngsters to elders, he held that children as well as adults have rights, and that these rights should always be respected. I was present on one occasion when he expressed himself indignantly over the conduct of a woman who, coming late into a public assembly, pulled a child out of a seat that she desired to occupy. He said nothing at the time, but took note of the occurrence, and at a subsequent meeting in the same place made it the text of a powerful discourse upon the principle of justice and the rules of propriety.

I have known him to leave his place upon a railroad train to speak a word of comfort to a poor old lady whose feelings had been hurt by an ill-mannered conductor in some matter pertaining to her ticket. Once I saw him, when an excursion was just about to start, walk the full length of the crowded train, with no apparent object but to satisfy himself that everybody was comfortably seated; and not until every man and woman . . . and child was provided for, did the President of the Church take his seat. More than once his brethren in council have writhed impatiently over his nonappearance at the time appointed, only to learn that his tardiness had been caused by some poor old creature who had . . . detained him past the hour, listening . . . and administering comfort and encouragement.

Orson F. Whitney. "President Joseph F. Smith As I Knew Him," *Juvenile Instructor*, 53 (Dec. 1918): 622.

◄—◆—►

JOSEPH F. SMITH

"Something Went Wrong with the Train"

. . . **V**ery few in this dispensation have been more gifted with spiritual insight than he [Joseph F. Smith]. As we were returning from an eastern trip some years ago on the train, just east of Green River, I saw him go out to the end of the car on the platform, . . . immediately return and hesitate a moment, and then sit down in the seat just ahead of me. He had just taken his seat when something went wrong with the train. A broken rail had been the means of ditching the engine and had thrown most of the cars off the track. Those in the sleeper were shaken up pretty badly, but our car remained on the track.

The President immediately said to me that he had gone on the platform when he heard a voice saying, "Go in and sit down."

He came in, and I noticed him stand a moment. And he seemed to hesitate, but he sat down.

He said further that as he came in and stood in the aisle he thought, "Oh, . . . perhaps it is only my imagination," when he heard the voice again say, "Sit down," and he immediately took his seat. And the result was as I have stated.

He, no doubt, would have been very seriously injured had he remained on the platform of that car, as the cars were all jammed up together pretty badly. He said, "I have heard that voice a good many times in my life, and I have always profited by obeying it."

Charles W. Nibley, "Reminiscences of President Joseph F. Smith," *Improvement Era*, 22 (Jan. 1919): 197.

JOSEPH F. SMITH

"I Saw the Hosts of the Dead"

On the third day of October, in the year nineteen hundred and eighteen, I sat in my room pondering over the scriptures and reflecting upon the great atoning sacrifice that was made by the Son of God for the redemption of the world, and the great and wonderful love made manifest by the Father and the Son in the coming of the Redeemer into the world, that through his atonement and by obedience to the principles of the gospel, mankind might be saved.

While I was thus engaged, my mind reverted to the writings of the Apostle Peter to the primitive saints. . . . I opened the Bible and read the third and fourth chapters of the first epistle of Peter, and as I read I was greatly impressed, more than I have ever been before, with the following passages:

> For Christ also hath once suffered for sins, the just for the unjust, that he might bring us to God, being put to death in the flesh, but quickened by the Spirit:
>
> By which also he went and preached unto the spirits in prison;
>
> Which sometime were disobedient, when once the long suffering of God waited in the days of Noah, while the ark was preparing, wherein few, that is, eight souls were saved by water. (1 Peter 3:18-20.)
>
> For, for this cause was the gospel preached also to them that are dead, that they might be judged according to men in the flesh, but live according to God in the spirit. (1 Peter 4:6.)

As I pondered over these things which are written, the eyes of my understanding were opened, and the Spirit of the Lord rested upon me, and I saw the hosts of the dead, both small and great. And there were gathered together in one place an innumerable company of the spirits of the just, who had been faithful in the testimony of Jesus while they lived in mortality. . . . All these had departed the mortal life, firm in the hope of a glorious resurrection through the grace of God the Father and his Only Begotten Son, Jesus Christ.

I beheld that they were filled with joy and gladness, and were rejoicing together because the day of their deliverance was at hand. They were assembled awaiting the advent of the Son of God into the spirit world, to declare their redemption from the bands of death. Their sleeping dust was to be restored into its perfect frame, bone to his bone, and the sinews and flesh upon them, the spirit and the body to be united never again to be divided, that they might receive a fulness of joy.

While this vast multitude waited and conversed, rejoicing in the hour of their deliverance from the chains of death, the Son of God appeared, declaring liberty to the captives who had been faithful. And there he preached to them the everlasting gospel, the doctrine of the resurrection and the redemption of mankind from the fall, and from individual sins on conditions of repentance. But unto the wicked he did not go, and among the ungodly and the unrepentant who had defiled themselves while in the flesh, his voice was not raised, neither did the rebellious who rejected the testimonies and the warnings of the ancient prophets behold his presence, nor look upon his face. Where these were, darkness reigned, but among the righteous there was peace, and the saints rejoiced in their redemption, and bowed the knee and acknowledged the Son of God as their Redeemer and Deliverer from death and the chains of hell. Their countenances shone, and the radiance from the presence of the Lord rested upon them, and they sang praises unto his holy name.

And as I wondered, my eyes were opened, and my understanding quickened, and I perceived that the Lord went not in person among the wicked and the disobedient who had rejected the truth, to teach them; but behold, from among the righteous he organized his forces and appointed messengers, clothed with power and authority, and commissioned them to go forth and carry the light of the gospel to them that were in darkness, over to all the spirits of men. And thus was the gospel preached to the dead. And the chosen messengers went forth to declare the acceptable day of the Lord and proclaim liberty to the captives who were bound even unto all who would repent of their sins and receive the gospel.

The Prophet Joseph Smith, and my father, Hyrum Smith, Brigham Young, John Taylor, Wilford Woodruff, and other choice spirits who were reserved to come forth in the fulness of times to take part in laying the foundations of the great latter-day work, including the building of the temples and the performance of ordinances therein for the redemption of the dead, were also in the spirit world. I observed that they were also among the noble and great ones who were chosen in the beginning to be rulers in the Church of God. . . .

I beheld that the faithful elders of this dispensation, when they depart from mortal life, continue their labors in the preaching of the gospel of repentance and redemption, through the sacrifice of the Only Begotten Son of God, among those who are in darkness and under the bondage of sin in the great world of the spirits of the dead. The dead who repent will be redeemed, through obedience to the ordinances of the house of God; and after they have paid the penalty of their transgressions, and are washed clean, shall receive a reward according to their works, for they are heirs of salvation.

Thus was the vision of the redemption of the dead revealed to me. And I bear record, and I know that this record is true, through the blessing of our Lord and Savior, Jesus Christ, even so. Amen.

Joseph Fielding Smith, *Life of Joseph F. Smith,* 466-71.

Biographical Sketch

HEBER J. GRANT

Heber Jeddy Grant was born on November 22, 1856. He was the first and only child of Rachel Ivans Grant. At the time of his birth, his father, Jedediah M. Grant, lay critically ill and just nine days later was dead at the age of 41. His loss was mourned by a multitude. He was truly a remarkable individual. At his death he was a counselor to President Brigham Young and mayor of Salt Lake City. At his funeral services, President Young paid him a unique tribute. He mentioned that "Brother Jedediah had been in the church a total of twenty-five years, but in those twenty-five years he had given the Lord one hundred years of Church service." That simple tribute eloquently described Heber J. Grant's valiant father. He was not privileged to know his father, but his father's influence was present in his life.

President Grant told of an experience he had in 1891. He asked a president of a bank, a respected man who was not a member of the Church, to sign some bonds. He promptly declined to do so. Just a few minutes later he sent a messenger and asked president Grant to return. As President Grant entered the office, the influential businessman said:

189

"Young man, give me those bonds." He signed them and then said, "When you were here a few moments ago, I did not know you. I have met you on the street now and then for a number of years and have spoken to you, but really did not know you. After you went out, I asked who you were. Learning that you were a son of Jedediah M. Grant, I at once sent for you. It gives me pleasure to sign your bonds. I would almost be willing to sign a bond for a son of Brother Jedediah if I knew I would have to pay it. In this case, however, I have no fears of having that to do."

President Grant continues, "Although my father died when I was a babe nine days old, . . . years after his death I was reaping the benefits of his honesty and faithful labors."[1]

Rachel Ivans Grant, Heber's outstanding mother, never remarried and devoted her life to supporting and training her son. She struggled to support herself and her son by sewing and having people board in her house. Heber slept in a large closet that had been ventilated so that his room could be rented.

On one occasion President Grant said:

I thank the Lord for that mother of mine. . . . She became converted to the restored gospel. The men who converted her were the Prophet Joseph Smith himself and Erastus Snow. And my mother's brothers who were well to do financially offered to settle an annuity upon her for life if she would renounce her religion. One of her brothers said to her: "Rachel, you have disgraced the name of Ivins. We never want to see you again if you stay with those awful Mormons,"—this was when she was leaving for Utah—"but," he continued, "come back in a year, come back in five years, come back in ten or twenty years, and no matter when you come back, the latchstring will be out, and affluence and ease will be your portion."

Later, when poverty became her lot, if she actually had not known that Joseph Smith was a prophet of God and that the gospel was true, all she needed to do was to return east and let her brothers take care of her. But rather than return to her wealthy relatives in the east where she would have been amply provided for, with no struggle for herself or her child, she preferred to make her way among those to whom she was more strongly attached than her kindred who were not believers in her faith.[2]

Rachel Ivins Grant was certain her son was going to grow up and become an apostle, and this he did at age twenty-five in the year 1882. The remarkable relationship between President Grant and his mother is truly inspirational.

---

[1]*Improvement Era*, 3:190-91.
[2]*Improvement Era*, 39:267.

President Grant organized and presided over the Japanese mission and also presided over the European mission.

At age sixty he became the president of the Council of Twelve. In 1918, at age sixty-two, he became the President of the Church. Speaking of this, President Grant said:

> On the day that Brother Joseph F. Smith bade me goodbye, and he died that very night, he told me that the Lord never makes a mistake. He said: "You have a great responsibility resting upon you. The Lord knows whom he wants to preside over his Church, and he never makes a mistake."[3]

Truly the Lord did call President Grant, and he directed him in his long years as the prophet, seer, and revelator. Elder Harold B. Lee has said:

> I heard President Clark, shortly after he came into the First Presidency, make an interesting public statement. He said that when President Grant called him to be a counselor in the First Presidency, he was worried. He had always thought of the President of the Church as the "mouthpiece" of the Lord. But he hadn't been long in the Presidency until he discovered his place.
>
> President Grant would say to each of his counselors, when they were discussing a serious matter, "What do you think about it?" and "What do you think about it?" And the counselors would respond. Sometimes their opinions were in contradiction or in conflict with what the President had thought. There was then the business of resolving the different points of view, but there would always come a time after a sufficient discussion when the President would say: "Now brethren, I feel that this is the thing we ought to do." Then President Clark remarked, "When he said that, I quit counseling because, to me, that was the prophet of the Lord speaking."[4]

President Grant served as President of the Church for twenty-seven years—longer than any other President except Brigham Young. During his devoted administration he dedicated three temples: Hawaiian, Canadian, and the Arizona Temple. The creation of the Church welfare program is one of a multitude of important contributions during his long and successful administration.

President Heber J. Grant died at age eighty-nine on May 14, 1945. He was a brilliant, persistent, devoted man. He was

---

[3]*Conference Report*, April 1942, p. 8.
[4]*Conference Report*, April 1963, p. 81.

candid, and his life was open to inspection. One can readily identify with President Grant, and he has been and will always be a great example to those who want to live better before the Lord.

HEBER J. GRANT

"Behave Yourself, Heber"

For years, Heber J. Grant's mother cherished in her heart promises which were made to her son in childhood. She had implicit faith in the fulfillment of those promises, provided he lived worthy of them. Referring to his mother, President Grant said: "My mother always told me, 'Behave yourself, Heber, and some day you will be an apostle. If you do not behave yourself, you will not be, because we have a revelation recorded in the Doctrine and Covenants which specifically states "there is a law irrevocably decreed in heaven before the foundations of the world upon which all blessings are predicated, and when we obtain any blessing from God, it is by obedience to that law upon which it is predicated." [D&C 130:20.] I said, 'Mother, I do not want to be an apostle. I do not want to be a bishop. I do not want to be anything but a businessman. Just get it out of your head.'"

When he was called to the apostleship, she asked him if he remembered a meeting where certain blessings were promised him. He replied: "No, I do not remember anything, only that when Aunt Zina was talking she said, 'You will become a great man in The Church of Jesus Christ of Latter-day Saints and one of the apostles of the Lord, Jesus Christ.'"

His mother said: "That is the reason I have told you to behave yourself. I knew it would not come true if you did not live worthily, but it has come true." Then she asked, "Do you remember Heber C. Kimball picking you up when you were a young boy and putting you on a table and talking to you at a great dinner he was having for a lot of his friends?" "Yes." "Do you remember anything that he said?"

"No, I only remember that he had the blackest eyes I have ever looked into. I was frightened. That is all I can remember."

"He prophesied in the name of the Lord Jesus Christ that you would become an apostle of the Lord Jesus Christ and become a greater man in the Church than your own father; and your father, as you know, became one of the counselors to President Brigham Young. That is why I have told you to behave."

Bryant S. Hinckley, *The Faith of Our Pioneer Fathers* (Salt Lake City: Deseret Book Co., 1956), pp. 69-71.

———◆——◆———

HEBER J. GRANT

"Throw It Here Sissy"

As I was an only child, my mother reared me very carefully. Indeed, I grew up more or less under the principles of a hothouse plant, a growth which is long and lengthy but not substantial. I learned to sweep and to wash and wipe dishes but did little stone throwing and little indulgence in works which are interesting to boys, which develop their physical frames. Therefore, when I joined the baseball club, the boys of my own age and a little older played in the first nine, those younger than I played in the second, and those still younger, in the third, and I played with them. One of the reasons for this was that I could not throw the ball from one base to another, and another reason was that I lacked the strength to run or bat the ball. When I picked up the ball, the boys would generally shout, "Throw it here, sissy!" So much fun was engendered on my account by my youthful companions that I solemnly vowed that I would play baseball in the nine that would win the championship in the territory of Utah. My mother was keeping boarders for a living at the time, and I shined their boots until I saved a dollar, which I invested in a baseball, and spent hours and hours throwing the ball at Bishop Edwin D. Woolley's barn, which caused him to refer to me as the laziest boy in the Thirteenth Ward. Often my arm would ache so that I could scarcely go to sleep at night, but I kept on practicing and finally succeeded in getting into the second nine of our club. Subsequently, I joined a better club and eventually played in the nine that won the championship in California, Colorado, and Wyoming, and thus made good my promise to myself and retired from the baseball arena."

When he could not sleep because his arm ached as a result of throwing the ball, his mother would wrap it with bandages dipped in cold water to relieve the pain.

Bryant S. Hinckley, *Highlights in the Life of a Great Leader* (Salt Lake City: Deseret Book Co., 1951), pp. 37-39.

HEBER J. GRANT

"It Looks As If Lightning Had Struck an Ink Bottle"

One day Heber was playing marbles with some other boys when the bookkeeper from the Wells Fargo Company Bank was walking down the other side of the street. One of the boys remarked, "That man gets $150.00 a month." Heber figured to himself that, not counting Sundays, that man made $6.00 a day, and that at five cents a pair, he would have to black 120 pairs of boots to make $6.00. He there and then resolved that some day he would be a bookkeeper in the Wells Fargo and Company's bank. In those days all the records and accounts of the bank were written with a pen, and one of the requisites of a good bookkeeper was the ability to write well. To learn to write well was his first approach to securing this job and the fulfillment of his resolve; so he set to work to become a penman.

At the beginning his penmanship was so poor that when two of his chums were looking at it one said to the other, "That writing looks like hen tracks." "No," said the other, "it looks as if lightning had struck an ink bottle." This touched Heber's pride and, bringing his fist down on his desk, he said, "I'll some day be able to give you fellows lessons in penmanship"; and he was.

Hinckley, *Heber J. Grant*, pp. 39-40.

HEBER J. GRANT

"The Laziest Boy in the Whole Thirteenth Ward"

"**R**eferring to that wonderful mother of mine, I remembered that one day we had at least a half-dozen, if not more, buckets on the floor catching the rain that came from the roof. It was raining very heavily, and Bishop Edwin D. Woolley came into the house and said, 'Why, Widow Grant, this will never do. I shall take some of the money from the fast offering and put a new roof on this house.'

"'Oh, no, you won't,' said Mother. 'No relief money will ever put a roof on my house. I have sewing here, and,' she said, 'I have supported myself and my son with a needle and thread for many years' and later with a Wheeler and Wilcox sewing machine . . . Then Mother said, 'When I get through with this sewing that I'm doing now, I will buy some shingles and patch the holes in the roof, and this house will take care of me until my son gets to be a man and builds me a new one. Bishop Woolley went away and said he was very sorry for Widow Grant and that if she waited for that boy to build a house she would never have one, for he was the laziest boy in the whole Thirteenth Ward. He went on to tell how I wasted my time throwing a ball across the fence behind the house hour after hour, day after day, and week after week at his adobe barn. Thank the Lord for a mother who was a general as well as a Latter-day Saint, who realized that it is a remarkable and splendid thing to encourage a boy to do something besides, perhaps, milking cows if he was on a farm, or encourage him if he had ambitions along athletic lines."

Hinckley, *Heber J. Grant,* pp. 38-39.

HEBER J. GRANT

*"Bishop, I Have Made Two Hundred
Eighteen Dollars and Fifty Cents"*

"I remember as a young man, I
had fifty dollars in my pocket on one occasion which I intended
to deposit in the bank. When I went on Thursday morning to
fast meeting—the fast meeting used to be held on Thursday
instead of Sundays—the Bishop made an appeal for donations.
I walked up and handed him fifty dollars. He took five dollars
of it and put it in the drawer and gave the forty-five dollars
back to me and said that was my full share. I said: 'Bishop
Woolley, by what right do you rob me of putting the Lord in
my debt? Didn't you preach here today that the Lord would
reward fourfold? My mother is a widow and she needs two
hundred dollars.' He said: 'My boy, do you believe that if I
take this other forty-five dollars you will get your two hundred
dollars quicker?' I said: 'Certainly.' Well, he took it."

While walking from the fast meeting to the place where he
worked, an idea suddenly came to him. He sent a telegram
to a man asking him how many bonds of a certain kind he
would buy at a specified price within forty-eight hours, allow-
ing Heber to draw a draft on him through Wells Fargo's Bank.
He did not know the man. He had never spoken to him in his
life but had seen him a time or two on the streets of Salt Lake.
The man wired back that he wanted as many as he could get.
Heber's profit on the transaction was two hundred eighteen
dollars and fifty cents.

The next day he walked down to the Bishop and said:
"Bishop, I have made two hundred eighteen dollars and fifty
cents after paying that fifty dollars donation the other day, and
so I owe twenty-one dollars and eighty-five cents in tithing.
I will have to dig up the difference between twenty-one dollars
eighty-five cents and eighteen dollars fifty cents. The Lord

did not quite give me the tithing in addition to his 'four to one' income."

Hinckley, *Faith of Our Pioneer Fathers*, pp. 71-72.

◄—•—►

H E B E R J . G R A N T

*"Would You Like to Go to
the Naval Academy?*

"**I** met President George Q. Cannon, then our delegate to Congress, and he said: 'Would you like to go to the Naval Academy, or to West Point?'

"I told him I would.

"He said: 'Which one?'

"I said, 'The Naval Academy.'

" 'All right, I will give you the appointment without competitive examination.'

"For the first time in my life I did not sleep well; I lay awake nearly all night long rejoicing that the ambition of my life was to be fulfilled. I fell asleep just a little before daylight; my mother had to awaken me.

"I said: 'Mother, what a marvelous thing it is that I am to have an education as fine as that of any young man in all Utah. I could hardly sleep; I was awake until almost daylight this morning.'

"I looked into her face; I saw that she had been weeping.

"I have heard of people who, when drowning, had their entire life pass before them in a few seconds. I saw myself an admiral, in my mind's eye. I saw myself traveling all over the world in a ship, away from my widowed mother. I laughed and put my arms around her and kissed her and said, 'Mother, I do not want a naval education. I am going to be a businessman and shall enter an office right away and take care of you and have you quit keeping boarders for a living.'

"She broke down and wept and said that she had not closed her eyes, but had prayed all night that I would give up my life's ambition so that she would not be left alone.

"Her prayers were answered, and her appeal to the Almighty was inspired by promises made to her son in his childhood by those she looked upon as being the servants of God."

After declining the appointment to Annapolis he made up his mind to be a businessman and went to work. That was the end of his formal schooling. He soon became absorbed in his business affairs, but he utilized every spare moment of his time reading and improving his mind. As he read, it was his practice to mark passages that impressed him and to pass the book along to some friends. Many books that he gave away were "marked copies," which added to their value. When he became an apostle, he had more and better opportunities for reading. He often had one of his daughters or his secretary read to him, especially in his later years. Thus he kept well-informed on current issues. While he had but few scholastic credentials, Heber J. Grant was well educated.

Hinckley, *Heber J. Grant*, pp. 33-34.

"I Ran Out of Ideas in Seven and One-half Minutes"

Do we not often take the credit when we excel instead of giving it to God? We are not yet humble enough, and therefore, when we offer a fine prayer or speech, or whatever it may be, we allow Satan to flatter us, and say, "How beautiful." To the Lord alone is due the praise.

I shall make a confession. When I was made the president of the Tooele Stake of Zion and made my maiden speech I ran out of ideas in seven and a one-half minutes by the watch. That night I heard in a very contemptuous voice in the dark, "Well, it is a pity if the General Authorities of the Church had to import a boy from the city to come out here to preside over us they could not have found one with sense enough to talk ten minutes." So you see he held his stop watch on me, he knew I did not take ten minutes. I knew I did not, because I timed myself—seven and one-half minutes was the limit. The next speech, and the next, and the next were the same. One of them was only five minutes. The next speech was at a little town called Vernon, sometimes called Stringtown, as it spread over twelve miles as I remember it.

As we were going to the meeting I was with the bishop, Brother John C. Sharp, and I did not see anybody going to meeting. The Bishop said, "Oh, there will be somebody there." We were going up a little hill, and when we got to the top of the hill we found a number of wagons and white tops at the meetinghouse—it was a log meeting house—but did not see anybody going in.

I said: "There doesn't seem to be anybody going to meeting."

He said, "Oh, I think you'll find somebody there."

When we got inside, the meetinghouse was crowded. We

went in at two minutes to two and nobody else came in afterwards. I congratulated the Bishop after the meeting on having educated his people to be so prompt.

He said: "Most of them have to hitch up a team to come here, and I have told them they could just as well hitch it up a few minutes earlier and be here at two minutes to two o'clock, so there will be no disturbance."

I had taken a couple of brethren with me that day to do the preaching. I got up expecting to take five or six minutes and talked forty-five minutes with as much ease, if not more, than I have ever enjoyed since. I shed tears of gratitude that night to the Lord for the inspiration of his Spirit.

The next Sunday I went to Grantsville, the largest town in Tooele County, and got up with all the assurance in the world and told the Lord I would like to talk forty-five minutes, and ran out of ideas in five. I not only ran out of ideas in five minutes, but I was perspiring, and [I] walked fully two and one-half, if not three, miles, after that meeting, to the farthest haystack in Grantsville, and kneeled behind that haystack and asked the Lord to forgive me for my egotism in that meeting. And [I] made a pledge to the Lord that never again in my life would I stand before an audience without asking for his Spirit to help me, nor would I take personally the credit for anything I said; and I have kept this pledge.

Heber J. Grant, "Honoring Dr. Karl G. Maeser," *BYU Quarterly*, 31 (Nov. 1934): 24-26.

"One Hundred and Fifteen Songs in One Day"

When I first commenced to write for the *Era*, it was my intention to become a frequent contributor, but during the past few months I have neglected writing for the reason that my spare time has been devoted to practicing singing.

Believing there are quite a number who have never sung who perhaps would be benefited by reading an account of my efforts, and who might be encouraged thereby in learning to sing, I have decided to give my experience to the readers of the *Era*. My mother tried to teach me when a small child to sing, but failed because of my inability to carry a tune. Upon joining a singing class taught by Professor Charles J. Thomas, he tried and tried in vain to teach me when ten years of age to run the scale or carry a simple tune, and finally gave up in despair. He said that I could never, in this world, learn to sing. Perhaps he thought I might learn the divine art in another world. Ever since this attempt, I have frequently tried to sing when riding alone many miles from anyone who might hear me, but on such occasions could never succeed in carrying the tune of one of our familiar hymns for a single verse, and quite frequently not for a single line.

When about twenty-five years of age, I had my character read by Professor Sims, the renowned physiognomist, and he informed me that I could sing, but added, "I would like to be at least forty miles away while you are doing it."

Nearly ten months ago, while listening to Brother Horace S. Ensign sing, I remarked that I would gladly give two or three months of my spare time if by so doing it would result in my being able to sing one or two hymns. He answered that any person could learn to sing who had a reasonably good voice and who possessed perseverance and was willing to do plenty of practicing. My response was that I had an abundance of voice and considerable perseverance. He was in my employ at the time, and I jokingly remarked that while he had not been hired as a music teacher, however, right now I would take my first music lesson of two hours upon the hymn "O My Father." Much to my surprise, at the end of four or five days, I was able to sing this hymn with Brother Ensign without any mistakes. At the end of two weeks, I could sing it alone, with the exception of being a little flat on some of the high notes. My ear, not being cultivated musically, did not detect this, and the only way I knew of it was by having Brother Ensign and other friends tell me of the error.

One of the leading Church officials, upon hearing me sing, when I first started to practice, remarked that my singing reminded him very much of the late Apostle Orson Pratt's poetry. He said Brother Pratt wrote only one piece of poetry, and this looked like it had been sawed out of boards, and sawed off straight.

Once, while practicing singing in Brother Ensign's office in the Templeton Building (his rooms are next to a dentist's), some of the students of the Latter-day Saints' College who were in the hall remarked that it sounded like somebody was having his teeth pulled.

One would think that the following item from a letter from one of my nearest and most intimate friends would be very discouraging, but, like the uncomplimentary remarks above referred to, it only increases my determination to learn to sing. Referring to my daughter, he says: "I see Lutie is making quite a name as a singer; I don't think, though, that this fact need encourage you to try to become the George Goddard of the Church. I admit that your point is a good one; i.e., if *you* can learn to sing, *nothing* need discourage *anybody*—but the fact that success ultimately must be reached by taveling along the borderland of ridicule makes the task a difficult and delicate one, particularly for an apostle, who, unlike the ordinary musical crank, cannot afford to cultivate his thorax at the expense of his reputation as a man of judgment."

One Sunday, at the close of a meeting in the Thirteenth Ward, upon telling Professor Charles J. Thomas that Brother Ensign informed me that I could sing, he said: "Didn't you tell him I said no?" I answered, "Yes." He said, "Why you can't even run the scale." I said, "I am aware of that fact, having tried for half an hour this morning and failed." My voice at ten years of age must have made a very deep impression upon Brother Thomas, seeing that he had remembered it for thirty-three years. Noticing that he seemed quite skeptical, I asked him to walk over with me into the corner of the building, so as not to disturb the people who had not yet left the meetinghouse, when I sang to him in a low voice, "God Moves in a Mysterious Way." At the close he said: "That's all right."

At the end of two or three months, I was able to sing not only "O My Father," but "God Moves in a Mysterious Way," "Come, Come, Ye Saints," and two or three other hymns. Shortly after this, while taking a trip south, I sang one or more hymns in each of the Arizona stakes and in Juarez, Mexico. Upon my return to Salt Lake City, I attempted to sing "O My Father" in the big tabernacle, hoping to give an object lesson to the young people, and to encourage them to learn to sing. I made a failure, getting off the key in nearly every verse, and instead of my effort encouraging the young people, I fear that it tended to discourage them.

When first starting to practice, if some person would join in and sing base, tenor or alto, I could not carry the tune. Neither could I sing if anyone accompanied me on the piano or organ, as the variety of sounds confused me.

I am pleased to be able to say that I can now sing with piano or organ accompaniment, and can also sing the lead in "God Moves in a Mysterious Way" in a duet, a trio, or quartet. I have learned quite a number of songs and have been assured by Brother Ensign, and several others well versed in music, to whom I have sung within the past few weeks, that I succeeded without making a mistake in a single note, which I fear would not be the case were the attempt to be made in public. However, I intend to continue trying to sing the hymn "O My Father" in the Assembly Hall or big tabernacle until such time as I can sing it without an error.

How did I succeed so far? Brother Ensign adopted the plan of having me sing a line over and over again, trying to imitate his voice. He kept this up until the line was learned and could be "pronounced musically" on the same principle as learning the sound of a word. The child may be taught to pronounce correctly the word "incomprehensibility," notwithstanding the length, even if the child does not understand the phonetic sounds. I learned to sing upon the same principle, starting, figuratively speaking, in the eighth grade, with not even a knowledge of the contents of the primary. It required a vast amount of practice to learn, and my first hymn was sung many hundreds of times before I succeeded in getting it right.

Upon my recent trip to Arizona I asked elders Rudger Clawson and J. Golden Kimball if they had any objections to my singing one hundred hymns that day. They took it as a joke and assured me that they would be delighted. We were on the way from Holbrook to St. Johns, a distance of about sixty miles. After I had sung about forty times, they assured me that if I sang the remaining sixty they would be sure to have nervous prostration. I paid no attention whatever to their appeal, but held them to their bargain and sang the full one hundred. One hundred and fifteen songs in one day, and four hundred in four days, is the largest amount of practicing I ever did.

Today my musical deafness is disappearing, and by sitting down to a piano and playing the lead notes, I can learn a song in less than one-tenth the time required when I first commenced to practice. Where a person has a low voice—as in my case—he should ask some kind friend, who understands music, to transpose his songs to a lower key. It is impossible for me to sing a majority of our hymns in the keys in which they are written in our psalmody. The above points are mentioned for the special benefit of my musically deaf friends whc desire to be cured and are willing to do a goodly amount of hard work in order to accomplish that very pleasant result.

Heber J. Grant, "Learning to Sing," *Improvement Era* 3 (Aug. 1900): 886-90.

"That Which We Persist in Doing Becomes Easier for Us to Do."

I propose to sing the "Holy City" in the big tabernacle before I get through with it, and I propose to sing it without a mistake. I do not say this boastingly, because I believe what Alma of old said, in the twenty-ninth chapter of his book, that "God granteth unto men according to their desires, whether they be for good or evil, for joy or remorse of conscience." I desire to sing, and I expect to work at it and stay right with it until I learn. The most I ever worked was to sing four hundred songs in four days; that is the heaviest work I have ever done in the singing line. There are a great many people who can learn to sing very easily. When I started to learn to sing, it took me four months to learn a couple of simple hymns, and recently I learned one in three hours by the watch and then sang it without a mistake.

"That which we persist in doing becomes easier for us to do; not that the nature of the thing itself is changed, but that our power to do is increased." I propose to keep at it until my power to do is increased to the extent that I can sing the songs of Zion. Nobody knows the joy I have taken in standing up in the tabernacle and other places and joining in the singing, because it used to be a perfect annoyance to me to try and to fail, besides annoying those around me, because I loved the words of the songs of Zion, and would sing.

I am very sorry now for having persecuted people as I used to. In our meetings in the temple the brethren would say, "That is as impossible as it is for Brother Grant to carry a tune," and that settled it. Everybody acknowledged that was one of the impossibilities.

I believe what the Lord says: "For my soul delighteth in the song of the heart; yea, the song of the righteous is a prayer unto me, and it shall be answered with a blessing upon their heads." (D&C 25:12.) I desire to serve the Lord and pray unto him in the songs of Zion; and I know that it produces a good influence.

Heber J. Grant in *Conference Report*, April 1901, pp. 63-64.

HEBER J. GRANT

"I Sat There and Wept for Joy"

From October 1882, when I was called to be one of the Council of the Twelve, until the following February, I had but little joy and happiness in my labors. There was a spirit following me that told me that I lacked the experience, that I lacked the inspiration, that I lacked the testimony to be worthy of the position of an apostle of the Lord Jesus Christ. My dear mother had inspired me with such a love of the gospel and with such a reverence and admiration for the men who stood at the head of this Church, that when I was called to be one of them I was overpowered; I felt my unworthiness, and the adversary taking advantage of that feeling in my heart. Day and night the spirit pursued me, suggesting that I resign. And when I testified of the divinity of the work we are engaged in, the words would come back, "You haven't seen the Savior; you have no right to bear such a testimony," and I was very unhappy.

But in February 1883, while riding along on the Navajo Indian reservation with Elder Brigham Young, Jr., and fifteen or twenty other brethren, including the late President Lot Smith of one of the Arizona stakes, on our way to visit the Navajos and Moquis—as we were traveling that day, going through a part of the Navajo reservation to get to the Moqui reservation —as we were traveling to the southeast, suddenly the road turned and veered almost to the northeast. But there was a path, a trail, leading on in the direction in which we had been traveling. There were perhaps eight or ten of us on horseback and the rest in wagons. Brother Smith and I were at the rear of our company. When we came to the trail I said, "Wait a minute, Lot; where does this trail lead to?"

He said, "Oh, it leads back into the road three or four miles over here, but we have to make a detour of eight or nine miles to avoid a large gully that no wagons can cross."

I asked, "Can a horseman get over that gully?"

He answered, "Yes."

I said, "Any danger from Indians by being out there alone?"

He answered, "No."

I said, "I want to be alone, so you go on with the company and I will meet you over there where the trail and the road join."

One reason that I asked if there was any danger was because a few days before, our company had visited the spot where George A. Smith, Jr. had been killed by the Navajo Indians, and I had that event in my mind at the time I was speaking. I had perhaps gone one mile when in the kind providences of the Lord it was manifested to me perfectly so far as my intelligence is concerned—I did not see heaven, I did not see a council held there, but like Lehi of old I seemed to see; and my very being was so saturated with the information that I received, as I stopped my animal and sat there and communed with heaven, that I am as absolutely convinced of the information that came to me upon that occasion as though the voice of God had spoken the words to me.

It was manifested to me there and then as I sat there and wept for joy that it was not because of any particular intelligence that I possessed more than a testimony of the gospel, that it was not because of my wisdom that I had been called to be one of the apostles of the Lord Jesus Christ in this last dispensation, but it was because the prophet of God, the man who was the chosen instrument in the hands of the living God of establishing again upon the earth the plan of life and salvation, Joseph Smith, desired that I be called, and that my father, Jedediah M. Grant, who gave his life for the gospel while one of the presidency of the Church, a counselor to President Brigham Young, and who had been dead for nearly twenty-six years, desired that his son should be a member of the Council of the Twelve. It was manifested to me that the prophet and my father were able to bestow upon me the apostleship because of their faithfulness, inasmuch as I had lived a clean life, that now it remained for me to make a success or failure of that calling. I can bear witness to you here today that I do not believe that any man on earth from that day, February 1883, until now, thirty-five years ago, has had sweeter joy, more perfect and exquisite happiness than I have had in lifting up my voice and testifying of the gospel at home and abroad in every land and in every clime where it has fallen to my lot to go.

Heber J. Grant, "A Remarkable Manifestation," *Improvement Era*, 22 (Dec. 1918):97-99.

◆——————◆

HEBER J. GRANT

"I Was Willing to Vote for Myself"

I was made one of the apostles in October 1882. On the sixth of October, 1882, I met brother George Teasdale at the south gate of the temple. His face lit up, and he said: "Brother Grant, you and I"—very enthusiastically —and then he commenced coughing and choking, and went on into meeting and did not finish his sentence. It came to me as plainly, as though he had said the words: ". . . are going to be chosen this afternoon to fill the vacancies in the Quorum of the Twelve Apostles."

I went to the meeting, and my head swelled, and I thought to myself, "Well, I am going to be one of the apostles," and I was willing to vote for myself, but the conference adjourned without anyone being chosen.

Ten days later I received a telegram saying, "You must be in Salt Lake tomorrow without fail." I was then president of Tooele Stake. The telegram came from my partner, Nephi W. Clayton. When I got to the depot, I said: "Nephi, why on earth are you calling me back here? I had an appointment out in Tooele Stake."

"Never mind," he said, "it was not I who sent for you; it was Brother Lyman. He told me to send the telegram and sign my name to it. He told me to come and meet you and take you to the President's office. That is all I know.'

So I went to the President's office, and there sat Brother Teasdale, and all of the ten apostles, and the presidency of the Church, and also Seymour B. Young and the members of the Seven Presidents of the Seventies. And the revelation was read calling Brother Teasdale and myself to the apostleship, and Brother Seymour B. Young to be one of the Seven Presidents of the Seventies.

Brother Teasdale was blessed by President John Taylor, and George Q. Cannon blessed me.

After the meeting I said to Brother Teasdale, "I know what you were going to say to me on the sixth of October when you happened to choke half to death and then went into the meeting."

He said, "Oh, no, you don't."

"Yes, I do," and I repeated it: "You and I are going to be called to the apostleship."

He said, "Well, that is what I was going to say, and then it occurred to me that I had no right to tell it, that I had received a manifestation from the Lord." He said, "Heber, I have suffered the tortures of the damned for ten days, thinking I could not tell the difference between a manifestation from the

Lord and one from the devil, that the devil had deceived me."

I said, "I have not suffered like that, but I never prayed so hard in my life for anything as I did that the Lord would forgive me for the egotism of thinking that I was fit to be an apostle, and that I was ready to go into that meeting ten days ago and vote for myself to be an apostle."

Heber J. Grant in *Conference Report*, October 3, 1942, pp. 24-25.

◄—————►

HEBER J. GRANT

"Her Mother Died Before the Salt Lake Temple Was Completed"

I shall always be grateful, to the day of my death, that I did not listen to some of my friends when, as a young man not quite twenty-one years of age, I took the trouble to travel all the way from Utah County to St. George to be married in the St. George Temple. That was before the railroad went south of Utah County, and we had to travel the rest of the way by team. It was a long and difficult trip in those times, over unimproved and uncertain roads, and the journey each way required several days.

Many advised me not to make the effort—not to go all the way down to St. George to be married. They reasoned that I could have the president of the stake or my bishop marry me, and then when the Salt Lake Temple was completed, I could go there with my wife and children and be sealed to her and have our children sealed to us for eternity.

Why did I not listen to them? Because I wanted to be married for time and eternity—because I wanted to start life right.

Later I had cause to rejoice greatly because of my determination to be married in the temple at that time rather than to have waited until some later and seemingly more convenient time.

Some years ago the general board members of the Young Women's Mutual Improvement Association were traveling throughout the stakes of Zion speaking on the subject of marriage. They urged the young people to start their lives together in the right way by being married right, in the temples of the Lord.

I was out in one of the stakes attending a conference, and one of my daughters, who was the representative of the Young Women's general board at the conference, said: "I am very grateful to the Lord that I was properly born—born under the covenant, born of parents that had been properly married and sealed in the temple of the Lord."

Tears came into my eyes, because her mother died before the Salt Lake Temple was completed and I was grateful that I had not listened to the remarks of my friends who had tried to persuade me not to go to the St. George Temple to be married. I was very grateful for the inspiration and determination I had to start life right.

Why did it come to me? It came to me because my mother believed in the gospel, taught me the value of it, gave me a desire to get all of the benefits of starting life right and of doing things according to the teachings of the gospel.

I believe that no worthy young Latter-day Saint man or woman should spare any reasonable effort to come to the house of the Lord to begin life together. The marriage vows taken in these hallowed places and the sacred covenants entered into for time and all eternity are proof against many of the temptations of life that tend to break homes and destroy happiness.

Heber J. Grant, "Beginning Life Together," *Improvement Era*, 39 (April 1936): 198.

HEBER J. GRANT

"Judge Men and Women by the Spirit They Have"

There stand out in my life many incidents in my youth, of wonderful inspiration and power through men preaching the gospel in the spirit of testimony and prayer. I call to mind one such incident when I was a young man, probably seventeen or eighteen years of age. I heard the late Bishop Millen Atwood preach a sermon in the Thirteenth Ward. I was studying grammar at the time, and he made some grammatical errors in his talk.

I wrote down his first sentence, smiled to myself, and said: "I am going to get here tonight, during the thirty minutes that Brother Atwood speaks, enough material to last me for the entire winter in my night school grammar class." We had to take to the class for each lesson two sentences, or four sentences a week, that were not grammatically correct, together with our corrections.

I contemplated making my corrections and listening to Bishop Atwood's sermon at the same time. But I did not write anything more after the first sentence—not a word; and when Millen Atwood stopped preaching, tears were rolling down my cheeks, tears of gratitude and thanksgiving that welled up in my eyes because of the marvelous testimony which that man bore of the divine mission of Joseph Smith, the prophet of God, and of the wonderful inspiration that attended the Prophet in all his labors.

Although it is now more than sixty-five years since I listened to that sermon, it is just as vivid today, and the sensations and feelings that I had are just as fixed with me as they were the day I heard it. Do you know, I would no more have thought of using those sentences in which he had made grammatical mistakes than I would think of standing up in a class and profaning the name of God. That testimony made the first profound impression that was ever made upon my heart and soul of the divine mission of the Prophet. I had heard many testimonies that had pleased me and made their impression, but this was the first testimony that had melted me to tears under the inspiration of the Spirit of God to that man.

During all the years that have passed since then, I have never been shocked or annoyed by grammatical errors or mispronounced words on the part of those preaching the gospel. I have realized that it was like judging a man by the clothes he wore to judge the spirit of a man by the clothing of his language. From that day to this the one thing above all others that has impressed me has been the Spirit, the inspiration of the living God that an individual had when proclaiming the gospel, and not the language; because after all is said and done there are a great many who have never had the opportunity to become educated so far as speaking correctly is concerned. Likewise there are many who have never had an opportunity in the financial battle of life to accumulate the means whereby they could be clothed in an attractive manner. I have endeavored, from that day to this, and have been successful in my endeavor, to judge men and women by the spirit they have; for I have learned absolutely, that it is the Spirit that giveth life and understanding, and not the letter. The letter killeth.

Heber J. Grant, "The Spirit and the Letter," *Improvement Era*, 42 (April 1939): 201.

HEBER J. GRANT

*"The Next Sabbath He Applied
to Me for Baptism"*

I remember what to me was the greatest of all incidents in my life, in this tabernacle. I saw for the first time, in the audience, my brother who had been careless, indifferent, and wayward, who had evinced no interest in the gospel of Jesus Christ.

As I saw him for the first time in this building, and as I realized that he was seeking God for light and knowledge regarding the divinity of this work, I bowed my head, and I prayed that if I were requested to address the audience that the Lord would inspire me by the revelations of his Spirit, by that Holy Spirit in whom every true Latter-day Saint believes, that my brother would have to acknowledge to me that I had spoken beyond my natural ability, that I had been inspired by the Lord.

I realized that if he made that confession, then I should be able to point out to him that God had given him a testimony of the divinity of this work.

I took out of my pocket a book that I always carried, called a *Ready Reference,* and I laid it down on the stand in front of me when I stood up to speak. . . . I prayed for the inspiration of the Lord and the faith of the Latter-day Saints, and I never thought of the book from that minute until I sat down at the end of a thirty-minute address. . . .

I devoted the thirty minutes of my speech almost exclusively to a testimony of my knowledge that God lives, that Jesus is the Christ, and to the wonderful and marvelous labors of the Prophet Joseph Smith, bearing witness to the knowledge God had given me that Joseph was in very deed a prophet of the true and living God.

The next morning my brother came into my office and said, "Heber, I was at a meeting yesterday and I heard you preach."

I said, "The first time you ever heard your brother preach, I guess?"

"Oh, no," he said, "I have heard you many times."

He said, "I generally come in late and go into the gallery. I often go out before the meeting is over. But you have never spoken as you did yesterday. You spoke beyond your natural ability. You were inspired of the Lord." The identical words I had uttered the day before, in my prayer to the Lord!

I said to him, "Are you still praying for a testimony of the gospel?'

He said, "Yes, and I am going nearly wild."

I asked, "What did I preach about yesterday?"

"You preached upon the divine mission of the Prophet Joseph Smith."

I answered, "And I was inspired beyond my natural ability; and I never spoke before—at any time you have heard me—as I spoke yesterday. Do you expect the Lord to get a club and knock you down? What more testimony do you want of the gospel of Jesus Christ than that a man speaks beyond his natural ability and under the inspiration of God, when he testifies of the divine mission of the Prophet Joseph Smith?"

The next Sabbath he applied to me for baptism.

"The Conversion of a Wayward Brother," *Instructor,* 104 (July 1969): 241.

◆—◆—▶

HEBER J. GRANT

"One-half of One Percent a Day"

The story of how Heber J. Grant saved two Church banks during the prolonged and disastrous panic of 1891-93 is so characteristic of his faith that we give this account of it. He made a trip to New York City in 1891 to sell one hundred thousand dollars worth of Z.C.M.I. notes owned by one of the banks. Money was then lending on the New York Stock Exchange at one-half percent a day, one hundred eighty-two and one-half percent per year. These notes bore six percent interest. Think of it! He states:

"Before starting, I was talking with President Woodruff, who knew why I was going. He smiled and said, 'You are going east on a very difficult mission. Sit down and let me give you a blessing." I sat down and he gave me a wonderful blessing, stating that I would get all the money I needed and more would be offered to me if I needed it. I went out with a feeling of perfect assurance that I would be successful. I heard that the directors of the Deseret National Bank were laughing at the idea of my being foolish enough to think I could cash Z.C.M.I. notes in the East at six percent per annum when money was one-half of one percent a day."

He stopped, on the way, at Omaha and asked the president of the Omaha National Bank, a correspondent of one of his banks, to cash a note of twelve thousand dollars. The president smiled and said: "The idea of your coming down here, trying to get money when it is one-half of one percent a day. Your banks are as well fixed financially, if not better, than ours. Young man, let me give you some advice. Go home and call your bank friends together and decide to lend a little more than would be considered strictly safe and the money will circulate around and come back into you bank again to take care of your own bank."

Brother Grant told this gentleman he was not asking for advice, that he had to go east for one hundred thousand dollars, that he intended to get it and on his return he would call on him and tell him where he got it. The bank president said: "Well, Mr. Grant, it will be a long time before I will see you."

When Brother Grant got to Chicago, he asked the vice-president of a bank there to cash two notes for twelve thousand dollars each. This bank was also one of their correspondents. He did not even ask Brother Grant to come into the bank. He stood on the outside of the counter, smiled, and declined to cash the notes. He said: "Young man, have you read the morning papers?" "Certainly," Brother Grant replied. "Have you read the financial sheet?" "Yes." "What is money loaning for in New York?" Brother Grant answered: "One-half of one percent a day." "Well, do you expect to get any money at six percent per annum?" "Yes, I do," responded Brother Grant, "because that is a rate you charge your customers if their balances are good enough to justify your making loans." Again, he replied: "I did not come to Chicago to get advice. I had the same advice from the president of the Omaha Bank. I told him I would go on my way, then on my way home I would call and tell him how I got the money, and I'll do the same with you." The vice-president smiled and said that he did not expect to see him for a long time.

When he reached New York, he had not sold one of his notes, but from then on he was divinely guided. It is a long and interesting story, but this is what he said in conclusion: "I borrowed $336 thousand all told. Before going to the train to go home, I received a telegram saying that we needed forty-eight thousand dollars more. I felt sure it was a mistake, that they did not need it, and I started for Chicago and wired one of my insurance friends at Hartford, and he made arrangements to get forty-eight thousand dollars if I needed it after I got home. After I got home, it was not needed; therefore, it was never borrowed."

From the day President Woodruff blessed him and promised him that he would get all the money he wanted and more if he needed it, he proceeded with the most perfect assurance that this promise made by a prophet of God would be fulfilled; and it was fulfilled to the very letter. This is the same faith that heals the sick and works miracles, but its application is in a different way. On his return, he called on the banker in Chicago who didn't expect to see him for a long time. He had only been gone a short time, and had much more money than he expected. When he got to Omaha, he did the same thing. The banker was utterly astonished. He felt he was a marvel; he wondered how Brother Grant did it.

Bryant S. Hinckley, *The Faith of Our Pioneer Fathers* (Salt Lake City: Deseret Book Co., 1959), pp. 76-78.

HEBER J. GRANT

"I Was Just $91,000 Worse
off Than Nothing"

Never but once in all my life have
I stood up in a meeting and prophesied in the name of the Lord
Jesus Christ, and that once was many, many years ago up in
Idaho, at Paris. I was preaching that we should judge things
not by the exception but by the general average, and that the
most prosperous, the most successful, the best financial men
were those that were honest with God. And it seemed as though
a voice said to me: "You lie, you lie. You will never live to pay
your debts, although you have been an honest tithe-payer." If
I had had a bucket of cold water poured over me, it could not
have made a greater impression.

I stopped a moment, then I said, "I prophesy in the name
of the Lord Jesus Christ that what I have said to you people is
true, and that the Lord rewards us when we do our duty; and I
prophesy that although I am a ruined man in the estimation
of many men, I will yet live to pay my debts." And I was just
$91,000 worse off than nothing. . . . But from that very day my
prophecy was fulfilled. The Lord blessed everything I touched,
and in only three short years I was even with the world, financially speaking.

Heber J. Grant in *Conference Report*, April 6, 1941, p. 130.

"Darn You, Heber Grant."

I have related the wonderful blessing that my dear friend Richard W. Young received by obeying the advice and counsel of President John Taylor. But the remarkable record of good fortune that resulted from following the advice of President Taylor was no more wonderful than the result of Richard's obeying the counsel of President Wilford Woodruff, successor to President Taylor.

Richard W. Young, like me and many others, invested quite heavily in Utah-Idaho Sugar stock which, at the time, paid a very generous dividend. . . .

When the trouble broke out between the United States and Spain I was visiting Richard in his office. He remarked that as a graduate of West Point it was his duty to volunteer again to enter the army. He thought that he would probably have the rank and pay of a major and stated that his compensation as a major would not pay one-half of the interest on his debts, but honor and duty demanded his return to the army.

I replied that it would take ten times as much courage to remain home and not enter the army, and I advised him to consult President Wilford Woodruff and take his advice, stating that if President Woodruff advised him to remain at home, I felt he ought to accept that advice, notwithstanding the ridicule that might come to him by doing so. I said: "There may be some special labor that the Lord has for you to perform that is of more importance than for you to volunteer and go to the Philippines where perhaps you might lose your life."

He said that he would not think of such a thing as to speak to President Woodruff about returning to the army, and further remarked: "He is one of the most tender-hearted men in the world. He is as tender-hearted as a woman. I feel sure he would not advise me to volunteer."

I replied: "Do you accept me, Richard, as an apostle of the Lord Jesus Christ, with authority to call people on missions?"

He answered: "I certainly do."

I said: "All right, as an apostle, I call you on a mission to go to President Wilford Woodruff and ask for his advice as to your returning to the army, and your mission is to follow that advice and counsel, no matter how much you dislike to do so. I will stay right here in your office until you return and report."

He said: "Darn you, Heber Grant." He picked up his hat and went to see President Woodruff, looking anything but happy.

He returned smiling and said: "President Woodruff is as full of fight as an egg is full of meat. He remarked, 'If you don't go back to the army, Brother Young, after graduating from West Point, you will disgrace the name you bear, and it will be a reflection upon your dear, dead grandfather, President Brigham Young.' "

Richard was very happy. He took President Woodruff's advice, joined the army, and went to the Philippines, notwithstanding the fact that he was heavily in debt and was very much concerned about leaving his unsettled obligations. But while he was still in the Philippines, one of the corporations in which Richard had twelve thousand dollars' worth of stock at par value, and which was worth only nine thousand when he joined the army, paid a special cash dividend of one hundred percent and during Richard's absence paid dividends of from ten to twenty percent regularly. Soon after his return home it paid a special dividend of forty percent. These two special dividends, to say nothing of the large regular dividends that were paid, netted him enough to cancel all of his debts and leave him a home and some other valuable property in addition.

The increase in the value of Richard's securities while he was in the Philippine Islands was very remarkable. The war with Spain lasted but a short time. After the war he was appointed by the governor-general of the Philippine Islands, William H. Taft (afterwards president of the United States), one of the supreme court judges of the Islands, and he was also appointed to write the code for the islands. He made an excellent record while in the Philippines and gained the love and confidence of that splendid man, William H. Taft, who ever afterwards was a friend not only of Richard W. Young, but of the Mormon people.

When Richard returned to Utah, he resumed his law practice and was one of the prosperous, successful lawyers of our state. Subsequently, as we all know, he was blessed of the Lord by being chosen to preside over the Ensign Stake of Zion, one of the important stakes of the Church; and he made a splendid stake president.

When the World War broke out, he again returned to the army and was made a brigadier-general. Because of his experience and education at West Point, he was detailed to train soldiers and was in charge of one of the large training camps, Fort Kearney. I had the pleasure of visiting with him and the late Brigham H. Roberts, the chaplain, while they were at Kearney.

Richard was only a short time in Europe when he wrote a fine article for the *Improvement Era*. The armistice having been signed almost immediately after Richard's arrival overseas, he did not actively participate in the World War, except in the training camp. In my former article regarding Richard W. Young, I quoted from the hymn, "God Moves in a Mysterious Way." Certainly God did move in a very wonderful and mysterious way in blessing my near and dear friend when he followed the advice of President Taylor, and also I feel to a much greater extent when he followed the advice of President Woodruff.

Faith is a gift of God, and when people have faith to live the gospel and to listen to the counsel of those who preside in the wards and stakes and of the General Authorities of the Church, it has been my experience that they have been abundantly blessed of the Lord, and that many of them have come out of great financial and other difficulties in a most miraculous and wonderful way.

"Obedience is better than sacrifice, and to hearken than the fat of rams." [1 Samuel 15:22.]

Heber J. Grant, "Further Facts on Following Counsel," *Improvement Era*, 39 (June 1936): 331-32.

———◆———

HEBER J. GRANT

"In the Death of Your Mamma the Will of the Lord Will Be"

My wife Lucy was very sick for nearly three years prior to her death. At one time I was in the hospital with her for six months. When she was dying, I called my children into the bedroom and told them their mamma was dying. My daughter Lutie said she did not want her mamma to die and insisted that I lay hands upon her and heal her, saying that she had often seen her mother, when sick in the hospital in San Francisco, suffering intensely, go to sleep immediately and have a peaceful night's rest when I had blessed her. I explained to my children that we all had to die some time, and that I felt that their mamma's time had come. The children went out of the room, and I knelt down by the bed of my dying wife and told the Lord that I acknowledged his hand in life or in death, in joy or in sorrow, in prosperity or adversity; that I did not complain because my wife was dying, but that I lacked the strength to see my wife die and have her death affect the faith of my children in the ordinances of the gospel. I therefore pleaded with him to give to my daughter Lutie a testimony that it was his will that her mother should die. Within a few short hours, my wife breathed her last. Then I called the children into the bedroom and announced that their mamma was dead. My little boy Heber commenced weeping bitterly, and Lutie put her arms around him and kissed him, and told him not to cry, that the voice of the Lord had said to her, "In the death of your mamma the will of the Lord will be." Lutie knew nothing of my prayers, and this manifestation to her was a direct answer to my supplication to the Lord, and for it I have never ceased to be grateful.

Heber J. Grant, "When Great Sorrows Are Our Portion," *Improvement Era,* 15 (June 1912): 726-27.

HEBER J. GRANT

"Her Pulse Beat Only Twenty-eight Times to the Minute"

When my wife died I took my oldest three daughters to Boston, New York, and other places in the hope that the sorrow caused by the death of their mother might be forgotten. When we reached Washington two of them were taken ill with diphtheria. They were as sick as any children I have ever seen. The younger of the two was so low that her pulse beat only twenty-eight times to the minute, and I felt sure she was going to die. I knelt down and prayed God to spare her life, inasmuch as I had brought my children east to relieve the terrible sorrow that had come to them, and prayed that I should not have the additional sorrow of taking one of my children home in a coffin. I prayed for her life, and shed bitter tears of humiliation. While praying, the inspiration came to me that if I would administer to her, she would live. Some people say we cannot know for a certainty that we receive manifestations from the Lord. Well, I know that I was shedding tears of sorrow, fear, and anguish while I was praying, and I know that immediately thereafter I received the witness of the Spirit that my little girl should live, and I shed tears of unbounding joy and gratitude and thanksgiving to God, thanking him for the inspiration that came to me to send for the elders that they might administer to my little girl.

Hiram B. Clawson and George Q. Cannon were in Washington at the time, and I sent for them. When George Q. Cannon laid his hands upon my daughter's head to seal the anointing wherewith she had been anointed, he made a statement that I have never heard before or since in all my life, in any prayer. He said, in substance: "The adversary, the destroyer, has decreed your death and made public announcement that you shall die; but by the authority of the priesthood of the Living God, we rebuke the decree of the adversary, and say that you shall live and not die; that you shall live to become a mother in the Church of Christ." She did live to become a mother, and in the providences of the Lord her children are the great-grandchildren of the man who held the priesthood of God and gave her that blessing.

Heber J. Grant in *Conference Report* October 3, 1941, pp. 12-13.

————◆◆————

HEBER J. GRANT

"My Last Son Died of a Hip Disease"

I have been blessed with only two sons. One of them died at five years of age and the other at seven.

My last son died of a hip disease. I had built great hopes that he would live to spread the gospel at home and abroad and be an honor to me. About an hour before he died I had a dream that his mother, who was dead, came for him, and that she brought with her a messenger; and she told this messenger to take the boy while I was asleep. In the dream I thought I awoke and I seized my son and fought for him and finally succeeded in getting him away from the messenger who had come to take him, and in so doing I dreamed that I stumbled and fell upon him.

I dreamed that I fell upon his sore hip, and the terrible cries and anguish of the child drove me nearly wild. I could not stand it, and I jumped up and ran out of the house so as not to hear his distress. I dreamed that after running out of the house I met Brother Joseph E. Taylor and told him of these things.

He said: "Well, Heber, do you know what I would do if my wife came for one of her children—I would not struggle for that child; I would not oppose her taking that child away. If a mother who had been faithful had passed beyond the veil, she would know of the suffering and anguish her child may have to suffer. She would know whether that child might go through life as a cripple and whether it would be better or wiser for that child to be relieved from the torture of life. And when you stop to think, Brother Grant, that the mother of that boy went down into the shadow of death to give him life, she is the one who ought to have the right to take him or leave him."

I said, "I believe you are right, Brother Taylor, and if she comes again, she shall have the boy without any protest on my part."

After coming to the conclusion, I was waked by my brother, B. F. Grant, who was staying that night with us.

He called me into the room and told me that my child was dying.

I went in the front room and sat down. There was a vacant chair between me and my wife who is now living, and I felt the presence of that boy's deceased mother sitting in that chair. I did not tell anybody what I felt, but I turned to my living wife and said: "Do you feel anything strange?" She said:

"Yes, I feel assured that Heber's mother is sitting between us, waiting to take him away."

Now, I am naturally, I believe, a sympathetic man. I was raised as an only child with all the affection that a mother could lavish upon a boy. I believe that I am naturally affectionate and sympathetic and that I shed tears for my friends—tears of joy for their success and tears of sorrow for their misfortunes. But I sat by the deathbed of my little boy and saw him die, without shedding a tear. My loving wife, my brother, and I upon that occasion experienced a sweet, peaceful, and heavenly influence in my home, as great as I have ever experienced in my life. And no person can tell me that every other Latter-day Saint that has a knowledge of the gospel in his heart and soul, can really mourn for his loved ones; only in the loss of their society in this life.

Heber J. Grant, *Gospel Standards* (Salt Lake City: *Improvement Era*, 1969), pp. 364-65.

Biographical Sketch

George Albert Smith was born in Salt Lake City just across the street from Temple Square. He had an unusually noble parentage. President Smith's great-grandfather was John Smith, a brother to Joseph Smith, Sr. He was the first stake president in Salt Lake Valley and later served as the Patriarch to the Church. Following is an account of the conversion of John Smith and his son, George A. Smith.

. . . Solomon Humphries and Joseph Wakefield preached in Potsdam, St. Lawrence County, New York. Among those to become interested in their message was the family of John Smith, the uncle of the Prophet Joseph Smith. John Smith had been in poor health for several years and for six months before his baptism, on January 9, 1832, was too incapacitated to walk to the barn. When he decided to be baptized the neighbors were sure such a venture would kill him. His son George, then fourteen years of age, broke a road to the creek where he cut the ice, and as the neighbors gazed with astonishment expecting John Smith to die in the water, Elder Solomon Humphries performed the holy ordinance, and John Smith walked out of the water invigorated. From that hour his health improved. (Ivan J. Barrett, *Joseph Smith and the Restoration*, p. 228.)

John Smith's son George, who was baptized on that day is the original George Albert Smith, the grandfather of President

George Albert Smith, and the person for whom President Smith was named. He is usually referred to as "George A." He was a cousin of the Prophet Joseph and was called to be an apostle at age twenty-one. No one else in this dispensation has been called at such a young age. George A. Smith was also a counselor to Brigham Young.

George A. Smith's son was John Henry Smith, who also served in the Quorum of the Twelve and later in the First Presidency as a counselor to President Joseph F. Smith. John Henry Smith was one of President George Albert Smith's ideals; in speaking of him President Smith remarked, "I have never met a greater man than my father. . . ."

In light of this information there is a great significance in the promises made in the patriarchal blessing given to George Albert Smith when he was fourteen years of age. Four years after John Henry Smith was called to the Quorum of the Twelve, a patriarch pronounced the following blessings upon Elder Smith's son, George Albert:

". . . Thou shalt become a mighty prophet in the midst of the sons of Zion. And the angels of the Lord shall administer unto you, and the choice blessings of the heavens shall rest upon you. . . .

"And thou shalt be wrapt in the visions of the heavens, and thou shalt be clothed with salvation as with a garment, for thou art destined to become a mighty man before the Lord, for thou shalt become a mighty apostle in the Church and kingdom of God upon the earth, for none of thy father's family shall have more power with God than thou shalt have, for none shall exceed thee; . . . and thou shalt become a man of mighty faith before the Lord, even like unto that of the brother of Jared; and thou shall remain upon the earth until thou art satisfied with life, and shall be numbered with the Lord's anointed and shall become a king and a priest unto the Most High. . . ."[1]

President Smith was twenty-two years old when he married Lucy Emily Woodruff in 1892. Shortly after his marriage he filled a mission to the Southern States. He was sustained as a member of the Quorum of the Twelve at age thirty-three in 1903. He presided over the European Mission from 1919 to 1921 and became the general superintendent of the YMMIA in 1921.

He was prominent in the National Society of the Sons of the American Revolution and was a member of the national executive board of the Boy Scouts of America. On the death of Heber J. Grant in 1945 he was sustained as President of the

---

[1]*Church History*, Student Supplement, 1969, pp. 75-76.

Church. He presided over the Church in some important and critical years just after World War II.

He was known throughout the world for his great humanity. He loved everyone and treated everyone with love and kindness. The following is taken from a conference address given by President George Albert Smith. The occasion was his seventy-eighth birthday, and by reading it one can gain insight to the greatness of President Smith and the conviction of a man beloved by the Lord and by millions of people.

I am celebrating my birthday. Seventy-eight years ago today, right across the street, I was born. My life has been spent very largely in this community and traveling for the Church. I don't know of any man in all the world that has more reason to be grateful than I. People have been kind and helpful to me, members of the Church and nonmembers alike. Wherever I have gone, I have found noble men and women. Therefore on this my birthday, after having traveled approximately a million miles in the world in the interests of the gospel of Jesus Christ, one of the frailest of my mother's eleven children, I testify that the Lord has preserved my life, and I have had joy beyond expression, and I have enjoyed the results of loving my neighbor as myself, and all this brings happiness.

After all these years of travel in many parts of the world, associating with many of the great and good men and women of the world, I witness to you, I know today better than I ever knew before that God lives; that Jesus is the Christ; that Joseph Smith was a prophet of the Living God; and that the Church that he organized under the direction of our Heavenly Father, the Church that received divine authority, The Church of Jesus Christ of Latter-day Saints, the Church that was driven into the wilderness and with headquarters now in Salt Lake City, Utah, is still operating under the guidance of the same priesthood that was conferred by Peter, James, and John upon Joseph Smith and Oliver Cowdery. I know that, as I know that I live, and I leave that testimony with you, and I pray that our Heavenly Father will continue to guide us and help us and inspire us and bless us, which he will if we are righteous. I am so thankful to be here with you this morning, and to look into your faces, hundreds of whom I have met in different parts of the country, and I take this occasion to thank you for your kindness to me as I have traveled among you.

May the Lord add his blessings. Thankful for the comforts that we have today, I pray that his peace and his love will abide with us forever, and that we may be the means under his guidance of bringing millions of his children to an understanding of his truths that they, too, may be blessed and are blessed this day. This is my testimony to you, that this is the gospel of Jesus Christ, the power of God unto salvation to all those who believe and obey it, and I bear that witness in the name of Jesus Christ, our Lord. Amen.[2]

President George Albert Smith died at age eighty-one on April 4, 1951.

---

[2]*Conference Report,* April 1948, pp. 17-18.

GEORGE ALBERT SMITH

"That Was My First Prayer"

One of the first things I remember was when my mother took me by the hand and led me upstairs to the bedroom. I can remember it as if it were yesterday. She sat down by my little trundle bed and had me kneel in front of her. She folded my hands and took them in hers and taught me my first prayer. I shall never forget it. I do not want to forget it. It is one of the loveliest memories that I have in life.

It was such a simple prayer that I can repeat it today:

Now I lay me down to sleep,
I pray the Lord my soul to keep.
If I should die before I wake,
I pray the Lord my soul to take.

That was my first prayer; it opened for me the windows of heaven. That prayer extended to me the hand of my Father in heaven. From that day, wherever I have been, I have felt close to my Heavenly Father.

I have often said no man in the world has been more blessed than I. From my childhood, ever since I can remember, I have never been compelled to associate with evil individuals. I have been very fortunate in having my life so adjusted that I could choose the very finest men and women that could be found in the world to be my companions. This has enriched my life and I am grateful.

Alice K. Chase, comp., *Sayings of a Saint* (Salt Lake City: Deseret Book Co., 1951), pp. 6-7.

◄—◆—►

GEORGE ALBERT SMITH

"Don't You Want to Bear Your Testimony?"

It doesn't seem very long since I bore my first testimony. It was at the time of my baptism, or when I was being confirmed. I had been reared in a Latter-day Saint home and had been taught to pray by a devoted mother. I was made to understand that we are children of our Heavenly Father. Then I was baptized, when eight years of age, and became a member of the Church. And, by the way, I was baptized in old City Creek on the north side of this block.

At the fast meeting that was held after I had been confirmed a member of the Church, a dear old aunt, who long since has gone home, asked me, "Don't you want to bear your testimony?" I had heard others bear their testimonies, but I had never thought of bearing mine. I arose to my feet and told the congregation that I was grateful that I belonged to the true church, and I was just as sure then that I belonged to the Church of the Lamb of God as I am today."

George Albert Smith, *Sharing the Gospel with Others* (Salt Lake City: Deseret Book Co., 1948), p. 27.

GEORGE ALBERT SMITH

"She Was Unusually Anxious about Me"

When I was a child I became very ill. The doctor said I had typhoid fever and should be in bed for at least three weeks. He told mother to give me no solid food, but to have me drink some coffee.

When he went away, I told mother that I didn't want any coffee. I had been taught that the Word of Wisdom, given by the Lord to Joseph Smith, advised us not to use coffee.

Mother had brought three children into the world and two had died. She was unusually anxious about me.

I asked her to send for Brother Hawks, one of our ward teachers. He was a worker at the foundry and a poor and humble man of great faith in the power of the Lord.

He came, administered to me, and blessed me that I might be healed.

When the doctor came the next morning I was playing outside with the other children. He was surprised. He examined me and discovered that my fever was gone and that I seemed to be well.

I was grateful to the Lord for my recovery. I was sure that he had healed me.

Jeremiah Stokes, *Modern Miracles* (Salt Lake City: Bookcraft, 1945), p. 135.

GEORGE ALBERT SMITH

"I Would Like to Know What You Have Done with My Name"

A number of years ago I was seriously ill; in fact, I think everyone gave me up but my wife. With my family I went to St. George, Utah, to see if it would improve my health. We went as far as we could by train, and then continued the journey in a wagon, in the bottom of which a bed had been made for me.

In St. George we arranged for a tent for my health and comfort, with a built-in floor raised about a foot above the ground, and could roll up the south side of the tent to make the sunshine and fresh air available. I became so weak as to be scarcely able to move. It was a slow and exhausting effort for me even to turn over in bed.

One day, under these conditions, I lost consciousness of my surroundings and thought I had passed to the other side. I found myself standing with my back to a large and beautiful lake, facing a great forest of trees. There was no one in sight, and there was no boat upon the lake or any other visible means to indicate how I might have arrived there. I realized, or seemed to realize, that I had finished my work in mortality and had gone home. I began to look around, to see if I could not find someone. There was no evidence of anyone living there, just those great, beautiful trees in front of me and the wonderful lake behind me.

I began to explore, and soon I found a trail through the woods which seemed to have been used very little, and which was almost obscured by grass. I followed this trail, and after I had walked for some time and had traveled a considerable distance through the forest, I saw a man coming towards me. I became aware that he was a very large man, and I hurried my steps to reach him, because I recognized him as my grandfather. In mortality he weighed over three hundred pounds, so you may know he was a large man. I remember how happy I was to see him coming. I had been given his name and had always been proud of it.

When Grandfather came within a few feet of me, he stopped. His stopping was an invitation for me to stop. Then—and this I would like the boys and girls and young people never to forget—he looked at me very earnestly and said:

"I would like to know what you have done with my name."

Everything I had ever done passed before me as though it were a flying picture on a screen—everything I had done. Quickly this vivid retrospect came down to the very time I was standing there. My whole life had passed before me. I smiled and looked at my grandfather and said:

"I have never done anything with your name of which you need be ashamed."

He stepped forward and took me in his arms, and as he did so, I became conscious again of my earthly surroundings. My pillow was as wet as though water had been poured on it—wet with tears of gratitude that I could answer unashamed.

I have thought of this many times, and I want to tell you that I have been trying, more than ever since that time, to take care of that name. So I want to say to the boys and girls, to the young men and women, to the youth of the Church and of all the world: Honor your fathers and your mothers. Honor the names that you bear, because some day you will have the privilege and the obligation of reporting to them (and to your Father in heaven) what you have done with their name.

George Albert Smith, *Sharing the Gospel*, pp. 110-12.

GEORGE ALBERT SMITH

"The Product of My Thoughts"

. . . **A**s a child thirteen years of age, I went to school at the Brigham Young Academy. It was fortunate that part of my instruction came under Dr. Karl G. Maeser, that outstanding educator who was the first builder of our great Church schools. . . . I cannot remember much of what was said during the year that I was there, but there is one thing that I will probably never forget. Dr. Maeser one day stood up and said:

"Not only will you be held accountable for the things that you do, but you will be held responsible for the very thoughts you think."

Being a boy, not in the habit of controlling my thoughts very much, it was quite a puzzle to me what I was to do, and it worried me. In fact, it stuck to me just like a burr. About a week or ten days after that it suddenly came to me what he meant. I could see the philosophy of it then. All at once there came to me this interpretation of what he had said: Why, of course, you will be held accountable for your thoughts because when your life is complete in mortality, it will be the sum of your thoughts." That one suggestion has been a great blessing to me all my life, and it has enabled me upon many occasions to avoid thinking improperly because I realize that I will be, when my life's labor is complete, the product of my thoughts.

Church News, 16 Feb. 1946, p. 1.

GEORGE ALBERT SMITH

"I Felt Absolutely No Terror"

While laboring as a missionary in the Southern States, President Smith had this experience.

We were in a wooded rural area. During the day we had held meetings with the people in the neighborhood who were very friendly and very receptive to our message. One of the local Saints had invited us to accept the hospitality of his home for the night. It was a humble home, built of split logs. It consisted of two rooms and a small log lean-to. There were six missionaries in the group, so it strained the capacity of the little house to be there.

About midnight we were awakened with a terrible shouting and yelling from the outside. Foul language greeted our ears as we sat up in bed to acquaint ourselves with the circumstances. It was a bright moonlight night and we could see many people on the outside. President Kimball jumped up and started to dress. The men pounded on the door and used filthy language, ordering the Mormons to come out, that they were going to shoot them. President Kimball asked me if I was going to get up and dress and I told him 'No, I was going to stay in bed, that I was sure the Lord would take care of us.' In just a few seconds the room was filled with shots. Apparently the mob had divided itself into four groups and they were shooting into the corners of the house. Splinters were flying over our heads in every direction. There were a few moments of quiet, then another volley of shots was fired and more splinters flew. I felt absolutely no terror. I was very calm as I lay there, experiencing one of the most horrible events of my life; but I was sure that as long as I was preaching the word of God and following his teachings that the Lord would protect me. And he did.

Primary Association General Board and Deseret Sunday School Union General Board, comps. *A Story to Tell* (Salt Lake City: Deseret Book Co., 1945), pp. 155-56.

GEORGE ALBERT SMITH

"Just One More Step"

The following also occurred during President Smith's labors in the Southern States Mission.

Late one evening in a pitch-dark night, Elder Stout and I were traveling along a high precipice. Our little walk was narrow; on one side was the wall of the mountain, on the other side, the deep, deep river. We had no light and there were no stars and no moon to guide us. We had been traveling all day and we knew that we would have hospitality extended to us if we could reach the McKelvin home, which was on the other side of a high valley. We had to cross this mountain in order to reach the home of Mr. McKelvin. Our mode of travel of necessity was very halting. We walked almost with a shuffle, feeling each foot of ground as we advanced, with one hand extended toward the wall of the mountain. Elder Stout was ahead of me and as I walked along I felt the hard surface of the trail under my feet. In doing so I left the wall of the mountain which had acted as a guide and a steadying force. After I had taken a few steps away I felt impressed to stop immediately, that something was wrong. I called to Elder Stout and he answered me. The direction from which his voice came indicated I was on the wrong trail, so I backed up until I reached the wall of the mountain and again proceeded forward. He was just a few steps in front of me, and as I reached him we came to a fence piling. In the dark we carefully explored it with our hands and feet to see whether it would be safe for us to climb over. We decided that it would be secure and made the effort. While I was on the top of this big pile of logs, my little suitcase popped open and the contents were scattered around. In the dark I felt around for them and was quite convinced I had recovered practically everything. We arrived safely at our destination about eleven o'clock at night. I soon discovered I had lost my comb and brush, and the next morning we returned to the scene of my accident. I recovered my property and while there my curiosity was stimulated and aroused to see what had happened the night before when I had lost my way in the dark. As missionaries, we wore hob-nails in the bottom of our shoes to make them last longer, so that I could easily follow our tracks in the soft dirt. I retraced my steps to the point where my tracks left and wandered to the edge of a deep precipice. Just one more step and I would have fallen over into the river and had been drowned. I felt very ill when I realized how close I had come to death. I was also very grateful to my Heavenly Father for protecting me. I have always felt that if we are doing the Lord's work and ask him for his help and protection, he will guide and take care of us.

A Story to Tell, pp. 156-58.

GEORGE ALBERT SMITH

"The Lord Had Again Spared My Life"

I was considered a very good swimmer and thoroughly enjoyed the sport. This particular day the tide was very high and very swift. As I left the shore and swam out into the ocean, I dived through the big breakers as they would crest and spray over me. My objective was the large swells beyond the breakers, where I could lie on my back and ride the big swells up and down. While engaging in this interesting sport, one very huge wave crested and broke before I could right myself following the dive through the previous one.

The second one caught me and threw me to the floor of the ocean. I could feel myself being dragged out by the undertow. At this particular time many waves came in rapid succession and I was not able to right myself before I had to dive from one into another. I realized that my strength was rapidly leaving me, that it was going to be necessary for me to find some means of help. As I rode to the crest of one high wave, I saw the underpilings of a pier close at hand, and I thought if with super-human effort I could reach the security of the pilings that I would be able to save my life. I silently asked my Heavenly Father to give me the strength to reach my objective. As I was washed into arm's length of the pier, I reached out and put my arms around one of the posts. They were covered with sharp, dark blue barnacles, and as I wound my arms and legs around its security, they cut my chest, legs, and thighs. I hung on as long as I could stand the pain and watched for a big friendly swell to come my way that I might throw myself on it and travel closer to shore. Each time with a prayer in my heart I would make the effort traveling from one pile to another with the aid of the rolling swell. Slowly but surely, and with great difficulty, I made my way to the shore where the water was shallow enough for me to walk to the beach. I was so weak, and so nearly drowned, I was unable to walk home until I had rested for some time. Lying on the sand with its warmth and security, I thought of the harrowing experience that I had just endured and my heart was filled with gratitude and humility that the Lord had again spared my life.

A Story to Tell, pp. 158-59.

GEORGE ALBERT SMITH

"It's What You Feel That Makes You Happy"

It is not the things we have that make us happy. It is what we feel. This was illustrated to me one day by an earnest brother who came from Holland. He could not speak English. I helped him get a modest position and a place where he could live, with a small garden, in the ward in which I lived. He used to come to fast meetings and hear the brethren and sisters bear their testimonies in English, although he could not understand what was being said. Then, to return the compliment, he and his wife would get up and bear their testimonies in Dutch, which we could not understand. One day after fast meeting, with the aid of many motions, I asked him: "Brother Folkers, why do you come to an English-speaking meeting when you cannot understand what is said?" At length it dawned on him what I was trying to say. "Ik versta," I think he said, to let me know he understood. Then he did this: he touched his eye and he said, "It is not what you see," and touched his ear and said, "It is not what you hear, but what you feel that makes you happy."

I have thought of this a good many times. It is what we feel; and the more we feel, under the inspiration of the Spirit of God, the happier we are. And at this season, as children of our Father in heaven, blessed above the world many times over, possessed of opportunities and privileges that the world knows nothing about, we may well be earnestly grateful for the goodness of the Lord to us, and we may well show our gratitude by honoring him and keeping his commandments.

George Albert Smith, *Sharing the Gospel,* pp. 108-9.

GEORGE ALBERT SMITH

"All Fear and Anxiety Left"

I remember, as a young man and missionary in the Southern States (1892-94) the first conference I attended. It was out in the woods on a farm in Mississippi. We didn't have comfortable seats to sit on. The brethren had been permitted to cut down a few trees and lay the trunks of those trees across the stumps which were left. We balanced ourselves on these, or else sat on the ground.

Our meeting started right after breakfast time, and we didn't even think it was necessary to have anything more to eat until evening. We stayed and enjoyed the blessings of the inspiration of the Almighty, and we certainly were blessed, notwithstanding the inconveniences and discomforts which surrounded us.

At that time there was considerable hostility manifested in Mississippi and other states in the South, but we just felt as though we had walked into the presence of our Heavenly Father, and all fear and anxiety left. That was my first experience in a mission field, attending a conference, and from that time until now I have appreciated the fact that the companionship of the Spirit of the Lord is an antidote for weariness, for fear, and all those things that sometimes overtake us in life.

George Albert Smith, *Sharing the Gospel*, pp. 16-17.

GEORGE ALBERT SMITH

"Doctor, Won't You Pray for Me?"

A little boy was upon the operating table, ready to undergo an operation for appendicitis—an orphan boy, about eight years of age. It was a rather unusual case, and by the way a charity case. As the boy lay there he looked up at the surgeons—there were several of them present—and addressing the surgeon in charge he said: "Doctor, before you begin to operate, won't you pray for me?" The surgeon looked at the boy amazed and said, "Why, I can't pray for you." Then the little fellow turned his eyes from one to the other, asking each if they would pray for him. Each in turn declined. Then the little man said: "If you won't pray for me, won't you please wait while I pray for myself?" The little fellow got up on the operating table on his knees, folded his hands, and uttered a prayer. He said to the Lord: "Heavenly Father, I am only a little orphan boy, but I am awful sick, and these doctors are going to operate. Will you please help them that they will do it right? And now, Heavenly Father if you will make me well I will be a good boy. Thank you for making me well." He then turned over and laid on his back and looked up at the doctors and nurses who were all standing around, but he was the only one in the room who could see because the others had tears in their eyes. He said: "Now I am ready."

A few days after that a man went into the office of the chief surgeon and asked him to tell him the story of the little boy he had operated on a few days before. The surgeon said: "I have operated on a good many little boys."

"Yes, I know, but this was an unusual case—tell me about it."

Then the doctor looked at him for some time and said, "I don't know whether I will tell you or not. I am not sure but what it is too sacred to talk about."

"Please tell me," he replied; "I will treat it as sacred, too."
Then the doctor told the story as I have related it, and when he
got through the visitor said, "My, that was a remarkable experience, wasn't it?"

The doctor said, "Remarkable? That was the most remarkable experience of my whole life. I have operated on hundreds
of men, women, and children, and I have known some of them
to pray, but never until I stood in the presence of that little
boy, have I heard anyone talk to their Heavenly Father face
to face."

George Albert Smith, *Sharing the Gospel*, pp. 144-45.

◄—◆—►

GEORGE ALBERT SMITH

"My Father Had Fallen into the River"

He [George Albert Smith] said at a
conference held in Provo: "I am standing on what to me is
sacred ground. My grandparents and my parents and many other
relatives lived here in Provo, and some still live here. My
father, as a young man, came near losing his life in the Provo
River, not far from where we are now. His father, who was in
Salt Lake City, felt impressed to go into a room that had been
set apart for prayer. He clothed himself in temple robes, knelt
down at the altar, and said: 'Heavenly Father, I feel that there
is something seriously wrong with my family in Provo. Thou
knowest that I cannot be with them there and be here. Heavenly
Father, wilt thou preserve and safeguard them, and I will be
grateful to thee and honor thee.'

"At the time when he was praying, just as near as it
was possible to indicate by checking the time, my father had

248

fallen into the river. It was at flood time. Logs and rocks were pouring down from the canyon, and he was helpless. Those who were near saw his predicament, but they could not reach him. The turbulance of the water was such that nobody could live in it. They just stood there in horror. Father was doing everything he could to keep his head above water, but he was being thrown up and down and being dashed against the rocks and logs. All at once a wave lifted him bodily from the water and threw him upon the shore. It was a direct answer of the prayer of a servant of the Lord."

George Albert Smith, *Sharing the Gospel*, pp. 216-217.

GEORGE ALBERT SMITH

"You Are a Very Generous Man with Someone Else's Property"

One day on the street I met a friend whom I had known since boyhood. I had not visited with him for some time, and I was interested in being brought up to date concerning his life, his problems, and his faith; therefore, I invited him to go to a conference in Utah County with me. He drove his fine car (the make of car I was driving had not been received into society at that time). He took his wife and I took mine.

At the conference, I called on him to speak. I did not know what it might do to him, but I thought I would take a chance. He made a fine talk. He told of his trips to the East, how he explained the gospel to the people he met, and how grateful he was for his heritage. He stated that his opportunities in the world had been magnified and multiplied because his father and mother had joined the Church in the Old World.

As we drove home, he turned to me and said: "My, this has been a wonderful conference. I have enjoyed it."

I thought to myself, he had enjoyed it because he himself had participated. I was glad he had. Then, he said: "You know I have heard many things in this conference, but there is only one thing that I do not understand the way you do."

I said: "What is it?"

"Well," he said, "it is about paying tithing."

He thought I would ask him how he paid his tithing, but I did not. I thought if he wanted to tell me, he would. He said: "Would you like me to tell you how I pay my tithing?"

I said, "If you want to, you may."

"Well," he said, "if I make ten thousand dollars in a year, I put a thousand dollars in the bank for tithing. I know why it's there. Then when the bishop comes and wants me to make a contribution for the chapel or give him a check for a missionary who is going away, if I think he needs the money, I give him a check. If a family in the ward is in distress and needs coal or food or clothing or anything else, I write out a check. If I find a boy or girl in the East, I send a check. Little by little I exhaust the thousand dollars, and every dollar of it has gone where I know it has done good. What do you think of it?"

"Well," I said, "do you want me to tell you what I think of it?"

He said, "Yes."

I said: "I think you are a very generous man with someone else's property." And he nearly tipped the car over.

He said, "What do you mean?"

I said, "You have an idea that you have paid your tithing?"

"Yes," he said.

I said: "You have not paid any tithing. You have told me what you have done with the Lord's money, but you have not told me that you have given anyone a penny of your own. He is the best partner you have in the world. He gives you everything you have, even the air you breathe. He has said you should take one-tenth of what comes to you and give it to the Church as directed by the Lord. You haven't done that; you have taken your best partner's money and have given it away."

Well, I will tell you there was quiet in the car for some time. We rode on to Salt Lake City and talked about other things.

About a month after that I met him on the street. He came up, put his arm in mine, and said: "Brother Smith, I am paying my tithing the same way you do." I was very happy to hear that.

Alma P. Burton and Clea M. Burton, comps., *Stories from Mormon History* (Salt Lake City: Deseret Book Co., 1960), pp. 70-72.

GEORGE ALBERT SMITH

"Let Us Bring to You More Good"

I remember upon one occasion a man said to me, after we had talked for some time, "Well, from all I can learn your church is just as good as any other church." I presume he thought he was paying us a great compliment, but I said to him: "If the church I represent here is not of more importance to children of men than any other church, then I am mistaken in my duty here. We have come not to take away from you the truth and virtue you possess. We have not come to find fault with you nor to criticize you. We have not come here to berate you because of things you have not done; but we have come here as your brethren. We are giving our time and our means voluntarily, and have come to your land with love in our hearts, with the desire to do you good, to encourage you to repent of your sins wherein you are sinful, and encourage you to retain your virtues wherein you are virtuous, and to say to you: 'Keep all the good that you have, and let us bring to you more good, in order that you may be happier and in order that you may be prepared to enter into the presence of our Heavenly Father.' "

George Albert Smith, *Sharing the Gospel*, pp. 12-13.

GEORGE ALBERT SMITH

"And Just Because I Tried To Be Polite to Someone"

In Chicago a number of years ago, during the Century of Progress Exposition, I went into our Church booth one day and inquired of the missionaries as to who had charge of the great cultural and scientific fair.

They told me the man's name was Dawes, and I asked, "Is he the brother of Charles G. Dawes, who was vice president of the United States and also ambassador to Great Britain?"

And they answered, "Yes."

"I am delighted to know that," I said. "I happen to know him."

To myself I said: "I think I will go and call on him. He will be Henry Dawes." His secretary answered the telephone, and I inquired, "Is Mr. Dawes there?"

"Yes, sir."

"May I come over and see him?" I asked.

She said: "There are already a hundred people ahead of you, and they all want a job."

I smiled and said: "Well, that may be true, but I am probably the one man he would like to see because I have a job."

"Do you know him?"

"Yes. I am from Salt Lake City. I just want to pay my respects."

She told Mr. Dawes that George Albert Smith of Salt Lake City was there and wanted to meet him, and he told her to have me come over. So, instead of running me behind a hundred people to wait my turn, she took me to a side door, and there stood before me a tall man whom I had never seen before in my life.

He said, "I am Mr. Dawes."

He was very pleasant, but you can imagine how embarrassed I was. He was Mr. Dawes, and he was Ambassador Dawes' brother, but he was Rufus Dawes. I did not know there was a Rufus Dawes in the world.

"I have only come to tell you that this is a wonderful fair." I said, "and to express to you my appreciation for what you have done in organizing and seeing it through. It is marvelous what has been accomplished, and what an education it is to so many people. That is all I wanted to come and say, and to congratulate and thank you."

"That is very considerate," he said. "Come in."

"No, that is all I came to say. There are a hundred people waiting to see you."

"None of them will say anything as nice as what you have said," he replied.

So, I went in, out of ideas and out of breath, almost. He insisted on my sitting down, and the next thing I said was: "By the way, Mr. Dawes, where do your people come from?"

"Do you mean in America?" he asked.

"I mean anywhere."

"Are you interested in genealogy?" he questioned.

"I certainly am," I answered. "We have one of the finest genealogical libraries in Salt Lake City."

He said, "Excuse me just a moment," and he walked out of his office and came back with a carton about the size of an old family Bible. He took his knife, opened the carton, and took out a package wrapped in white tissue paper. He took the tissue paper off and put on the table one of the most beautifully bound books I have ever seen. It was well printed and profusely illustrated, and the cover was elegantly embossed with gold.

As I looked it over, I said, "Mr. Dawes, that is a beautiful piece of work."

"It ought to be. It cost me twenty-five thousand dollars."

"Well," I said, "it is worth it."

He said, "Is it worth anything to you?"

"It would be if I had it."

"Alright, you may have it!" Twenty-five thousand dollars worth of genealogy placed in my hand by a man whom I had met only five minutes before! I was amazed. Our visit continued but a short while longer. I told him how delighted I was to have it and that I would place it in the genealogical library in Salt Lake City.

Before I left the room, he said, "Mr. Smith, this is my mother's genealogy, the Gates genealogy. We are also preparing my father's genealogy—the Dawes family. It will be one just like this. When it is finished, I would like to send you a copy of that also."

Fifty thousand dollars worth of genealogy! And just because I tried to be polite to someone.

I do not think that was an accident. The Dawes family is one of the most prominent families in the United States, and in that line is the Gates family, including Jacob Gates, one-time member of the First Council of the Seventy. Other Church families also run through these books.

The man Rufus Dawes died before the second volume was finished. He left word with Charles G. Dawes, his elder brother, to be sure to send me a copy of that book when it was finished. I was afraid that Charles G. Dawes didn't know anything about it, so about a year later I called on him and told him how I had obtained the other volume.

"I know all about it," he said, "and we will have another of my father's line for you as soon as it is completed." And this second volume, according to promise, came to me.

Albert L. Zobell, *Topic Echoes* (Salt Lake City: Bookcraft, 1964), pp. 41-45.

GEORGE ALBERT SMITH

*"I Wonder If You Appreciate
the Richness of Your Life"*

I am reminded of a conversation with a gentleman who was not a member of the Church. He was a judge of the supreme court of Oregon (and, by the way, nominated one of the vice-presidents of the United States, who later became president of the United States). He had been among our people, had come to know a number of them, and he and I became quite well acquainted. We were riding together in an automobile from Nashville, Tennessee, out to the old Jackson Hermitage, and he surprised me by turning in the car and saying:

"I wonder if you appreciate the richness of your life?"

I said, "I think I do."

He said, "I wonder if you do."

"Well," I said, "just what do you have in your mind?"

"Why," he said, "to have been reared as you were in a home where they believed in God, and where they had family prayers, where they were familiar with the Bible, and where they did not partake of good without thanking the Lord for it.

"Furthermore, wherever you go everybody knows you are a member of the Mormon Church, and this does not seem to be any disadvantage to you; in fact, they seem to want to do more for you because of it. Here in this great convention you are the only member of your Church, everybody knows who you are. And you can't get off the train in any large city in the United States in which you do not have a friend who would meet you, if he knew you were coming."

He continued: "Think of it: think of your forebears and of the lineage of the blood that is in your veins."

Then he climaxed it all when he said: "And your sublime faith—I wonder if you appreciate it."

I have thought of this many times. With all that God gives us, do we appreciate it?

George Albert Smith, *Sharing the Gospel*, pp. 107-8.

———◆———

GEORGE ALBERT SMITH

"Brother Smith, the Governor of New York Wants to Talk to You"

During World War I, I was in Washington, D.C., and wrote New York's Governor Charles Seaman Whitman telling him that on my way home I would like to stop and pay my respects to him. I received a telegram: "Come right along. I will receive you here."

But I found myself in Albany a day early. The Governor was out of town. I left the telephone number of my hotel with the Governor's secretary and then contacted the missionaries. They were going to visit the home of one of the families of Saints that evening, and I was invited to go along. I left that telephone number with the hotel clerk.

About nine o'clock that evening the telephone rang. The sister answered it and reported, "Brother Smith, the governor of New York wants to talk to you."

"You are certainly coming to see me, aren't you?" the voice on the telephone asked.

"I stopped here for that purpose," I said. "What time shall I come?"

"Ten o'clock."

"Ten o'clock tomorrow morning?"

"Ten o'clock tonight—at the Governor's mansion, not at the office."

I went back to the missionaries, saying that one of them would have to come and help me find the governor's mansion. One of them offered to come, and we said good-bye to those Saints who had entertained us in their home.

The mansion was surrounded by guards as a wartime precaution. We had a little difficulty convincing them that we had an appointment at that hour, but finally were past the gate and introduced to the governor, who said: "Come with me and we will go up to my den, and we will have a good time together; no one will bother us up there."

Surrounded by the governor's library, the three of us talked. Finally, the conversation turned to the war, and the governor was happily surprised at the number of LDS boys that I told him were in the services. And of how we had supported the bond drives.

"You have done better than we have done. But, how is this war coming out?"

"Don't you know, Governor?" I asked.

"No, I don't know who is going to win it."

"Well," I said, "where is your Book of Mormon?"

He turned around in his swivel chair and reached into the book cupboard behind him, and laid a copy of the Book of Mormon on the table in front of me. And the young missionary's eyes fairly popped out of his head. Here we were in the home of the governor of the State of New York, and he had a Book of Mormon.

"Governor," I said, "I am not going to take a lot of time, but you can find out right in here how this war is coming out. We are going to win the war." I read to him what is found in the Book of Mormon with reference to this people and this nation, in which the Lord told us: "There shall be no kings upon this land which shall rise up unto the Gentiles. . . . I, the Lord, the God of heaven, will be their king," and then he refers to the fact that if we keep his commandments we have the promise from him of his preservation and his watchcare.

"I had not seen that," the governor said.

I replied, "You are not doing a very good job reading your Book of Mormon."

I laid the book down, and our visit continued. Out of the corner of my eye I saw the young missionary pick up that book. I knew what he was wondering—just how the governor had a copy. The missionary turned to the first page, and there he read the inscription: "To the Honorable Charles Seaman Whitman, Governor of New York, with compliments and best wishes of George Albert Smith."

Albert L. Zobell, *Story Gems* (Salt Lake City: Bookcraft, 1953), pp. 23-26.

GEORGE ALBERT SMITH

"It's All Ready"

At the war's end President Smith set to work. In November he called on Harry S. Truman. "When I called on him," President Smith reported later, "he received me very graciously—I had met him before—and I said: 'I have just come to ascertain from you, Mr. President, what your attitude will be if the Latter-day Saints are prepared to ship food and clothing and bedding to Europe.'

"He smiled and looked at me, and said: 'Well, what do you want to ship it over there for? Their money isn't any good.'

"I said: 'Of course; we would give it to them. They are our brothers and sisters and are in distress. God has blessed us with surplus, and we will be glad to send it if we have the cooperation of the government.'

"He said, 'You are on the right track,' and added, 'we will be glad to help you in any way we can.'

"I have thought of that a good many times. After we had

sat there a moment or two, he said again: 'How long will it take you to get this ready?'"

"I said: 'It's all ready.'

The government, you remember, had been destroying food and refusing to plant grain during the war, so I said to him:

"Mr. President, while the administration at Washington were advising the destroying of food, we were building elevators and filling them with grain, and increasing our flocks and our herds, and now what we need is the cars and the ships in order to send considerable food, clothing, and bedding to the people of Europe who are in distress. We have an organization in the Church that has over two thousand homemade quilts ready."

Robert B. Day, *They Made Mormon History* (Salt Lake City: Deseret Book Co., 1968), pp. 332-33.

Biographical Sketch

DAVID O. MCKAY

When David Oman McKay was born in Huntsville, Utah, on September 8, 1873, to David McKay and Jennette Evans McKay, Brigham Young was the President of the Church.

While he was a young boy a double tragedy struck the McKay household. His two older sisters, Margaret, age eleven, and Ellena, age nine, died within four days of each other. Margaret died of the effects of rheumatic fever, and Ellena died of pneumonia. Joint funeral services were held, and the grave that had been dug for Margaret was enlarged and the sisters were placed side by side. One year passed, and David McKay received a mission call to Scotland. The call followed very closely the deaths of his two daughters, and in addition, his wife, Jennette, President McKay's mother, was expecting a baby. But the Lord had called. Sister McKay insisted that her husband go, and David McKay said to his son David O., "Take care of Mama." Ten days after David McKay left for Scotland, the baby, a daughter, was born. It was during this absence that a humorous incident took place. President McKay, age eight, was assisting his mother in feeding the cattle. He had carried several arm loads of hay, but each time as he returned with another the previous armload had disappeared. He quickly threw in another and said to his mother, "Let's give them two large armfulls of hay and run to the house before they eat it."

Jennette McKay worked hard and she and her children were blessed greatly during her husband's absence. After two years, when David McKay walked up the lane toward his Huntsville home, he saw a long-hoped-for addition to the house. He had known nothing of it. It was Sister McKay's surprise.

President McKay's mother received a small inheritance, but it was sufficient to send her children to school. David O. McKay played on the University of Utah's first football team and was valedictorian of his graduating class; he planned to be a school teacher. And then there was Emma Ray Riggs, a lovely young lady whom he had grown very fond of. He looked to his future with joy and anticipation, and then the unexpected—a call to serve the Lord in Scotland.

David O. McKay, at age twenty-three, received an unexpected and inconvenient call to serve the Lord. It had been only fifteen years since his own father had received an unexpected and inconvenient call to the same mission. What if David McKay had not accepted that call from God? What if David O. McKay had not seen the strength of his father and the courage of his mother that day fifteen years before. It was in the mission field that great spiritual growth took place and his future as an extraordinary servant of the Lord Jesus Christ became assured.

He returned to marry Emma Ray Riggs in the Salt Lake Temple on January 2, 1901. He served as an instructor at the Church-owned Weber Academy in Ogden, Utah. This was near his childhood home. He became the principal of that institution, stake Sunday School superintendent, and then in 1916 at the early age of thirty-one, he became a member of the Quorum of the Twelve. He served faithfully in a great many capacities —general superintendent of the Sunday Schools, Church commissioner of education, president of the European Mission, and then at age sixty-one he was chosen as a counselor to President Heber J. Grant. Upon Heber J. Grant's death, he was chosen to the same position by President George Albert Smith and continued in that position until the death of President Smith.

April, 1951, at the age of seventy-eight, David Oman McKay stood in the tabernacle on Temple Square and spoke to those assembled. He had just been unanimously sustained as the Prophet, Seer and Revelator by the Saints. As he brushed back the tears he said, "No one can preside over the church without first being in tune with the head of the Church, our Lord and Savior, Jesus Christ. He is our head. This is his church. Without his divine guidance and constant inspiration, we cannot succeed. With his guidance, with his inspiration, we cannot fail." (*Conference Reports*, April, 1951, p. 157.)

President McKay's administration, like his life before, was dramatic. He and Sister McKay went to nation after nation to visit and bless both members and nonmembers. Temple building commenced in many countries. Missionary activities expanded, and the Church population grew. President David O. McKay looked like a prophet—tall, handsome, distinguished, gentle, and filled with love and universally loved by his people and all who were privileged to know him.

On Sunday, January 18, 1970, word went throughout the world that David Oman McKay was dead. Tens of thousands came to pass by his body and pay their last respects. They were only representative of millions throughout the world who mourned. All who knew him will forever be better individuals, because they had known greatness. Perhaps few men had been loved like President David O. McKay. All responded to his keen wit, his brilliant mind and the greatness of his soul. David O. McKay, prophet, seer and revelator, will ever live in the memory of those who knew and loved him.

DAVID O. MCKAY

"Nothing Will Hurt You"

One night while his father was gone, David had a dream about Indians. It was so real that he became dreadfully frightened. It seemed that those Indians were right in the house. Then, on another night, he heard noises around the house and felt sure there were burglars. He knew his mother would be frightened, too, if she heard them, and he hoped that she would not. As he lay there wide awake, with his brother Thomas sleeping by his side, he decided to do what his parents had taught him to do—pray. He had always said his prayers kneeling at his bedside, so he felt that now too he must get out of bed and kneel down to pray. Climbing out of bed was a terrible test; it took all his strength and willpower because he was so frightened. But he did it!

As he knelt down by the side of the bed, he prayed earnestly and with real faith. Then, just as clearly as one person speaks aloud to another, he heard a voice say to him, "Don't be afraid. Nothing will hurt you." David then climbed back into bed and fell fast asleep.

Marie F. Felt, "David—A Boy of Promise," *Instructor,* 104 (Sept. 1969): 330.

DAVID O. MCKAY

"The Best Is None Too Good for the Lord"

What does it mean to obey the law of sacrifice? Nature's law demands us to do everything with self in view. The first law of mortal life, self-preservation, would claim the most luscious fruit, the most tender meat, the softest down on which to lie. Selfishness, the law of nature, would say, "I want the best; that is mine." But God said: "Take of the firstlings of your herds and of your flocks." (Deut. 12:6.)

The best shall be given to God; the next you may have. Thus should God become the center of our very being.

With this thought in view, I thank my earthly father for the lesson he gave to two boys in a hayfield at a time when tithes were paid in kind. We had driven out to the field to get the tenth load of hay, and then over to a part of the meadow where we had taken the ninth load, where there was "wire grass" and "slough grass." As we started to load the hay, father called out, "No, boys, drive over to the higher ground." There was timothy and redtop there. But one of the boys called back, (and it was I) "No, let us take the hay as it comes!"

"No, David, that is the *tenth* load, and the best is none too good for God."

That is the most effective sermon on tithing I have ever heard in my life, and it touches, I found later in life, this very principle of the law of sacrifice. You cannot develop character without obeying that law. Temptation is going to come to you in this life. You sacrifice your appetites; you sacrifice your passions for the glory of God; and you gain the blessing of an upright character and spirituality. That is a fundamental truth.

Clare Middlemiss, comp., *Cherished Experiences* (Salt Lake City: Deseret Book Co., 1955), pp. 19-20.

266

DAVID O. MCKAY

"Again It Was Christmas Eve"

Christmas experiences in the Old Home were always joyous occasions. Perhaps the finest description of these days is contained in a letter written in 1938 by President McKay to his brother, Thomas E., who was at that time presiding in the Swiss-German Mission of the Church.

> Salt Lake City, Utah
> December 12, 1938

My Dear Brother and Playmate, Thomas E.,

I went to Huntsville the other day and visited the Old Home. It was a typical wintery day, so you can easily imagine how cold the rooms were in which no fires were burning, and in which none had been for weeks. The house was just like a large refrigerator.

There were a few things which I wanted to do so I threw your old coonskin coat over my shoulders, and soon felt warm and comfortable. For a few moments I strolled leisurely from room to room, and, being in a reminiscent mood, I let my mind wander at will down the lanes of memory. I saw "Tommy" and "Dadie" go upstairs to bed, and felt the tender touch of the dearest, sweetest mother that ever lived as she tenderly tucked the bed-clothes around her two roguish boys and gave them goodnight kisses.

Again it was Christmas Eve. Our stockings having been hung where Santa couldn't help but see them, we lay half expecting to hear the jingle of the sleigh bells announcing the approach of good old St. Nick to the chimney top—sleep came tardily, but finally the sandman succeeded in closing our eyes.

Christmas morning. I can see those boys creeping down the stairs before daybreak—no electric switch to press and flood the room with light; no flashlight at hand. They didn't even light the old kerosene lamp. Step by step they groped their way in the dark, and sought the nail (or chair) on which each had hung respectively his empty stocking. Who can ever forget the thrill of that first touch of the stocking filled with Santa's treasures! Apple in the toe, sticks of red and white candy protruding from the top, and trinkets and presents hidden in between! Perhaps a trumpet stuck out with the candies; but the drum and sled were standing near by.

The air in the room was cold even though the last embers in the kitchen were still smouldering—evidence, if the boys had stopped to think, that father and mother had sat up late enough to welcome St. Nick to our house.

Soon the girls were awake also, and the lamp was lit—then the "oh's" and the "ah's," and the medley of sounds of drums, jewsharp, harmonica, and music box!

As the sun came smiling over those snow-capped mountains, he turned the frost into diamonds that sparkled from the leafless trees and seemed to dance on the twelve-inch blanket of pure white snow.

Then came the playmates with their merry cry "Christmas Gift."

In the afternoon the children's dance! (One of those boys danced with a sweet little girl eleven successive times!) Oh the romance of childhood!

Chores—evening shadows, supper and bed, and another Christmas was gone. Why, to childhood, is Christmas day so short, and the next far away?

Christmas again, anticipated by the trip up South Fork to get our own Christmas tree from the hillside. They were older then, those boys, but their stockings still were hung, and good old Santa never failed to fill them.

Summer time and the swimming hole in Spring Creek; baseball on the "square." Boys and girls strolling "across the Creek," over on the knoll plucking flowers—daisies, blue bells, and the modest forget-me-nots, then leisurely back to town where we played croquet—parlor games in the evening where we had to redeem the forfeits!

Later came school and missions, yet still the tender ties that radiated from a devoted father and loving mother ever pulled us back to the Old Home, the dearest, sweetest spot on earth.

It is only an old country home, but no palace was ever filled with truer love and devotion on the part of parents, brothers, and sisters, than those which pervaded the hearts of the loved ones in that family circle.

Hanging your coat in its accustomed place, I walked out of the front door; as the night-latch clicked, I thought it might have been the click of the lid of a treasure chest that held the wealth of memories that no money could buy.

Well, my brother and pal of youthful days, I just wanted you to share with me this glimpse of happy memories, and to say as the yuletide now approaches, my heart is full of loving wishes to you, that you and yours may enjoy the happiest Christmas ever, and that the New Year may come laden with happiness and joy supreme.

Jeanette McKay Morrell, comp., *Highlights in the Life of President David O. McKay* (Salt Lake City: Deseret Book Co., 1966), pp. 29-51.

◄—◆—►

DAVID O. MCKAY

"Just the Same 'Old Boy' That I Was Before I Prayed"

One day in my youth I was hunting cattle. While climbing a steep hill, I stopped to let my horse rest, and there, once again, an intense desire came over me to receive a manifestation of the truth of the restored gospel. I dismounted, threw my reins over my horse's head, and there under a serviceberry bush I prayed that God would declare to me the truth of his revelation to Joseph Smith. I am sure that I prayed fervently and sincerely and with as much faith as a young boy could muster.

At the conclusion of the prayer, I arose from my knees, threw the reins over my faithful pony's head, and got into the saddle. As I started along the trail again, I remember saying to myself: "No spiritual manifestation has come to me. If I am true to myself, I must say I am just the same 'old boy' that I was before I prayed."

The Lord did not see fit to give me an answer on that occasion, but in 1899, after I had been appointed president of the Scottish conference, the spiritual manifestation for which I had prayed as a boy in my teens came as a natural sequence to the performance of duty.

Middlemiss, *Cherished Experiences,* pp. 19-20.

DAVID O. MCKAY

"Brethren, There Are Angels in This Room"

On May 29, 1899, a memorable priesthood meeting was held in Glasgow in connection with the Scottish conference, and it illustrates the spirit of this mission and the love and sympathy existing among those who labored there. President McKay records the events in his diary, excerpts from which follow:

A peaceful, heavenly influence pervaded the room. Some of the elders were so affected by it that they expressed their feelings in tears.

Just as Brother Young sat down after giving his report, Elder Charles

Woolfenden said, "Brethren there are angels in this room," and everyone present, impressed with the spirit of the occasion, and sensing the divine influence, could testify to the truth of his remarks. Elders wept for joy; sobs came from different parts of the room, and they were fitting, too, for it seemed manly to weep there.

At the conclusion of the reports, all joined in a prayer of thanksgiving to the Lord for his blessings and manifestations. President James L. Mc-Murrin then addressed the meeting and said, among other things, "The Lord has accepted our labors, and at this time we stand pure before him." He continued, "Yes, brethren, there are angels in this room;" and the announcement was not startling, but seemed wholly proper. Designating two of the brethren, he said their guardian angels were present, then turning to me he continued, "Let me say to you, Brother David, Satan has desired you that he may sift you as wheat; but God is mindful of you, and if you will keep the faith, you will yet sit in the leading councils of the Church."

It was no coincidence that on July 17, 1887, when David was thirteen years old, Patriarch John Smith had also said, in his blessing, "For the eye of the Lord is upon thee—the Lord has a work for thee to do, in which thou shalt see much of the world. It shall be thy lot to sit in council with thy brethren, and preside among the people, and exhort the saints to faithfulness."

Morrell, *Highlights*, pp. 37-38.

DAVID O. MCKAY

"In Spite of All Odds"

Father has always had the courage to stand up for his convictions. Even when a boy, his determination to hold his ground when he was convinced he was right was always evident. An incident is told by Thomas E. McKay that happened during a Fourth of July baseball game between

Huntsville and Eden. Keen rivalry had always existed between these two teams, and on this holiday the grandstand was packed and feelings were tense. During the seventh inning one of the Huntsville players was forced to leave the game because of an injury, and David O. was drafted to take his place although he was much younger than the players on the regular team. It was an exciting moment for him because the score was tied and had been for several innings. David O. was a good batter and received a cheer when his turn came around. As the playing proceeded, the umpire called the second strike. The pitcher on the Eden team, however, claimed that it was the third strike. He was a large, burly fellow with a quick temper, and he was known to be a bully and quite a pugilist. He picked up a baseball bat, and coming up to David O. he waved the bat menacingly and demanded, "Get out of there, kid, or I will crack this on your head!"

Immediately a hush came over the spectators, who anxiously awaited the outcome. Thomas E. claims that he was shaking in his boots to see his brother in such a predicament. However, his older brother was up to the situation. In a cool tone he said, "The umpire called only two strikes; so go back to your pitcher's box and try to get me out; you have one more chance!" By this time John Allen, one of the best players, came strolling over with a bat in his hand as though he were waiting for his turn at the plate. The pitcher looked at the determination on David O.'s face and at John Allen's warning glance and decided to continue the game. His next throw was a swift straight ball. David O. connected and made a two-base hit. The next batter hit a single, and father was able to make home plate safely. This brought a thunderous applause from the spectators because this was the deciding run of the game. Although father's friends congratulated him on making the run, the true congratulations were in their hearts because he stood up to a bigger man in spite of all odds and because he refused to be bullied when he knew that he was right.

Llewelyn R. McKay, *Home Memories of President David O. McKay* (Salt Lake City: Deseret Book Co., 1956), pp. 162-63.

DAVID O. MCKAY

"One Little Bird Was Outside Trying to Get In"

Several years ago someone broke into the farm and stole the President's best saddles from the saddle house. One of these was a hand-carved Mexican saddle and was prized very highly by President McKay. When the unfortunate incident became known, a group of stake presidents in Weber and Davis counties presented him with the best saddle available, so that he could still enjoy riding his horses while in Huntsville. Care was taken that this new saddle was kept in a safe place. Other saddles were later purchased to replace the ones that were stolen, and these were kept in the saddle house, but under lock and key. One day, during hot weather, when members of the family were at the home in Huntsville, two of President McKay's sisters were out for a drive and decided to check on things at the farm. They found the door to the saddle house locked, but one of the windows open. They immediately corrected what they felt was a bit of carelessness and went on their way with a feeling of satisfaction that another theft had been averted.

That afternoon President McKay drove up to keep an appointment at Huntsville, with barely enough time to return to Salt Lake City for a later engagement. Upon being told of the open window, he said, "I left that window open purposely because there is a bird's nest inside, and that is the only entrance the parent birds have to carry food to their babies. I think I shall just have time to run over."

When the sisters said they would correct the mistake, he insisted on doing it, saying, "I must pick up a halter that needs repairing, anyway." When he returned to the house after the two-mile drive, he said in his gracious way, "It was just as I expected—one little bird was outside trying to get in, and the mother was inside attempting to get out."

His kindness to everyone and to everything has given him a benign demeanor that is one of his great characteristics. It has made him more like the One who "marks the sparrow's fall."

Morrell, *Highlights*, pp. 294-95.

DAVID O. MCKAY

"They Don't Show As Much Sense As the Horses"

Father hates to see an animal mishandled, or to know that one is suffering or killed unnecessarily. As a small boy, I observed my first lesson in this regard. We were walking up the hill on 21st Street, Ogden, and were half-way up the block after leaving Washington Avenue. There we observed a man whipping his horses unmercifully as the team vainly attempted to pull a wagonload of coal out of a rut in the road. The driver swore and cursed as he cracked his whip over their heads and cut the creatures' backs. Father watched only for a second before he strode up to the driver and said, "Hold on there a minute, young man; you can't expect these horses to pull with their heads held up so high!" And without waiting for an answer, he unhooked the checkreins, loosened them several inches, then turned to the driver who was still swearing—but in lower tones: "Now turn your team to the left, keep a tight hold on the reins, and command the team sternly—but without the whip!"

The man was about to answer, but thought better of it after looking into father's determined eyes and did as he was told.

The faithful horses lowered their heads and pulled the load out of the hole. Father came back to where I was standing on the sidewalk and said, "Some people shouldn't be allowed to drive horses, because they don't show as much sense as the horses!"

Llewelyn R. McKay, *Home Memories*, p. 126.

DAVID O. MCKAY

"Caesar in Chicken Coop. Water Him!"

Caesar was a full-blooded boar. We children were a little apprehensive of him because he was large and had ferocious-looking tusks. He responded to father's kindness and took every opportunity to stay by him in hope of having his back scratched with a stick.

On a Sunday morning, just as father was leaving for Ogden to catch a train, Caesar broke out of his enclosure. There was no time to repair the fence, and not wanting him to run loose, father put him in the chicken coop with the intention of writing a note of instructions to one of us boys.

That night at two a.m. the telephone rang incessantly, waking up the whole household. Uncle Tommy answered the phone and was told that a telegram had arrived for Lawrence, my older brother. Lawrence was called out of bed. By this time everyone was alerted to the fact that a telegram was to be read over the phone. Naturally all were concerned, wondering what had happened: sickness? an accident? a death? All members gathered around the phone as Lawrence wrote down the following message:

"Caesar in chicken coop. Water him!"

Llewelyn R. McKay, *Home Memories*, p. 127.

DAVID O. MCKAY

*"He Was Allowed to Share
in the Expense"*

On another occasion, when the boys were playing with their baseball, it inadvertently went through a basement window. As was the custom, the culprit went immediately to his father, saying, "It was an accident and I am very sorry." The wise father replied, "I am sorry, too, but just being sorry will not repair the damage."

The boy asked, "How much will a new window cost?"

"I do not know," replied his father, "but we shall have a repairman come up, and he can tell us the exact amount."

The child offered, "I haven't much money, but I am willing to pay what I have."

He was allowed to share in the expense, and when his mother remonstrated, "How could you take his money when he has such a small allowance?" David O. replied, "He has received a valuable lesson in the cost of keeping up a home, and now he has a monetary interest in this home which he will protect." It may have been a coincidence, but there were no more windows shattered by baseballs.

Morrell, *Highlights,* pp. 44, 47.

—◄—▶—

DAVID O. MCKAY

"I, Too, Was Praying"

Sunday morning, April 24, 1921, dawned in a cloudless east and promised a clear day.

We held the usual prayers and scripture repeating exercises, and at ten a.m. met in the Sunday School session of conference.

Having wet my feet yesterday, I have aggravated my cold. As a result, I'm so hoarse I can scarcely speak above a whisper, a condition that forebodes difficulty and disappointment for me and for the people on this the heaviest day of our tour!

Ten a.m. I managed to tell the children a story, but my voice was weak and husky. However, Brother Cannon was at his best, so we had an excellent meeting.

A thousand people—Maoris and Pakehas, sitting, reclining, and standing—assembled for the afternoon service. They came with curiosity and high expectation. It was my duty to give them a message, but I was not only too hoarse to speak and be heard by that crowd, but I was also ill!

However, with a most appealing prayer in my heart for divine help and guidance, I arose to perform my duty. My voice was tight and husky. Five minutes after I began, someone shouted from the group standing on my right, "Joseph Smith didn't receive the revelation on polygamy!"

Evidently the emissaries of the devil had chosen an opportune moment to obtain some free advertising. I hesitated a moment, turned my head in his direction, saw some men scuffling, and the crowd beginning to sway towards them. Motioning to the audience to remain quiet, I said with as much good nature as I could muster, "When the sons of God met, the devil came also." Many grasped the application and broke into laughter. Some began to clap, but I motioned for order, and continued with my discourse.

Then happened what had never before happend to me. I entered into my theme with all the earnestness and vehemence I could muster and spoke as loud as possible. Feeling my voice getting clearer and more resonant, I soon forgot I had a voice and thought only of the truth I wanted my hearers to understand and accept. For forty minutes I continued with my address, and when I concluded, my voice was as resonant and clear as it ever was!

Brother Cannon concluded with a fervent testimony; and thus our fifth meeting closed with thanksgiving and rejoicing in every heart!

When I told Brother Cannon and some other brethren how earnestly I had prayed for the very blessing I had received, he said, "I, too, was praying—never prayed more fervently for a speaker in my life."

Middlemiss, *Cherished Experiences*, pp. 85-86.

DAVID O. MCKAY

"Brother Cannon, I Think We Should Return and Leave Our Blessing"

The month spent in Samoa passed all too quickly, with some of the largest conferences yet held, in preparation for which every detail had been carefully arranged. Missionary meetings were as satisfactory as the larger meetings, attended by members, investigators, and friends. When the time for farewells arrived, genuine friendships had been formed, and the parting was a sad one for the people who had never before had the privilege of meeting one of the General Authorities.

At the last party there were beautiful interpretations of the island dances in native costume, singing, and instrumental selections, and then, as they returned to the mission home, fathers and mothers brought their children to be blessed, occupying the last moments before the necessary departure. Of these last experiences Elder McKay recorded the following:

> As we came out, we found the people standing in a double column from our door out across the lawn to the street. They had prepared a farewell song for us and all began to sing. As we passed through the lines, shaking hands with them, sobs interrupted the singing. Staunch old Papo, the head of the village, sobbed like a child and clung to us as though we were his son. As we mounted our horses, we looked back and saw the crowd, headed by the band, coming toward us for one more parting handshake.
>
> From that spot to the dugway leading to the ocean, there was a straight, grassy roadway, lined with tall native trees and tropical vines. As we rode slowly up the gentle incline, the band leading, the people followed as though they could not yield to parting. We had gained, perhaps, a quarter of a mile ahead of them, when I felt tempted to say, "Brother Cannon, I think we should return and leave our blessing with them here in this beautiful grove."
>
> As we approached the sobbing crowd, I was thrilled with the picturesque setting. Hanging my folded umbrella on an overhanging limb, Kippin, our interpreter, told them why we had come back. Their sobs were louder than my voice when I commenced the prayer, but they became more subdued as I continued, and their "Amen" was distinct and impressive at the end.

An elder who remained with the crowd reported what happened after the visitors left:

> The villagers watched as long as they could see their friends, then returned sadly to their homes. Kippin, the interpreter, immediately sat down and wrote the prayer as he remembered it. He and some of the others then conceived the idea of burying a copy of it on the spot where Apostle McKay had stood and covering it with a pile of stones to mark the place. The town bell was rung, the people reassembled, and the plan was presented and approved. A copy of the prayer, together with an account of the entire proceedings, was sealed in a bottle and placed in a hole which was covered with stones, each of the heads of families throwing a handful of soil to assist in the covering. The branch on which the umbrella was hung was taken back to the village as a souvenier, and steps were taken to erect a monument at the sacred spot.

Morrell, *Highlights*, 69-70.

DAVID O. MCKAY

"Brethren, I Feel Impressed. . . ."

It happened in 1921, while President McKay and Elder Hugh Cannon were making a tour of the missions of the world. After a day of inspiring conference meetings in Hilo, Hawaii, a night trip to the Kilauea volcano was arranged for the visiting brethren and some of the missionaries. About nine o'clock that evening, two carloads, about ten of us, took off for the then very active volcano.

We stood on the rim of that fiery pit watching Pele in her satanic antics, our backs chilled by the cold winds sweeping down from snowcapped Mauna Loa and our faces almost blistered by the heat of the molten lava. Tiring of the cold, one of the elders discovered a volcanic balcony about four feet down inside the crater where observers could watch the display without being chilled by the wind. It seemed perfectly sound, and the "railing" on the open side of it formed a fine protection from intense heat, making it an excellent place to view the spectacular display.

After first testing its safety, Brother McKay and three of the elders climbed down into the hanging balcony. As they stood there warm and comfortable, they teased the others of us more timid ones who had hesitated to take advantage of the protection they had found. For quite some time we all watched the ever-changing sight as we alternately chilled and roasted.

After being down there in their protected spot for some time, suddenly Brother McKay said to those with him, "Brethren, I feel impressed that we should get out of here."

With that he assisted the elders to climb out, and then they in turn helped him up to the wind-swept rim. It seems incredible, but almost immediately the whole balcony crumbled and fell with a roar into the molten lava a hundred feet or so below.

It is easy to visualize the feelings of those who witnessed this terrifying experience. Not a word was said—the whole thing was too awful, with all that word means. The only sound was the hiss and roar of Pele, the fire goddess of old Hawaii, screaming her disappointment.

None of us, who were witnesses to this experience could ever doubt the reality of "revelation in our day!" Some might say it was merely inspiration, but to us it was a direct revelation given to a worthy man.

Middlemiss, *Cherished Experiences*, pp. 55-56.

DAVID O. MCKAY

"Isn't This Brother McKay"

Another month was spent in visiting the missions of Australia, then on to Java, India, Egypt, and Palestine. Traveling through the Holy Land was like passing familiar towns, villages, rivers, lakes, mountains, and gardens because of Elder McKay's long and intimate association with these places in Old Testament history, and especially because of his love of the life of Christ and his apostles.

President Grant had expressed a hope that in their travels the two could visit the Armenian Mission, which had received such harsh treatment during the great World War. On a special fast day, several thousand dollars had been contributed for the relief of these suffering people, but almost a year had passed since the brethren had left home, and they had no recent information about conditions in this part of the world. Cablegrams to the president of the European Mission and to the United

States Consul at Aleppo brought only information that J. Wilford Boothe was on his way to Aleppo. Elder McKay's diary, under date of November 2, 1921, reads:

> We have no idea where President Boothe is. We shall leave Jerusalem for Haifa, enroute to Aleppo, tomorrow morning. We have concluded to go by auto through Samaria, visiting Bible scenes. At three-thirty p.m. of the same day, we ascended the Mount of Olives, and, choosing a secluded spot, near where Jesus is supposed to have stood, we knelt in humble supplication and thanksgiving to God, asking that we might be led by inspiration on our trip to the Armenian Mission.
>
> Upon returning to the hotel, I felt strongly impressed that we should go to Haifa by train instead of by auto. When I said as much to Brother Cannon, be replied, "If you feel that way we had better take the train." Our greatest desire as we neared this mission was to meet Elder Boothe. Indeed, it seemed that our trip to Syria would be useless unless we should meet him. We were strangers. We knew no one. The branches of the Church in Syria were disorganized, and the members were scattered.
>
> During all our travels, besides giving excellent addresses at every meeting, Brother Cannon had assumed the responsibility of arranging for train and boat tickets and hotel accommodations, and had never failed in a single instance; but shortly after leaving Jerusalem, when asked if he had the name of a hotel in Haifa, he said he had forgotten to ask about it, but would contact the Allenby Hotel runner when the train stopped at Lud.

When they changed trains at that station, and were again on their way, they both realized that they had forgotten to speak to the hotel representative.

Arriving at Haifa, Brother Cannon remained with the luggage while Brother McKay left to make inquiry regarding a suitable hotel. After some difficulty, he returned in about ten minutes reporting that there seemed to be two fairly good ones, and they would take the one whose runner appeared first. The delay caused by locating a hotel brought them to the station office door just at the same moment that another traveler reached it. He said, "Isn't this Brother McKay?" Elder McKay then records in his diary:

> Astounded beyond expression to be thus addressed in so strange a town, I turned and recognized Elder Joseph Wilford Boothe, the one man above all others that we were most desirous of meeting. We had met, too, at the most opportune time and place. Having known nothing of our whereabouts, he had come from the western part of the world, hoping in

his heart to meet us. We had come from the east, praying that we might meet him, and there we had met at the very time and place best suited to our convenience and to the success of our mission to Armenia.

As we recounted to each other our experiences, we had no doubt but that our coming together was the result of divine interposition. If we had taken an auto from Jerusalem, or if we had remembered to secure the name of a hotel before we left the Allenby, or if we had thought to ask at Lud, we should not have met Elder Boothe. It is true we would have been in town that same day, but we had intended to stay at a hotel across the city from the one he decided upon, where we never should have met him; and our visit to Armenia would have failed.

Morrell, *Highlights*, pp. 70-72.

DAVID O. MCKAY

"The Gift of Interpreting Tongues Was Given to Me"

On Friday, June 13, there was a mission-wide conference of missionaries and members in Rotterdam, attended by 1,024, which represented one third of the membership of the mission. At this meeting there was a presentation of a Delft blue china plate to President and Mrs. McKay, and one also to Elder and Mrs. David Lawrence McKay.

During his remarks, the President said:

Today, Sister McKay and I stood on the ruins of the place where thirty years ago a very remarkable experience occurred to me. I was speaking to an audience here in Rotterdam, and President Zappey was interpreting, when it happened that the gift of interpreting tongues was given to me. There may be some here today who were present at that time. President Zappey was making a statement following my remarks, and even though

I could not understand the language, I knew that he had given the wrong interpretation, and I told him so and corrected him. He turned to me and said that I really had no need for an interpreter since I understood the language so well. This is an illustration of the spirit directing the minds of each.

Now that building is gone—destroyed by the power of man. May the Lord hasten the day when there shall be no more war. Nobody is helped by it. The victors are losers and the innocent suffer.

As I stood on that barren spot, I felt moved to offer a prayer to the Lord to hasten the day when peace may once more come to the world.

Morrell, *Highlights*, pp. 110-11.

DAVID O. MCKAY

"The Maoris Corrected Him"

One of the most important events on my world tour of the missions of the Church was the gift of interpretation of the English tongue to the Saints of New Zealand at a session of their conference, held on the twenty-third day of April, 1921, at Puke Tapu Branch, Waikato District, Huntly, New Zealand.

The service was held in a large tent, beneath the shade of which hundreds of earnest men and women gathered in anxious anticipation of seeing and hearing an apostle of the Church, the first one to visit that land.

When I looked over that vast assemblage and contemplated the great expectations that filled the hearts of all who had met together, I realized how inadequately I might satisfy the ardent desires of their souls, and I yearned, most earnestly, for the gift of tongues that I might be able to speak to them in their native language.

Until that moment I had not given much serious thought to the gift of tongues, but on that occasion I wished with all my heart that I might be worthy of that divine power.

In other missions I had spoken through an interpreter, but, able as all interpreters are, I nevertheless felt hampered—in fact, somewhat inhibited—in presenting my message.

Now, I faced an audience that had assembled with unusual expectations, and I then realized, as never before, the great responsibility of my office. From the depth of my soul, I prayed for divine assistance.

When I arose to give my address, I said to Brother Stuart Meha, our interpreter, that I would speak without his translating sentence by sentence what I said, and then to the audience I continued:

"I wish, oh, how I wish I had the power to speak to you in your own tongue, that I might tell you what is in my heart; but since I have not the gift, I pray, and I ask you to pray, that you might have the spirit of interpretation, of discernment, that you may understand at least the spirit while I am speaking, and then you will get the words and the thought when Brother Meha interprets."

My sermon lasted forty minutes, and I have never addressed a more attentive, a more respectful audience. My listeners were in perfect rapture—this I know when I saw tears in their eyes. Some of them at least, perhaps most of them, who did not understand English, had the gift of interpretation.

Brother Sidney Christie, a native New Zealander who had been a student at Brigham Young University, at the close of my address whispered to me, "Brother McKay, they got your message!"

"Yes," I replied, "I think so, but for the benefit of some who may not have understood, we shall have Brother Meha give a synopsis of it in Maori."

During the translation, some of the Maori corrected him on some points, showing that they had a clear conception of what had been said in English.

Middlemiss, *Cherished Experiences*, pp. 73-74.

DAVID O. MCKAY

"It Was the City Eternal"

On Tuesday, May 10, 1921, we sailed all day on the smoothest seat of our entire trip. The slightly undulating waves had been so free from even signs of unrest that the slight ripples discernible appeared on the surface like millions of little squares—like plaited cloth with the rich design of the same deep blue material as the body.

Nearing Savali, we could see with the aid of field glasses the "Spouting Horns," which looked like geysers. On our right we caught a glimpse of the little village nestling safely in the mouth of an extinct volcano on the little island of Apolima.

Towards evening, the reflection of the afterglow of a beautiful sunset was most splendid! The sky was tinged with pink, and the clouds lingering around the horizon were fringed with various hues of crimson and orange, while the heavy cloud farther to the west was sombre purple and black. These various colors cast varying shadows on the peaceful surface of the water. Those from the clouds were long and dark, those from the crimson-tinged sky, clear but rose-tinted and fading into a faint pink that merged into the clear blue of the ocean. Gradually, the shadows became deeper and heavier, and then all merged into a beautiful calm twilight that made the sea look like a great mirror upon which fell the faint light of the crescent moon!

Pondering still upon this beautiful scene, I lay in my berth at ten o'clock that night, and thought to myself: Charming as it is, it doesn't stir my soul with emotion as do the innocent lives of children, and the sublime characters of loved ones and friends. Their beauty, unselfishness, and heroism are after all the most glorious!

I then fell asleep and beheld in vision something infinitely sublime. In the distance I beheld a beautiful white city. Though far away, yet I seemed to realize that trees with luscious fruit, shrubbery with gorgeously-tinted leaves, and flowers in perfect bloom abounded everywhere. The clear sky above seemed to reflect these beautiful shades of color. I then saw a great concourse of people approaching the city. Each one wore a white flowing robe and a white headdress. Instantly my attention seemed centered upon their Leader, and though I could see only the profile of his features and his body, I recognized him at once as my Savior! The tint and radiance of his countenance were glorious to behold! There was a peace about him which seemed sublime—it was divine!

The city, I understood, was his. It was the City Eternal; and the people following him were to abide there in peace and eternal happiness.

But who were they?

As if the Savior read my thoughts, he answered by pointing to a semicircle that then appeared above them, and on which were written in gold the words:

These Are They Who Have Overcome the World—Who Have Truly Been Born Again!

When I awoke, it was breaking day over Apia harbor.

Middlemiss, *Cherished Experiences*, pp. 101-2.

◄━●━►

D A V I D   O .   M C K A Y

---

*"The Storm Had Suddenly
Changed Its Course"*

In 1954 the general authorities approved the building of a temple at once somewhere in the South

Pacific. The location could not be determined so easily, since there were many Church members in all of the islands, as well as on the continent of Australia. All must be given consideration, but since only one temple could be built it would have to be located where it could serve the most people to the best advantage.

Accordingly, it was decided by the General Authorities that President McKay should visit all the missions involved and make a careful survey of conditions and needs and then determine the location of the new temple.

Such a trip was planned, and on January 1, 1955, President and Sister McKay left Salt Lake City by plane, accompanied by President Franklin J. Murdock of the Highland Stake who was to serve as secretary of the tour. Plans called for them to visit all of the missions of the Pacific Islands and make the trip a missionary tour as well as a fact-finding trip. Some of the islands had been visited by previous presidents of the Church, and President McKay had visited all of them in 1921. This visit, however, would be the first to all of the missions by the President of the Church.

First stop was San Francisco, where the party remained until January 4, 1955, then leaving by plane for Honolulu, Hawaii. As they left the airport they were informed that a hurricane warning was posted for the mid-Pacific area and undoubtedly would alter their plans. Some concern was expressed about continuing the flight, but President McKay expressed no worry at all and insisted that they continue. He recounted his travels over almost all of the globe without any serious trouble and said he felt secure while on this important mission.

The flight to the Hawaiian Islands was made without any difficulty. Only a few hours were spent in Hawaii since they planned to tour these islands on their return trip. They left Honolulu in the evening, with President and Mrs. Wendell B. Mendenhall of the San Joaquin Stake joining their party there.

During the night a stop was made at Canton Island, a small spot in the Pacific, where they were warned of the dangers of hurricane weather. Their next scheduled stop was at Nandi, in the Fiji Islands, and the plane's route was directly in the path of the storm. The pilot was apprehensive about continuing, but while they were waiting, an unexplainable thing occurred. Reports were received that the storm had suddenly changed its course, almost reversing itself, and they could proceed to Fiji with no concern.

This peculiar action of the hurricane caused a good deal of comment at Nandi and Suva, on the Fiji Islands. Weather officials explained in detail the abrupt change of the storm's path, but could offer no explanation for it, and called the typhoon "The Screwball."

<hr>

Morrell, *Highlights,* pp. 178-79.

<hr>

DAVID O. MCKAY

"There Are No Scars"

In the latter part of March, 1916, Ogden River overflowed. It came through the Narrows a raging torrent.

Wednesday noon (about the middle of March, 1916) I drove three of my young children up there as far as the Narrows that they might see the river at floodtide and hear the grinding of the stones as they pushed against each other by the force of the water.

Wednesday night my brother Thomas E. called at the house. Unable to get through the canyon, he called his wife by telephone and asked if she would send a horse down with the road supervisor the next morning so that he (Thomas E.) might get up to the valley. As he hung up the telephone, he turned to my son Lawrence and said: "Will you please drive me up as far as where the road is washed out?" Having been up just that afternoon and knowing the danger, I said: "I think I had better drive you, Thomas E., if you will get up early in the morning so that I can get back in time to catch my train for Salt Lake City."

The next morning several things delayed us, and it was seven o'clock before we started for the canyon. My train left in one hour. I hesitated for a moment, thinking that I should not have time to drive up to the mouth of the canyon and return by eight o'clock. It was then that I received a strong impression to "go up to the bridge and back."

We jumped into a little Ford car, dashed through the rain and mud up 21st street toward the canyon road. Without my having said anything to Thomas E. about my impression, he said: "I think you had better not attempt to cross the bridge."

Notwithstanding these two warnings, as we approached the bridge I thought I could spend another five minutes and take him as far as I had taken the children the day before. I saw the pile of rocks there at the bridge, and it seemed to be intact just as it had been the day before. So jocularly I said, "I'm going across the bridge, can you swim?" With that I stepped on the gas and dashed across the bridge, only to hear Thomas E. say, "Oh, look out! There's a rope!" The watchman who left at seven o'clock had stretched the derrick rope across the road, and his successor, the day watchman, had not arrived. I reached for the emergency brake, but was too late. The rope smashed the window, threw back the top, and caught me just in the chin, severing my lip, knocking out my lower teeth, and breaking my upper jaw. Thomas E. ducked his head and escaped uninjured, but I was left partially senseless.

The engine of the car was unimpaired, and Thomas E. moved me over in the seat, turned the car around, and drove toward home. Just as we neared the top of the hill in Canyon Road, I heard him say, "I think I had better take you to the hospital." I opened my eyes and saw blood in my hand and some loose broken teeth. I said, "No, you had better take me home; something has happened."

About nine o'clock I was on the operating table in care

of Dr. Joseph R. Morrell and Dr. Robert S. Joyce. They sewed my upper jaw in place and took fourteen stitches in my lower lip and lacerated cheek.

One of the attendants remarked: "Too bad; he will be disfigured for life."

Certainly I was most unrecognizable. When I was wheeled back to my room in the hospital, one of the nurses consolingly remarked, "Well, Brother McKay, you can wear a beard," meaning that thus I might hide my scars.

Word of the accident soon spread throughout the city, and at ten o'clock Bishop A. E. Olson, President Thomas B. Evans, and Herbert Snowcroft, three very close friends, called and administered to me. In sealing the anointing, Bishop said, "We bless you that you shall not be disfigured and that you shall not have pain."

I repeat, that was Thursday morning.

Friday morning one of my dearest friends, Peter G. Johnston, came down from Blackfoot, Idaho. My face was so swollen and disfigured that he did not recognize me. He passed by the open door, thinking that I was the wrong patient. When he entered later and was leaving, he said, "Well, the eyes are the same, anyhow."

Saturday evening Dr. William H. Petty called to see if the teeth that were still remaining in the upper jaw might be saved. It was he who said, "I suppose you are in great pain?" I answered: "No, I haven't *any* pain." He said, "I cannot understand that—I should think that you would have neuralgia pains."

That evening I began to wonder whether or not my nerves were stunned. As I dozed, my arm that I evidently had up at my forehead dropped and hit some of the stitches of my face. Then I knew that my nerves were not stunned, as I felt the pain intensely, for I was aware of the contact of my hand on the stitches.

Sunday morning President Heber J. Grant came up from Salt Lake City. He was then President of the Council of the Twelve. Having noticed the sign on the door, "Visitors Not Allowed," he entered and said, "David, don't talk; I'm just going to give you a blessing."

Among other things he said, "I bless you that you shall not be scarred." Later when he took his hands off my head and looked at me he thought (as he afterwards told me), "My, I've made a promise that cannot be fulfilled!"

On the following Monday morning the doctors removed the stitches from my lower lip, the severed parts having joined together. When Dr. Joyce came in Tuesday morning to take out the stitches from my face, he said, "Well, Mr. McKay, it pays to live a clean life!" Wednesday morning I returned home.

The following October, at a banquet given to the General Authorities on the Roof Garden of the Hotel Utah, I sat at a table near where President Grant was sitting. I noticed that he was looking at me somewhat intently, and then he said, "David, from where I am sitting I cannot see a scar on your face!" I answered, "No, President Grant, there are no scars—your blessing was realized completely."

Middlemiss, *Cherished Experiences,* pp. 145-48.

———◆—◆———

DAVID O. MCKAY

"First Violets of Springtime"

William (not the boy's true name) was a lad who had been taught to pray. When he was about ten years old, his father was nearly killed in an automobile accident. It happened early in the morning, and so grief-stricken were the mother and children, including William, that none could eat a meal or cared to.

However, later in the day, after the doctors had sewed up the lacerations, repaired the broken bones, and given assurances that daddy was not fatally injured, the loved ones calmed their fears and began to resume the regular family routine.

As was the practice in that Mormon home, before the evening meal, all knelt in prayer. Following it, William started away from the table. Seeing this his mother said, "Come, Will, sit down and eat your dinner."

"No, mother," replied the lad, "I am not hungry."

"You must!" insisted the mother. "You haven't eaten all day. Don't worry any longer, Daddy will be all right."

"Please excuse me, Mother; I am fasting and want to go to my room."

He did go to his room, and there knelt in earnest prayer for his father's speedy and complete recovery.

Rising from his knees, he put on his hat, picked from his little garden the few first violets of springtime, walked to the hospital, and placed the flowers in his injured father's hand. As the father received them, he recognized in the lad's face an expression that reflected the yearning of his little soul for his father's recovery. There was no need for words. Father and son understood each other, and the Lord comforted both—the boy in the consolation, the father in the assurance that the Lord would answer the lad's prayer.

And he did in a miraculously speedy and prominent recovery.

> They never sought in vain
> That sought the Lord aright.

The incident related above is a true story of the automobile accident in which President McKay was injured; and the child called William, who prayed for his father, was in reality President McKay's own son.

Middlemiss, *Cherished Experiences*, pp. 28.

DAVID O. MCKAY

"His Last Request"

I was in President McKay's office one day in 1951 when he mentioned something about the increase in missionary volunteers. Then he fingered through some mail on his desk, picked out a letter, and asked me to read the hand-written note from a mother. She was enclosing the money sent by her son from Korea. She asked that it be used to help some worthy young man to finance his mission. Her boy, through his nurse, wrote her from his hospital bed in Korea that his own dream and hope to go on a mission might not be realized, and that if he "didn't get home" she was to use his savings for some other needy member. He died of his wounds, and she was fulfilling his last request. Some tears stole down the cheeks of President McKay.

F. E. Schluter, *A Convert's Tribute to President David O. McKay* (Salt Lake City: Deseret Book Co., 1964), p. 22.

DAVID O. MCKAY

"Please Find That Little Girl in the Blue Dress"

During the trip to Europe to dedicate the temple sites at Zollikofen, Switzerland, and at Chapel

Hill, England, I noticed that no matter how fatiguing it was for father, he always shook hands with everyone present. . . . After the dedication at Chapel Hill I observed that father looked tired, and I decided to spare him the autograph signing if at all possible. . . . The first in line was a sweet little girl about nine years of age.

"May I have President McKay's autograph?" she inquired of me.

I began to find excuses, not knowing that father was just behind me overhearing the conversation. He put his hand on my shoulder and said, out of the children's hearing distance, "My boy, never hurt or disappoint a child. Children are most sensitive to praise, to criticism, and to recognition than we realize. I can take the time to sign these few autographs—it means a lot to these youngsters, and I wouldn't disappoint them for anything."

He turned to the little girl and jokingly asked, "Do you think I can write plainly enough so you can read it?"

The young girl wasn't sure whether or not father was in earnest and became flustered. At that moment, President Reiser interrupted to ask a pressing question, and a minute or two of conversation between the two men ensued. When father turned to the table to begin writing autographs, the girl had disappeared.

I have never seen father more upset. "Llewelyn," he called, "please find that little girl in the blue dress. I'm sure she has the impression that I didn't wish to sign her book. She misinterpreted my remarks. You must find her. She must not go home with this false impression!"

Before long branch presidents and mission presidents were looking for a little girl in blue, but all search was in vain.

During the drive back to London, father mentioned the incident again. One of the elders riding with us said, "We think we know who the little girl is, and the branch president in the village where she lives is going to inquire and will phone you tonight in London."

Sure enough, a telephone call came that night, and this is what father instructed:

Tell that little girl I am sorry I missed her at New Chapel, and that I have asked the branch president to send her book to me by mail to Salt Lake City; I will sign my autograph and mail it directly back to her.

And he did!

Llewelyn R. McKay, *Home Memories*, pp. 133-35.

◄────◆────►

DAVID O. MCKAY

"With My Blessing"

On Sunday, June 29, 1952, Sister McKay and I were in Berlin, Germany, near the Iron Curtain. Arrangements had been made for a meeting of the Saints, investigators, and friends in the "Mercedes Palast" theater, the largest hall in North Berlin.

Prior to the meeting I had received word through the presidency of the East German Mission that one of the members of the Church in that mission—a sister—had lost her husband and eldest son under communist rule. She had been driven from her home, and was subsequently exposed to the rigors of the weather and lack of nutrition until she finally became paralyzed and had been confined to her bed for five years. She had heard of my coming to Berlin, and being unable to travel herself, she expressed the desire that her two little children—a boy and a girl about ten and twelve years of age—be sent over to meet the President of the Church. This good sister said, "I know if I send my children to shake hands with President McKay, and then they come home and take my hand—if I can hold their little hands in mine I know that I shall get better."

Arrangements were made for them to take the trip. Some of the Saints contributed to the clothing of the little children, and the missionaries contributed to pay their expenses.

I asked the mission president to point out these little children as they came to the meeting. Two little children among thousands who were assembled! Anticipating meeting them, I took a new handkerchief; and when that little girl and boy came along, I went to them and shook their hands, and said, "Will you take this handkerchief to your mother with my blessing?" I later learned that after I had shaken hands with them, they would not shake hands with anyone else, for they did not want to touch anyone with their hands until they got back to their mother.

We heard no more about it; however, the incident was well-known throughout the crowd. I saw the children again in the conference house that night. They were sleeping on the top floor of the mission home—sweet little darlings!

When Sister McKay returned to Salt Lake City, she wrote to the mission president's wife and asked her to find out how the mother of the two little children was getting along. In her reply, the mission president's wife said:

"This sister thanks the Lord every day for the blessing and the handkerchief which President McKay sent through her two children, and she had the faith that she will fully recover and I believe so, too. Immediately after the children came home, her feet and toes began to get feeling in them, and this feeling slowly moved up into her legs. And now she gets out of bed alone and seats herself on a chair, and then, with her feet and the chair, works all the way around to the kitchen sink, where she has the children bring her the dishes to wash, and other things, and is very thankful that she is able to help now."

That is the faith of a mother in the Russian zone. God bless her, and bless all who are over there!

Middlemiss, *Cherished Experiences,* pp. 149-51.

————◄—►————

DAVID O. MCKAY

"I Knew You Would Come"

When the travelers to the South Seas were at Suva (Fiji Islands) January 8, 1955, word was received at the office that a Mrs. Sally Skips, a patient of the leper colony (two miles from the city) was anxious to see father. She had met him when she was a little girl in Samoa thirty-four years ago when father and Hugh J. Cannon were touring missions. Of course it was impossible for her to leave the colony. Although other plans had been made, and father's appointments were full, he remarked, "This lady has as much right as anyone else to speak with me, and since she has expressed the desire to see me and cannot come to us, then we shall go to her."

Subsequently, a taxi was called which took father, mother, and Brother Murdock to a group of cottages on a hillside. The matron in charge of the colony sent an assistant to fetch the afflicted woman, but he soon returned with the explanation that Mrs. Skipps was too ill to leave her room.

"Well," said father, "if it is permitted, we shall go to her cottage."

Just off a corridor in a small ward waited a middle-aged Samoan woman sitting on her bed, and as she greeted her visitors, tears streamed down her face. . . . "I knew you would come, if it were at all possible," she said in good English.

After receiving a blessing from father, she gratefully waved farewell, but now a smile replaced her tears, for she was confident that she would soon join her family in New Zealand.

Llewelyn R. McKay, *Home Memories*, pp. 152-53.

→◆→

DAVID O. MCKAY

"The President of the Church Keeps His Appointments"

In Salt Lake City one Thursday, a Sunday School class had been granted the great favor of an appointment with the President. Unfortunately he was called to the hospital where his brother Thomas E. lay critically ill. The children were naturally disappointed. A member of the Council of the Twelve greeted the class and talked with them.

Many busy men would have considered the matter closed, but the next Sunday morning found President McKay driving eight miles to a small chapel south of the city. Entering the building he inquired where this particular class met. Imagine the thrill experienced in that little classroom when the door opened and the President walked in. After explaining why he was not in his office, he shook hands with the teacher and with each of the children and left his blessing.

"I want you children to know," he said, "that the President of the Church keeps his appointments if at all possible."

Glenn Snarr in "Memories of a Prophet," *Improvement Era,* 73 (Feb. 1970): 72.

◄―◄―►

DAVID O. MCKAY

"Today I Found a Prophet"

I remember being in New York when President McKay returned from Europe. Arrangements had been made for pictures to be taken, but the regular photographer was unable to go, so in desperation the United Press picked their crime photographer—a man accustomed to the toughest type of work in New York. He went to the airport, stayed there two hours, and returned later from the darkroom with a tremendous sheaf of pictures. He was supposed to take only two. His boss immediately chided him. "What in the world are you wasting time and all those photographic supplies for?"

The photographer replied very curtly, saying he would gladly pay for the extra materials, and they could even dock him for the extra time he took. It was obvious that he was very touchy about it. Several hours later the vice-president called him to his office, wanting to learn what happened. The crime photographer said, "When I was a little boy, my mother used to read to me out of the Old Testament, and all my life I have wondered what a prophet of God must really look like. Well, today I found one."

Arch L. Madsen in "Memories of a Prophet," *Improvement Era*, 73 (Feb. 1970): 72.

Biographical Sketch

JOSEPH FIELDING SMITH

April 6, 1970, the one-hundred-fortieth anniversary of the organization of the Church was a special, sacred occasion. It was on that day that Joseph Fielding Smith was sustained in a solemn assembly as Prophet, Seer, and Revelator and President of The Church of Jesus Christ of Latter-day Saints.

Joseph Fielding Smith was named for his father, President Joseph F. Smith, who presided over the Church from 1901 to 1918. Joseph Fielding Smith was also the grandson of Hyrum Smith, who died with his brother, the Prophet Joseph Smith, at the Carthage Jail in 1844. President Smith was rightly proud of his ancestry.

He said:

I am . . . proud to be a descendant of Latter-day Saint parentage, of the fifth generation. I am also proud to be a grandson of one of the original members of the Church, a man who was faithful to the end, and laid down his life for the truth; and I am glad to know that so many of his descendents are actively engaged in the cause, and are also faithful in the truth.[1]

On another occasion President Smith paid tribute as follows:

I have also been impressed this afternoon by the singing of this hymn, sacred to me, composed by President Taylor, who dearly loved the Prophet

---

[1]*Conference Report,* April 1913, p. 99.

Joseph Smith. I never read this hymn or hear it sung without being touched in my soul, and I shall take the liberty this afternoon, in my weak and imperfect way, to read it, for I realize that in the singing we do not always get the full comprehension of the words, which may not be impressed upon our souls, especially in a large gathering such as this, as we would like to have them:

O, give me back my Prophet dear,
And Patriarch, O give them back,
The Saints of Latter-days to cheer,
And lead them in the Gospel track!
But, O, they're gone from my embrace,
From earthly scenes their spirits fled,
Two of the best of Adam's race,
Now lie entombed among the dead.

Ye men of wisdom, tell my why—
No guilt, no crime in them were found—
Their blood doth now so loudly cry,
From prison walls and Carthage ground:
Your tongues are mute, but pray attend,
The secret I will now relate,
Why those whom God to earth did lend,
Have met the suffering martyrs' fate.

It is because they strove to gain,
Beyond the grave a heaven of bliss,
Because they made the gospel plain
And led the Saints to righteousness;
It is because God called them forth,
And led them by His own right hand,
Christ's coming to proclaim on earth,
And gather Israel to their land.

It is because the priests of Baal
Were desperate their craft to save,
And when they saw it doomed to fail,
They sent the Prophets to their grave.
Like scenes the ancient Prophets saw,
Like these the ancient Prophets fell,
And, till the resurrection dawn,
Prophet and Patriarch, farewell.

My heart is always touched when I hear this beautiful hymn, or when I read it. I understand the spirit that rested upon President Taylor when he wrote it; but I rejoice, my brethren and sisters, in this fact—although the prophet who stands at the head of the dispensation of the fulness of times, and the patriarch who stood with him have been taken from us, the Lord has not left us helpless. There has never been a time since the restoration of the gospel when we have not had a prophet, some one to lead us, to direct us, to teach the commandments of God that we might walk in the straight and narrow path. We are not without leaders. . . .[2]

President Smith further said:

The time shall never come when the Lord will not find some one that he can trust; in whom he has confidence, and who will be qualified to stand to represent him among the people. This is my testimony, and I rejoice in its truth.[3]

Joseph Fielding Smith was born on July 19, 1876.

In April of 1898 he married Louie Emyle Shurtliff, and a year later he was called to serve in the British Mission. He was ordained a seventy by his father on May 12, 1899, and left the next day for the mission field. He labored in the Nottingham Conference for two years, returning home in June, 1901.

Upon his return, President Smith accepted employment with the Church Historian's Office, where he ultimately devoted a greater part of his life. Further responsibility came to him in 1907 when he was appointed secretary of the Genealogical Society.

Two years before he became a member of the Council of the Twelve, President Smith lost his first wife, Louie Emyle. She died March 30, 1908. On November 2, 1908, he married Ethel Georgina Reynolds. She died August 26, 1937. President Smith married Jessie Evans, former contralto and concert singer and soloist with the Salt Lake Tabernacle Choir, April 12, 1938. 1938.

Two daughters were born to President Smith's first wife, and his second wife bore him five sons and four daughters. . . .[4]

President Smith was called to fill a vacancy in the Quorum of the Twelve in 1910 at the young age of thirty-three. At the time of his call, his father was the President of the Church and one of his brothers was a General Authority, which gives an

---

[2]Ibid., October 1912, pp. 124-25.
[3]Ibid., p. 124.
[4]*Church News*, January 24, 1970, p. 3.

indication of the quality of his family. President Smith served as an apostle for sixty years, longer than any other man in this dispensation. President Smith held the responsible position as President of the Quorum of the Twelve for nineteen years and for five years was a counselor in the First Presidency. In addition to his remarkable record as a General Authority, his service and contributions in other areas were almost unparalleled in the history of the Church. President Smith was Church Historian for forty-nine years and had twenty-four volumes of his writings and sermons published. He was recognized throughout the Church for his exceptional knowledge of Church history and Church doctrine.

In 1956, members of the Council of the Twelve published a tribute to President Joseph Fielding Smith. Among other things they said:

> . . . President Joseph Fielding Smith has inherited in rich measure the dauntless courage and the unswerving devotion to duty which have characterized the lives of his noble ancestors. . . . He has been a fearless defender of the faith and an untiring preacher of the gospel of repentance.
>
> We who labor in the Council of the Twelve under his leadership have occasion to glimpse the true nobility in his character. Daily we see continuing evidences of his understanding and thoughtful consideration of his fellow workers. . . . We only wish that the entire Church could feel the tenderness of his soul and his great concern over the welfare of the unfortunate and those in distress. He loves all the Saints and never ceases to pray for the sinner.
>
> With remarkable discernment, he seems to have but two measures in arriving at final decisions. What are the wishes of the First Presidency? Which is best for the kingdom of God? In his profound gospel writings and in his theological dissertations, he has given to his associates and to the Church a rich legacy which will immortalize his name among the faithful. . . .[5]

How fitting it is that the capable, beloved grandson of Hyrum Smith and son of Joseph F. became the Prophet, Seer, and Revelator in these latter-days.

After President Smith was sustained as President of the Church by the unanimous vote of the Church members he said:

---

[5]*Improvement Era*, 59 (July 1956): 495.

My beloved brethren and sisters:

I stand before you today in humility and in thanksgiving, grateful for the blessings which the Lord has poured out upon me, upon my family, upon you, upon all his people.

I know we are engaged in the work of the Lord and that he raises up men to do his work in every time and age of the earth's history. . . .

I desire to say that no man of himself can lead this Church. It is the Church of the Lord Jesus Christ; he is at the head. The Church bears his name, has his priesthood, administers his gospel, preaches his doctrine, and does his work.

He chooses men and calls them to be instruments in his hands to accomplish his purposes, and he guides and directs them in their labors. But men are only instruments in the Lord's hands, and the honor and glory for all that his servants accomplish is and should be ascribed unto him forever.

If this were the work of man, it would fail, but it is the work of the Lord, and he does not fail. And we have the assurance that if we keep the commandments and are valiant in the testimony of Jesus and are true to every trust, the Lord will guide and direct us and his Church in the paths of righteousness, for the accomplishment of all his purposes.[6]

President Smith died on Sunday, July 2, 1972. Funeral services were held in the Salt Lake Tabernacle on July 6, and burial was in the Salt Lake City cemetery.

---

[6]*Improvement Era*, 73 (June 1970): 26.

JOSEPH FIELDING SMITH

"A Mighty Man in Israel"

In the year 1896 President Smith received a patriarchal blessing from John Smith, the Patriarch to the Church. The following . . . is copied from that blessing:

Thou art numbered among the sons of Zion, of whom much is expected. Thy name is written in the Lamb's Book of Life and shall be registered in the chronicles of thy fathers with thy brethren. It is thy privilege to live to a good old age and the will of the Lord that you should become a mighty man in Israel. Therefore, I say unto thee, reflect often upon the past, present, and future. If thou shalt gain wisdom by the experience of the past, thou shalt realize that the hand of the Lord has been and is over thee for good, and that thy life has been preserved for a wise purpose. Thou shalt realize also that thou hast much to do in order to complete thy mission upon the earth. It shall be thy duty to sit in counsel with thy brethren and to preside among the people. It shall be thy duty also to travel much at home and abroad by land and water, laboring in the ministry; and I say unto thee, hold up thy head, lift up thy head, lift up thy voice without fear or favor as the Spirit of the Lord shall direct, and the blessing of the Lord shall rest upon thee. His Spirit shall direct thy mind and give thee word and sentiment that thou shalt confound the wisdom of the wicked and set at naught the councils of the unjust.

Early in the year 1910 President John R. Winder, a great and good man, passed from this life. His position as a counselor to President Joseph F. Smith was filled by the choosing and sustaining of Elder John Henry Smith as counselor. Also at this April conference of 1910 Elder Joseph Fielding Smith was chosen as apostle to fill the vacancy in the Quorum of the Twelve, thus fulfilling part of the inspired promise of the patriarch. Subsequently he became President of the Quorum, and on January 23, 1970, was called to serve the highest position in the Church, that of President—the Prophet, Seer, and Revelator to lead us in these troubled times.

A. William Lund, "Forty Years An Apostle," *Improvement Era*, 53 (April 1950): 315-16.

———◆———◆———

JOSEPH FIELDING SMITH

"At My Mother's Knee"

My beloved brethren and sisters, I feel like I had just passed through a tornado. (Laughter.) I did not say that to make you laugh. But the Lord never blessed me with a voice nor the quality to explode when I get up to deliver a discourse, so I am deficient in those things. I do wish to say, however, that I have a testimony of this truth. I am grateful for it. I do not remember the time when I did not believe in the mission of our Lord and Savior Jesus Christ nor in the mission of the Prophet Joseph Smith, and I hope you will forgive me if I get a little personal.

I was trained at my mother's knee to love the Prophet Joseph Smith and to love my Redeemer. I never knew my Grandmother Smith. I have always regretted that, because she was one of the most noble women who ever lived; but I did know her good sister, my Aunt Mary Thompson, and as a boy I used to go and visit her in her home and sit at her knee, where she told me stories about the Prophet Joseph Smith, And, oh, how grateful I am for that experience.

Brethren and sisters, teach your children from their infancy to believe in Jesus Christ as our Redeemer, in Joseph Smith as a prophet of God, and in his successors in this kingdom, and let them grow up with a knowledge of this truth in their hearts built upon faith and obedience to the commandments the Lord has given to us and through the guidance of that Holy Spirit which will not dwell in unclean tabernacles.

Conference Report, April, 1962, p. 44.

JOSEPH FIELDING SMITH

"I Can Remember Hearing My Father Sing"

I would like to say right here that it delights my heart to see our people everywhere improving their talents as good singers. Everywhere we go among our people we find sweet voices and talent for music. I believe that this is a manifestation to us of the purpose of the Lord in this direction toward our people, that they will excel in these things, as they should excel in every other good thing. I can remember, when I was a young boy, hearing my father sing. I do not know how much of a singer he was, for at that time I was not capable of judging as to the quality of his singing; but the hymns he sang became familiar to me in the days of my childhood.

When we listen to this choir, we listen to music, and music is truth. Good music is gracious praise of the Lord. It is delightsome to the ear, and it is one of our most acceptable methods of worshiping. And those who sing in the choir and in all the choirs of the Saints should sing with the Spirit and with understanding. They should not sing merely because it is a profession, or because they have a good voice; but they should sing also because they have the spirit of it, and can enter into the spirit of prayer and praise the Lord who gave them their sweet voices. My soul is always lifted up, and my spirit cheered and comforted, when I hear good music. I rejoice in it very much indeed.

Conference Report, October 5, 1969, pp. 109-10.

＜━●━●━►

JOSEPH FIELDING SMITH

"Born of Goodly Parents"

I am grateful that I have been born of goodly parents who taught me to walk in the light of the truth. From my earliest recollection, from the time I first could read, I have received more pleasure and greater satisfaction out of the study of the scriptures and reading of the Lord Jesus Christ, and of the Prophet Joseph Smith, and the work that has been accomplished for the salvation of men, than from anything else in all the world. The Lord has given me a testimony of the truth which I pray may abide with me forever. I know that Joseph Smith was and is a prophet of the living God, and that he holds the keys of this dispensation. More than this— and I hope I may be pardoned for the references I am about to make—I am grateful for my lineage. I am very thankful to my Father in heaven that I am the son of my father and the son of my grandfather. May I say to you that I am not boasting, but I am speaking, I hope and fully believe, in the spirit of humility in saying this. I cannot express my gratitude fully that my father remained faithful and obedient to the gospel and the Church all his days, and that he taught his children to love the truth and to be loyal to the message delivered through the Prophet Joseph Smith, and to honor the name they bear.

All my life I have prayed and hoped that the Lord would touch the hearts of the children of the Prophet Joseph Smith. I still pray that he may do so. No man would hold out the hand of fellowship more quickly than I would to welcome them into the fold of truth.

. . . May he bless the descendants of Hyrum Smith that they also may walk in the light of the everlasting gospel. May they never falter nor turn from the path in which their father walked, and may they honor and uphold his good name.

Conference Report, April 8, 1930, pp. 91, 94.

JOSEPH FIELDING SMITH

"Mixed Memories of Juny"

He [Joseph Fielding Smith] learned to work on the family farm in Taylorsville, Salt Lake County. An early memory is of milking the family cow without permission "before I was baptized." Milking was a task that had been given to an older sister, but apparently he did it well enough that he soon found himself given the job.

He learned early to work with animals, with nature, with men, and with God. His own growing testimony was aided by the faith and works of his father, who had been a full-time missionary at fifteen and an apostle ten years before Joseph Fielding was born, and who had been called as second counselor in the First Presidency when his namesake son was only four years of age.

Another of the family tasks that fell his lot was that of being stable boy for his mother in her capacity as a licensed midwife. At all hours of the night he was called from his deep boyhood sleep to harness a horse so she could go where she was needed. He would light a kerosene lantern and go to the barn, and soon the horse would be ready.

Reflecting on those early years, he has mixed memories of Juny, a fine horse that his father had purchased from President George Q. Cannon of the First Presidency:

> She was so smart she learned how to unlock one kind of corral fastener after another that I contrived, until father said to me, half humorously, that Juny seemed to be smarter than I was. So Father himself fastened her in with a strap and buckle. As he did so, the mare eyed him coolly; and, as soon as our backs were turned, she set to work with her teeth until she actually undid the buckle and followed us out, somewhat to my delight. I could not refrain from suggesting to father that I was not the only one whose head compared unfavorably with the mare's.

Albert L. Zobell, Jr., "President Joseph Fielding Smith," *Improvement Era,* 73 (March 1970): 5.

JOSEPH FIELDING SMITH

"Well, Here's My Finish"

In his patriarchal blessing, given by John Smith in 1896, Joseph Fielding Smith was promised that his life would be preserved and he would be privileged to live to "a good old age" that he might become a mighty man in Israel. An incident in his boyhood days illustrates how his life was once so preserved. Joseph and his brothers herded cows near the Jordan River and worked diligently on their father's farm. One day Joseph and his brother George were loading hay onto a wagon from the field to take it into the barn. They stopped on the road by a canal to stack some bales, and Joseph instructed George to stand by the heads of the team and hold their bridles until he, Joseph, could climb up and take the reins. But George failed to heed his brother's words, the skittish horses started up with a sudden jerk, and young Joseph fell down between the team. One thought went through his mind: "Well, here's my finish." But something turned them and he was thrown clear of their hoofs and the wheels of the wagon. He proceeded to give George a lecture and then hurried home, somewhat shaken but still in one piece. His father came out to meet him and wanted to know what difficulty he had encountered, because he had received the strong impression that his son was in some kind of danger.

From a talk by President Joseph Fielding Smith at a family reunion.

◄—◆—►

JOSEPH FIELDING SMITH

"The Best Company Is None Too Good"

The following story was told by President Smith's daughter, Amelia Smith McConkie.

Knowing full well that your associates can have great influence upon your actions, Joseph Fielding Smith counseled and cautioned his children to be wise in their choice of friends. He knew that their friends could determine the things they did, and the places they went and thereby determine whether they found lasting happiness in righteous living or momentary pleasures.

Often as he spoke to his family as they sat around the breakfast table or in their family home evenings he would tell them of the story of Alma pleading with his son, Corianton, to repent and do the things he had been taught, saying, "Remember, my son, wickedness never was happiness."

To impress these principles upon his children he related his experience in looking for employment upon his return from his mission to Great Britain.

He was married at this time, and the job he had did not pay enough to support himself and a wife, therefore he was desirous of improving his situation. About this time he was offered a job as a traveling representative for a company which would take him into an area covering much of the western states. The salary would be exceptionally good for those days. Thus it was a tempting offer even though it would necessitate associating with people whose standards were not always in keeping with his. On inquiring why they were offering him this position he was told the man who had it had been discharged, as he had succumbed to the temptations connected with the environment he was in. They were offering him the position because they felt he would be above temptation, and could be trusted.

Before giving the employer an answer Joseph Fielding Smith went to his father, President Joseph F. Smith, and explained the situation, asking for advice. Looking straight at him his father's immediate response was, "My boy, the best of company is none too good."

"That's all I wanted to know," was his reply, and he declined the job to the great astonishment of the man who made the offer. Not long after that he was employed in the Church Historian's Office where he remained until he became the tenth President of the Church.

JOSEPH FIELDING SMITH

"Ye May Stand Spotless"

When I was a small boy, too young to hold the Aaronic Priesthood, my father placed a copy of the Book of Mormon in my hands with the request that I read it. I received this Nephite record with thanksgiving and applied myself to the task which had been assigned to me. There are certain passages that have been stamped upon my mind, and I have never forgotten them. One of these is in the twenty-seventh chapter of third Nephi, verses 19 and 20. It is the word of our Redeemer to the Nephites as he taught them after his resurrection. It is as follows:

"And no unclean thing can enter into his kingdom; therefore nothing entereth into his rest save it be those who have washed their garments in my blood, because of their faith, and the repentance of all their sins, and their faithfulness unto the end.

"Now this is the commandment: Repent, all ye ends of the

earth, and come unto me and be baptized in my name, that ye may be sanctified by the reception of the Holy Ghost, that ye may stand spotless before me at the last day."

The other passage is in the tenth verse of chapter 41 in the book of Alma and is as follows:

"Do not suppose, because it has been spoken concerning restoration, that ye shall be restored from sin to happiness. Behold, I say unto you, wickedness never was happiness."

These two passages I have tried to follow all the days of my life, and I have felt to thank the Lord for this counsel and guidance, and I have endeavored to stamp these sayings on the minds of many others. What a wonderful guide these teachings can be to us if we can get them firmly fixed in our minds!

Conference Report, October 2, 1964, p. 6.

————◆——◆——

JOSEPH FIELDING SMITH

"We Lived on Bean Soup"

I was called to go on a mission March 17, 1899, by President Lorenzo Snow. I accepted and was set apart to fill a mission in Great Britain. My brother Richards was also called to go on a mission at the same time and place. We traveled together.

The afternoon of May 12, 1899, I was set apart and ordained a seventy by my father, President Joseph F. Smith. . . .

June 2, we reached the coast of Ireland and I saw my first view of part of the old country. Our actions on the ship had been a credit to us because we were asked by some why we didn't smoke or drink beer. We had a chance to tell them about the Word of Wisdom.

On June 3 we could see Ireland on one side and Wales on the other. We arrived in Liverpool just two weeks after we had left Philadelphia. We were taken to headquarters and then assigned to our different fields of labor. I was assigned to the Nottingham Conference. My brother Richards, who traveled with me, was sent to Leeds.

I left Liverpool at four P.M., June 4, and arrived in Nottingham at 7:30 that same evening. No elders were expecting me. I arrived at the mission home. The door was locked. I left my trunk on the outside and sat on it. A few youngsters who were in the street gathered around and began to sing,

> Chase me, girls, to Salt Lake City,
> Where the Mormons have no pity.

I went out into the street where they were, and they all ran away. But that was my first welcome in the mission field.

June 6 was a very important day in my life. I came from my home less than a month before for the purpose of preaching the gospel unto this nation, Great Britain. The streets were crooked and different from the ones at home, but we tracted and got along very well. I visited twenty-five homes on my first visit in the mission field, had many of the doors slammed in my face, and received a number of insults; but I think it all did me some good.

We held meetings on the streets. We would travel maybe six miles, or eight miles. Sometimes we would go fourteen miles. We didn't think anything about walking from one place to another. The longest walk that I ever had in the mission field —and we always walked; we never rode—was from Uttoxeter in Staffordshire, through Derby, to Nottingham. I left at six a.m., and I arrived in Nottingham at twelve that night, traveling on foot all that distance.

We thought nothing of walking twelve or fourteen miles to hold a meeting.

We had members of the Church in certain towns, ten or fifteen miles away from our headquarters, and we thought nothing of going to see them and walking all the distance. I don't remember ever riding on a bus while I was in the mission field. I walked. . . .

Several of us elders lived in the headquarters of the conference and we would take turns in cooking the meals. I got to be quite a cook. We had to wait upon ourselves. I taught them some things that they didn't know; one was that navy beans were very good. You could eat them boiled or in soup.

I went to the store one day to get some navy beans. (I was in charge at the headquarters.) The man reached down off the shelf a one-pound package and handed it to me. I said, "I don't want just one pound; I want eight or ten pounds." He looked at me in astonishment. He went to his shelf, looked up, and he took down eight one-pound packages and said, "This is all I've got." I took the eight packages home. We lived on beans boiled and bean soup. You don't know how good it is if you haven't tried it. . . .

I shall always be grateful that the Lord gave me this experience. I am grateful—and I have said this many times—that I wasn't born 500 years ago, or 1,000 years ago, when the gospel wasn't here upon the face of the earth.

I thank the Lord constantly that I am living in this day when the gospel is restored. The blessings are here: men and women can be baptized for the remission of their sins; men can be ordained to receive the Holy Priesthood and go forth into the mission field with divine authority to preach the gospel of Jesus Christ.

Joseph Fielding Smith, *My Missionary Experiences*, Brigham Young University, Speeches of the Year (Provo, 1966), pp. 3-7.

JOSEPH FIELDING SMITH

"The Lord Will Look After His Own"

One of many incidents will show how the inspiration of the Lord rests upon Joseph Fielding Smith with respect to this genealogical work. Shortly after the commencement of World War II, Brother Archibald F. Bennett reported to the board of directors of the Genealogical Society that efforts to continue negotiations with Denmark to obtain microfilm copies of vital records had been interrupted, and the outbreak of war had also caused England to refuse to the Church the privilege of copying its vital records. This report was very disturbing to the board, and expressions of concern for the preservation and obtaining of records were made. Elder Smith was very quiet and then expressed his feeling that the outcome of the war would render these records available to us which could not then be obtained. He said, "The Lord will look after his own." The collecting of millions of names from these and other countries of Europe shows the literal fulfillment of this inspiration.

A. William Lund, "Forty Years An Apostle," *Improvement Era*, 53 (April 1950): 312.

——◄━━►——

JOSEPH FIELDING SMITH

"Placed in Quarantine"

President Smith has always been deeply involved in genealogical work. Shortly after the death of

President Ivins, Brother Smith was appointed to succeed him as the president of the Genealogical Society. When permission was gained for the Society to publish a magazine to promote the growth of historical and genealogical work, Brother Smith was appointed its editor and manager. This magazine had its beginning in January of 1910. The preparation of the first publication had only begun when Brother Joseph and his family were placed in quarantine, as some of his children had contracted scarlet fever. Such a condition might have discouraged most men, but not this one. He prepared his manuscript, treated it with an antiseptic, and placed it in a box by his gate. From here it was gathered, taken to the printer, the galley proofs returned, read, fumigated, and then returned to the printer. The first publication of the magazine was thus put out on time and continued a successful career until the year 1940.

A. William Lund, "Forty Years an Apostle," *Improvement Era*, 53 (April 1950): 275.

—————◆—◆—————

JOSEPH FIELDING SMITH

"See If You Cannot Get the Spirit"

I know a man who went to school when I went to school; we played together, went to school together. When he grew up to be a man, he went East and became a scientist. He came back, and then he began to create a great deal of disturbance in the Sunday School classes, questioning the revelations that had been given through the Prophet Joseph Smith. This came to my attention when one of the members of the class came to see me and said, "This brother comes to our class, and he is just a disturbance." As I was well acquainted with him, I made it my duty to get hold of him and asked him why he did those things that were disturbing the members of the class.

"Well," he said, "I cannot accept all of the revelations that were given to the Prophet Joseph Smith."

"Are there any of them you can accept?"

"Yes," he said, "I can accept some of them," but he could not accept all of the doctrines that had come through the revelations of our Father in heaven and his Son Jesus Christ to the Church.

After we got through with the conversation, and I had a long conversation with him, he said, "Now, I am going to ask you one favor. Please do not take any step to have me excommunicated."

I said, "Why do you want to stay in the Church when you are opposing its doctrines?"

He said, "I will tell you why. I was raised in the Church, and my friends are members of the Church. I have few associations outside of the Church. If I should be excommunicated that means that I should be cut off from all communication, all fellowship with the people with whom I am now associating, and I do not want that to happen. So please do not take any steps to have me excommunicated."

I thought there was some hope for him so I did not take any such step; but I did talk to him kindly and try to get him to see the folly of his ways, to repent, and when he went to classes—and he could go to the classes—he should not go with the spirit of defiance or opposition to the doctrines which the others believed. I said, "If you don't believe them, then keep still and see if you cannot get the Spirit of the Lord so that you can accept them."

Well, he is dead now. I do not know whether he repented or not; but brethren, the gospel of Jesus Christ is the most vital thing in all the world to us. We should so live that we can accept every word that proceedeth forth from the mouth of God, and that is a commandment from him.

Conference Report, October, 1959, p. 18.

JOSEPH FIELDING SMITH

"I Keep Two of Your Faith with Me"

I suppose there are members in the congregation and who are listening in who are anxious to know something about their boys who are in the service of the country in the Far East. . . .

You fathers and mothers who have sons serving in the forces, be proud of them. They are fine young men. Some of our servicemen are converts who have been brought into the Church by the teachings, by precept, and by example—principally by example of the members of the Church who are also serving with them in the forces.

I met a number of young men who said, "We came in the Church because of the lives of these young men and because they taught us the principles of the gospel."

They are doing a good work. There might be one or two that may be careless, but those young men with whom I had the privilege of meeting, talking to, would bear their testimony of the truth and were walking humbly.

And as I met with the officers and chaplains (and unfortunately, at this time, we have no chaplain of the Church there) —but when I met with them, universally they said, "We like your young men. They are clean. They are dependable."

One of these chaplains, when I was talking with him, said, "I keep two of these young men of your faith with me all the time. If I lose one of them, if he is called away, I get another." While I was talking with him, a young man came in with a message, and when he was in there, he held out his hand and said, "I am Brother so-and-so." (I do not remember his name now.) He received the instruction given him and departed. A little later another one came. He likewise was a member of the Church. This man, not a member of the Church, said, "I keep them with me all the time because they are dependable."

Be proud of your boys. Be proud of your young men in the mission field. . . .

The Spirit of the Lord is leading them. The doors are opening for them to preach the gospel.

Now just one more word that I would like to say. This comes a little close to me; nevertheless I want to say it. Sister Smith's singing everywhere we went was a great help. When she could not go to Korea, we took a record of "The King of Glory," and we were able to broadcast the recording from the military grounds so it could be heard all over the city; so her voice was heard there, although she was not privileged to accompany me.

It was a glorious visit.

The Lord bless you.

Conference Report, October 1955, pp. 42-44.

—◆—◆—

JOSEPH FIELDING SMITH

"The Man I Know"

The following tribute was given to President Smith in 1932 by his now deceased wife Ethel G. Reynolds Smith.

You ask me to tell you of the man I know. I have often thought when he is gone people will say, "He is a very good man, sincere, orthodox, etc." They will speak of him as the public knows him; but the man they have in mind is very different from the man I know. The man I know is a kind, loving husband and father whose greatest ambition in life is to make his family happy, entirely forgetful of self in his efforts to do this. He is the man that lulls to sleep the fretful child, who tells bedtime stories to the little ones, who is never too tired or too busy to sit up late at night or to get up early in the morning to help the older children solve perplexing school problems. When illness comes, the man I know watches tenderly over the afflicted one and waits upon him. It is their father for whom they cry, feeling his presence a panacea for all ills. It is his hands that bind up the wounds, his arms that give courage to the sufferer, his voice that remonstrates with them gently when they err, until it becomes their happiness to do the thing that will make him happy.

The man I know is most gentle, and if he feels that he has been unjust to anyone the distance is never too far for him to go and, with loving words or kind deeds, erase the hurt. He welcomes gladly the young people to his home and is never happier than when discussing with them topics of the day—sports or whatever interests them most. He enjoys a good story and is quick to see the humor of a situation, to laugh and to be laughed at, always willing to join in any wholesome activity.

The man I know is unselfish, uncomplaining, considerate, thoughtful, sympathetic, doing everything within his power to make life a supreme joy for his loved ones. That is the man I know.

Bryant S. Hinckley, "Joseph Fielding Smith," *Improvement Era*, 35 (June 1932): 459.

----◆——▶—

JOSEPH FIELDING SMITH

"President Smith Kept His Appointments"

President Smith's unusual life span spread from the covered wagon to the jet plane. In his early years as a member of the Council of the Twelve he and his assigned companion would sometimes journey to stake conferences by starting out by train, then transferring to a wagon, and sometimes making even a third transfer and perhaps completing their journey on horseback.

This memory is in contrast to another experience of a few years ago. One weekend President Smith found himself with an appointment that would keep him in the Salt Lake City area for the greater part of Saturday. However, he had been assigned to conduct a quarterly stake conference in the San Francisco area Saturday evening and Sunday. This worried President Smith, who prides himself on the way his appointments seldom, if ever, are in conflict. But it looked as if, this time, one appointment would have to be cancelled.

He casually mentioned the problem to a young friend who was a jet pilot in the National Guard. The pilot replied, "You know, my crew is lacking some air time this month. We've got to fly some place to log out time. The Bay Area is just about the distance we need to keep our training record up to where it should be this month. Let's fly there late Saturday afternoon and return Sunday evening."

President Smith kept both of his Saturday appointments that week, and he and his younger friends enjoyed themselves at quarterly conference on Sunday.

Albert L. Zobell, Jr., "President Joseph Fielding Smith," *Improvement Era,* 73 (March 1970): 8.

JOSEPH FIELDING SMITH

"I Was in the Arms of the Prophet"

A large crowd gathered at the General Authorities' exit of the Tabernacle following the general conference. The visitors, many from out-of-town, were anxious to get a glimpse of President Joseph Fielding Smith or perhaps a warm handshake from the new Church president.

From the crowd, wiggling between legs, came a small girl who made her way to President Smith. Soon she was in his arms for a little hug, and then back into the crowd so quickly that the *Deseret News* photographer was unable to get her name.

The picture, unidentified, appeared in the *Church News*. However, her proud grandmother, Mrs. Milo Hobbs of Preston, Idaho, recognized her and promptly wrote a letter to President Smith to share the information.

"I am so happy that we can identify her as our granddaughter, Venus Hobbs. She has a birthday on April 17 when she will be four years old," Grandmother Hobbs wrote.

On her birthday, little Venus Hobbs, who lives in Torrance, Calif., received a surprise "happy birthday" call and song from President and Mrs. Smith. President Smith was spending the week in California when he made the call.

The call was a thrill to the W. Odell Hobbs family. Mrs. Hobbs was touched with tears to think that the President of the Church was so kind. Venus was delighted with the song.

The letter went on to explain, "She was with two of her aunts, but she slipped away. They feared they had lost her in the crowd. When they asked, "How did you get lost?"

"I wasn't lost!" she said.

"Who found you?" they asked.

"I was in the arms of the Prophet," was her reply.

"She Wasn't Lost, She Was With The Prophet," *Church News*, April 25, 1970, p. 3.

Biographical Sketch

HAROLD B. LEE

Harold B. Lee became president of The Church of Jesus Christ of Latter-day Saints on July 7, 1972, following the death of President Joseph Fielding Smith. He had been a member of the Council of the Twelve since April 6, 1941, and president of that council as well as first counselor to President Smith since January 23, 1970.

He was born March 28, 1899, in Clifton, Oneida County, Idaho, one of six children of Samuel Marion and Louisa Bingham Lee, and was reared on the family farm in Clifton. He attended the Oneida Stake Academy and Albion State College (which later was merged with the Idaho State University), receiving a teacher's certificate in 1917. At the age of 17 he became principal of an Idaho school, and after further study at the University of Utah in 1922-23, he was a principal in the Granite School District in Salt Lake County from 1923 to 1928. In November 1920 he was called to serve on a mission in the Western States Mission, with headquarters in Denver.

In 1928 President Lee resigned his school position to become intermountain manager for the Foundation Press, Inc. He was appointed to the Salt Lake City Commission on December 1, 1932, and won reelection in November 1933.

Meanwhile, as a stake president, he organized, with his

counselors, the Pioneer Stake Bishop's Storehouse early in 1932 to care for the needy and unemployed members of his stake. This was one of the beginnings of the Church's general welfare program. When the Church combined its various relief activities into the enlarged Churchwide welfare program, Harold B. Lee became managing director on January 1, 1937, a position he held for twenty-two years.

On November 14, 1923, he married Fern Lucinda Tanner in the Salt Lake Temple, and they had two daughters: Helen (Mrs. L. Brent Goates) and Maurine (Mrs. Ernest J. Wilkins). Sister Lee died September 24, 1962, and Maurine passed away in 1965. On June 17, 1963, President Lee married Freda Joan Jensen.

President Lee received three honorary doctorate degrees: the Doctor of Humanities from Utah State Agricultural College (now Utah State University) in 1953; the Doctor of Christian Service from Brigham Young University in 1955; and the Doctor of Humanities from the University of Utah in 1965.

He served on the boards of numerous corporations, including Zion's First National Bank, Beneficial Life Insurance Company, Utah-Idaho Sugar Company, ZCMI, Zions Securities Corporation, Union Pacific Railroad, and Equitable Life Assurance Society of the United States. He was also on the board of governors of the American Red Cross.

President Lee passed away following a sudden illness on December 26, 1973, at the age of seventy-four.

HAROLD B. LEE

"A Voice of Warning"

I have a believing heart that started with a simple testimony that came when I was a child—I think maybe I was around ten or eleven years of age. I was with my father out on a farm away from our home, trying to spend the day busying myself until my father was ready to go home. Over the fence from our place were some tumbledown sheds that would attract a curious boy, and I was adventurous. I started to climb through the fence, and I heard a voice as clearly as you are hearing mine, calling me by name and saying, "Don't go over there!" I turned to look at my father to see if he were talking to me, but he was way up at the other end of the field. There was no person in sight. I realized then, as a child, that there were persons beyond my sight, for I had definitely heard a voice. Since then, when I hear or read stories of the Prophet Joseph Smith, I too have known what it means to hear a voice, because I've had the experience.

Stand Ye in Holy Places (Deseret Book Co., 1974), p. 139.

HAROLD B. LEE

"The Faith of a Mother"

Since nine o'clock last night° I have lived an entire lifetime in retrospect and in prospect. I spent a sleepless night. I never closed my eyes one moment, and neither would you if you had been in my place. Throughout the night, as I thought of this most appalling and soul-stirring assignment, there kept coming to me the words of the Apostle Paul, which he spoke in explanation of the human qualities that were to be found in the Lord and Savior:

"For we have not an high priest which cannot be touched with the feeling of our infirmities; but was in all points tempted like as we are, yet without sin.

"Let us therefore come boldly unto the throne of grace, that we may obtain mercy, and find grace to help in time of need." (Hebrews 4:15-16.)

One could not have listened to the soul-stirring testimony of President Heber J. Grant, in bearing testimony as to his feelings when he was called to the apostleship, or his experiences in calling others to similar positions, without realizing that he has been close to his Heavenly Father in this experience. Therefore I shall take the word of the Apostle Paul. I shall come boldly unto the throne of grace, and ask for mercy and His grace to help me in my time of need. With that help I cannot fail. Without it I cannot succeed.

Since my childhood I have looked upon these men as the greatest men on the face of the earth, and now the contemplation of an intimate association with them is overwhelming and beyond my comprehension.

I thank God today for my parentage. My father and mother are listening, either in this great assembly or on the radio, if perchance they did not get into this meeting. I think perhaps this is my way of paying tribute to the two family names they gave me

---

°This address was given following President Lee's call to the Council of the Twelve.

at my birth, Bingham and Lee. I trust I shall not disgrace those names. I have been blessed with a splendid father and a grand and lovely mother, one who didn't display often her affection, but who showed her love in tangible ways that, as a child, I came early to recognize as true mother love.

As just a high school boy, I went away on a high school debating team trip. We won the debate. I came back and called Mother on the telephone only to have her say, "Never mind, son. I know all about it. I will tell you when you get home at the end of the week." When I came home she took me aside and said, "When I knew it was just time for this performance to start, I went out among the willows by the creekside, and there, all by myself, I remembered you and prayed God you would not fail." I have come to know that that kind of love is necessary for every son and daughter who seek to achieve in this world: my tribute to my parents.

Ye Are the Light of the World (Deseret Book Co., 1974), pp. 327-28.

HAROLD B. LEE

"Put the Priesthood of God to Work"

I had a lesson years ago as to the greatness of priesthood. A call came for me from the First Presidency, asking me to come to their office on a day that I shall never forget— April 20, 1935.

I was a city commissioner at the time, as well as a stake president. In our stake there were 4,800 of our 7,300 people who were wholly or partially dependent. There were few government work programs; the finances of the Church were low; and we had been told that not much could be done so far as outside help was concerned. We had only one place to go, and that was to apply the Lord's program as set forth in the revelations.

It was from our humble efforts in helping our people that the First Presidency, knowing of our experience, called me asking if I would come to their office. It was Saturday morning and they had no other appointments on their calendar, so for hours they talked with me. They told me they wanted me to resign from the city commission and they would release me from being stake president; they wished me now to head up the welfare movement to turn the tide from government relief and help put the Church in a position where it could take care of its own needy.

After that morning I drove my car up to the head of City Creek Canyon into what was then called Rotary Park, and there, all by myself, I offered one of the most humble prayers of my life.

There I was, just a young man in my thirties. My experience had been limited. I was born in a little country town in Idaho and had hardly been outside the boundaries of the states of Utah and Idaho. And now, to put me in a position where I was to reach out to the entire membership of the Church worldwide, was one of the most staggering contemplations I could imagine. How could I do it with my limited understanding?

As I knelt down, my petition was, "What kind of an organization should be set up in order to accomplish what the Presidency has assigned?" And there came to me on that glorious morning one of the most heavenly realizations of the power of the priesthood of God. It was as though something were saying to me, "There is no new organization necessary to take care of the needs of this people. All that is necessary is to put the priesthood of God to work. There is nothing else that you need as a substitute."

Conference Report, October 1972, pp. 123-24.

HAROLD B. LEE

"Acquiring That Special Witness"

I shall never forget my feelings of loneliness the Saturday night after I was told by the President of the Church that I was to be sustained the next day as a member of the Quorum of the Twelve Apostles. That was a sleepless night. There ran through my mind all the petty things of my life, the nonsense, the foolishness of youth. I could have told you about those against whom I had any grievances and who had any grievance against me. And before I was to be accepted the next day, I knew that I must stand before the Lord and witness before him that I would love and forgive every soul that walked the earth and in return I would ask Him to forgive me that I might be worthy of that position.

I said, as I suppose all of us would say as we are called to such a position, or any position, "President Grant, do you feel that I am worthy of this call?" And just as quick as a flash, he said, "My boy, if I didn't think so, you would never be called to this position."

The Lord knew my heart and He knew that I was not perfect and that all of us have weaknesses to overcome. He takes us with imperfections and expects us to begin where we are and make our lives conform fully with the principles and doctrines of Jesus Christ.

The following day I went to the temple where I was ushered into the room where the Council of the Twelve meet with the First Presidency each week in an upper room. I thought of all the great men who have occupied those chairs and now here I was, just a young man, twenty years younger than the next youngest of the Twelve, being asked to sit in one of those chairs. It was frightening and startling.

And then one of the Brethren, who arranged for Sunday evening radio programs, said, "Now you know that after having been ordained, you are a special witness to the mission of the Lord Jesus Christ. We want you to give the Easter talk next Sunday night."

The assignment was to bear testimony of the mission of the Lord concerning His resurrection, His life, and His ministry, so I went to a room in the Church Office Building where I could be alone, and I read the Gospels, particularly those that had to do with the closing days and weeks and months of the life of Jesus. And as I read, I realized that I was having a new experience.

It wasn't any longer just a story; it seemed as though I was actually seeing the events about which I was reading, and when I gave my talk and closed with my testimony, I said, "I am now the least of all my brethren and want to witness to you that I know, as I have never known before this call came, that Jesus is the Savior of this world. He lives and He died for us." Why did I know? Because there had come a witness, that special kind of a witness, that may have been the more sure word of prophecy that one must have if he is to be a special witness.

Joint Nottingham and Leicester conference, Nottingham England Stake, September 2, 1973. (See *Ensign*, February 1974, p. 18.)

→——→

HAROLD B. LEE

"Listening to the Right Sources of Power"

A very grievous case came before a high council and stake presidency that resulted in the excommunication of a man.

The very next morning I was visited in my office by the brother of this man. He said, "I want to tell you that my brother wasn't guilty of what he was charged with."

"How do you know he wasn't guilty?" I asked.

"Because I prayed, and the Lord told me he was innocent," the man answered.

I asked him to come into the office. As we sat down, I asked, "Would you mind if I ask you a few personal questions?"

He said, "Certainly not."

"How old are you?"

"Forty-seven."

"What priesthood do you hold?"

He said he thought he was a teacher.

"Do you keep the Word of Wisdom?"

"Well, no." He used tobacco, which was obvious.

"Do you pay your tithing?"

He said, "No"—and he didn't intend to as long as that blankety-blank-blank man was the bishop of the ward.

I said, "Do you attend your priesthood meetings?"

He replied, "No, sir!" and he didn't intend to as long as that man was bishop.

"You don't attend your sacrament meetings either?"

"No, sir."

"Do you have your family prayers?" and he said no.

"Do you study the scriptures?" He said well, his eyes were bad, and he couldn't read very much.

I then said to him: "In my home I have a beautiful instrument called a radio. When everything is in good working order we can dial it to a certain station and pick up the voice of a speaker or a singer all the way across the continent or sometimes on the other side of the world, bringing them into the front room as though they were almost right there. But after we have used it for a long time, the little delicate instruments or electrical devices on the inside called radio tubes begin to wear out. When one of them wears out, we may get some static—it isn't so clear. Another wears out, and if we don't give it attention, the sound may fade in and out. And if another one wears out—well, the radio may sit there looking quite like it did before, but because of what has happened on the inside, we can hear nothing.

"Now," I said, "you and I have within our souls something like what might be said to be a counterpart of those radio tubes. We might have what we call a 'go-to-sacrament-meeting' tube, a 'keep-the-Word-of-Wisdom' tube, a 'pay-your-tithing' tube, a 'have-your-family-prayers' tube, a 'read-the-scriptures' tube, and, as one of the most important—one that might be said to be the master tube of our whole soul—we have what we might call the 'keep-yourselves-morally-clean' tube. If one of these becomes worn out by disuse or inactivity—if we fail to keep the commandments of God—it has the same effect upon our spiritual selves that a worn-out tube has in a radio.

"Now, then," I said, "fifteen of the best-living men in that stake prayed last night. They heard the evidence and every man was united in saying that your brother was guilty. Now you, who do none of these things, you say you prayed and got an opposite answer. How would you explain that?"

Then this man gave an answer that I think was a classic. He said, "Well, President Lee, I think I must have gotten my answer from the wrong source." And, you know, that's just as great a truth as we can have. We get our answers from the source of the power that we wish to obey. If we're following the ways of Satan, we'll get answers from Satan. If we're keeping the commandments of God, we'll get our answers from God.

Stand Ye in Holy Places, pp. 135-38.

◄——►

HAROLD B. LEE

"A Son Worthy of My Daughter"

As I have thought of home evening, I have thought of my own family. When our older daughter was to be married to a fine Latter-day Saint boy, the two mothers were talking to each other, and the mother of our daughter said, "You know, from the time my little girl was born, I have been praying all my life that somewhere a mother would be preparing a son worthy to marry my daughter." And this other mother smiled and said, "Isn't that strange? This is my only son who is being married to your daughter, and ever since he was born, I, too, have been praying that somewhere there would be a mother preparing a daughter worthy to meet and to marry my son." That is the kind of home attention that will make us and our homes stronger today.

Ye Are the Light of the World, p. 83.

———◆——◆———

"Success in Rearing a Family"

Coming home on the train from California, I rode with a lovely mother whom I have known and who has reared an excellent family. We talked about practices that had helped to keep her family faithful. She said:

"Brother Lee, I made it a practice and rule, when my children came along, that I was going to make as many contacts with my children in the home as I possibly could. I was always there when they went to school. I planned to give up everything else, if necessary, to be there when they came home. I was there when they had their parties and their friends in the home. And I always waited up after the evening parties in order to greet my children when they came home from the party, because I found that at such moments I was able to encourage a frankness between us, and it permitted me to enjoy their confidences. Over the years this built a comradeship that kept them safe in times of difficulty."

What a blessing is such a wise mother! Such children, so taught, with whom mothers and fathers have made such comrades, in times of stress and storm will turn to mother and father as the ship that is laboring in the storm turns to the port for safety.

Conference Report, October 1948, p. 54.

———◆——◆———

HAROLD B. LEE

"Obey the Counsels of the Church"

In Kelsey, Texas, I once heard a group of anxious people asking, "Is now the day for us to come up to Zion. where we can come to the mountain of the Lord and be protected from our enemies?"

I pondered that question; I prayed about it. What should we say to those people who were so anxious? I studied the subject and learned something of what the Spirit has taught, and I know now that the place of safety in this world is not in any given place; it doesn't make much difference where we live. The all-important consideration is how we live. I have found that security can come to Israel only when the Saints keep the commandments, when they live so that they can enjoy the companionship, the direction, the comfort, and the guidance of the Holy Spirit of the Lord, when they are willing to listen to the men whom God has sent here to preside as His mouthpieces, and when they obey the counsels of the Church.

When a decision has been reached by the presiding councils of the Church and a majority of these councils has decided on a certain policy, and there then develops a minority vote contrary to that majority decision, one may know with a surety that that minority voice is not speaking the will of the Lord. I tremble when I think of that statement. I am greatly concerned when I now sit in one of the presiding councils of the Church and remember that in days gone by, some have fallen by the way because they went out in contradiction of the majority decision of that body. And so that places before us a safe guide. Should there be those, even though in high places, who may come among us who are not speaking the policy of the Church as declared by the men whom we sustain as prophets of the living God, the Church may know that those who thus speak are not speaking the mind of the Lord and the voice of the Lord and the power of God unto salvation.

Conference Report, April 1943, p. 129.

+———▶

"Why Do You Want to Go on This Mission, Son?"

While I was attending a stake conference, I was to interview some of the prospective missionaries. Before one boy came to see me, the stake president said, "Now here is a boy who has just come through a serious experience. He is just out of the service. He suffered shell-shock in battle, and I think we need to talk pretty carefully to him and make certain that he is prepared to go."

So as I talked with the young man, I said, "Why do you want to go on this mission, son? Are you sure that you really want to go, after all the harrowing experiences you have had?"

He sat thoughtfully for a few moments and then said, "Brother Lee, I had never been away from home when I went into the service, and when I got out into the camps, every waking hour I heard filthy, profane language. I found myself losing a certain pure-mindedness, and I sought God in prayer to give me the strength not to fall into that terrible habit. God heard my prayer and gave me strength. Then we went through basic training, and I asked Him to give me physical strength to continue, and He did. He heard my prayer. As we moved up toward the fighting lines and I could hear the booming of the guns and the crackling of the rifles, I was afraid. Again I prayed to God to give me the courage to do the task that I was there to do, and He heard my prayer and gave me courage.

"When I was sent up with an advance patrol to search out the enemies and to send back for the reinforcements, telling them where to attack—and sometimes the enemy would almost hedge me around until I was cut off, and it seemed that there was no escape—I thought that surely my life would be taken. I asked for the only force of power to guide me safely back, and God heard me. Time and again through the most harrowing experiences He led me back. Now," he said, "I am back home. I have recovered, and I would like to give thanks to that power to which I prayed—God, our Heavenly Father. Going out on a mission, I can teach others that faith which I was taught in Sunday School, in seminary, in my priesthood class, and in my home.

I want to teach others so that they will have that same strength
that guided me through this difficult experience."

_____
Ye Are the Light of the World, pp. 111-12.

◆━◆━◆

HAROLD B. LEE

"Faith to Hold to Church Standards"

I was asked to address a group of young girls a
few years ago at the Lion House, where they were being
shepherded under the direction of the great Young Women's
Mutual Improvement Association. At the close of our meeting
this lovely girl took me aside, and from her purse she unfolded a
picture of a handsome young soldier. Underneath the picture
was something about love, and his name signed. I asked, "Well,
what does this mean?"

Tears were swimming in her eyes. She replied, "I met that
young man here in an army camp. He was not a member of the
Church. He was clean and fine, and he had the ideals I had
longed for in a companion, all except one thing—he was not a
member of the Church. And when he proposed marriage to me, I
said, 'Only will I be married when I can be married in the house
of the Lord, because love means something more than just a
thing that pertains to this life. It is an eternal thing, and I want
to be married in the temple.' "

Well, he reasoned with her, he pleaded with her, he
scolded, and then he became angry; and finally, after repeated
efforts to break down her religious objection to a marriage out of
the temple, he left her. It was now time to go overseas, and she
cried her heart out the night he left, thinking that maybe she had
made a mistake because her heart had gone out to this fine young
man.

During a long ocean voyage over to Australia, where he was to be stationed and from where he was to go into combat, he began to think about this young woman. He began to think that he had been a little hasty in his judgment about her religious convictions. Perhaps it was her religion that had made her the fine girl that she was. With that on his mind, he began to seek companionship with our Latter-day Saint men. He finally met a Latter-day Saint chaplain there and became associated with the LDS boys of the camp, and he began to study the gospel. On her birthday he had sent her this picture, and behind the picture was a slip of paper which proved to be a certificate evidencing the fact that he had been baptized a member of The Church of Jesus Christ of Latter-day Saints. In the letter that accompanied the picture, he had said, "I am preparing now to live worthy so that when I come home, I can be ordained an elder and together we can be married in the house of the Lord."

There, young men, is the first thing that you must think of if you would have exaltation in the celestial kingdom. Marriage is eternal, and here was a young woman who realized the foundation on which she must build if she were to have a fulness of eternal happiness.

Stand Ye in Holy Places, pp. 374-75.

HAROLD B. LEE

"Healing of Body and Soul"

There is a power beyond the sight of man that heals not only sick bodies but sick souls. I met a young man in Tokyo, where we were holding a servicemen's conference. He had his right arm in a sling, and as he was introduced, he put out his left hand to acknowledge the introduction. "I am not a

member of the Church," he said, "but I understand you are going to be in Manila in a few weeks. We will be there with the
U.S. Seventh Fleet, and I hope to be able to tell you when you
get there that I have become a member of the Church."

The weeks went by and I had almost forgotten the incident
until, as we held a conference at Clark Field in Manila, I spotted
the same man whom I had met in Tokyo. In an interview we had
with him later he said, "You noticed when we met in Tokyo that
I had my arm in a sling. It was hurting me terribly all through
that service, but after we had shaken hands on the stand, suddenly the throbbing pain seemed to stop. I took my arm out of
the sling and began to flex it, and there was no more pain. When
I went back to the ship, I didn't need any treatment; the infec-
tion seemed to have gone. I sensed the fact that I had been in the
presence of a power that had taken away the pain from my body,
even healed my sick body. I am going back home now to prove
that I am worthy of the love of my sweet wife."

A few years later I was with a companion in Norfolk, Vir-
ginia, where we were organizing a new stake, and right down in
the front seat sat this same man with a beautiful woman by his
side, his wife. We sustained him as a member of the elders
presidency in that stake. Yes, the Lord can heal sick bodies, but
the greatest miracle we see is the healing of sick souls.

Baccalaureate Address, Ricks College, Rexburg, Idaho, May 6, 1970. (See also
Ensign, February 1974, p. 16.)

◄━━◆━━►

HAROLD B. LEE

"A Husband's Most Precious Gift"

In the old Provo Tabernacle some years ago,
we held a meeting of husbands and wives where we tried to
inspire those who were less active in the Church. . . .

A lovely sister was asked to come forward to tell about the

joy that had come into their home since her husband had now become active in the Church. They had gone to the temple, and now they had the joy of an eternal union. They had fallen in love when they were youngsters, but he had been careless and smoked and didn't go to his meetings. Thus, when they were ready to be married, he hadn't been advanced to the position of elder in the Melchizedek Priesthood and couldn't take her to the temple. But he said, "I promise you that if you will marry me in a civil marriage, I will take you to the temple. I will make myself worthy."

However, he was like the man who said he knew a man who could quit smoking because he had done it a thousand times; he would quit in the morning and smoke again before nightfall. Finally somebody took this man by the right hand, as Peter did the impotent man at the Gate Beautiful, and lifted him up, so to speak—taught him how to walk without tobacco smoke, without drink, and to walk straightforwardly. He was ordained an elder, and then came the day when the bishop gave him a temple recommend.

The wife told about that beautiful experience in the temple where, across an altar, they were sealed together for eternity. And then the doors opened and their five little girls, dressed in white, came in and joined them around that sacred altar, and a man of God pronounced them a family through the eternities.

As she spoke, she looked over the pulpit, and right down in front of her was her husband. As she looked at him, she seemed to forget that anyone else was present. She said to him, "Daddy, I don't know how to tell you how grateful the girls and I are for what you have done for us; because, you see, except for you who have the priesthood of God to unlock the key to an eternal home, none of us could be together in the hereafter. From the bottom of our hearts we thank you, our Daddy."

As the man sat there and sobs shook his body, I wished that all the careless daddies in this church could have heard the commendation that came from this woman, who was so grateful for the repentance of her husband.

Address at the Brigham Young University Sixth Stake quarterly conference, April 27, 1969.

HAROLD B. LEE

_____

"How to Receive Revelation"

A man came in to see me and said that he had heard that some man appeared mysteriously to a group of temple workers and told them, "You had better hurry up and store for a year, or two, or three, because there will come a season when there won't be any production." He asked me what I thought about it, and I said, "Well, were you in the April conference of 1936?" He replied, "No, I couldn't be there." And I said, "Well, you surely read the report of what was said by the Brethren in that conference?" No, he hadn't. "Well," I said, "at that conference the Lord did give a revelation about the storage of food. How in the world is the Lord going to get over to you what He wants you to do if you are not there when He says it, and you do not take the time to read it after it has been said?"

_____

Stand Ye in Holy Places, p. 159.

HAROLD B. LEE

_____

"Revelation: A Light from Heaven"

I was sent several years ago to New York to select a patriarch. We decided upon a certain man and went to his home. He had been out with his sons on the welfare farm, pitching manure all day, and was tired and weary. . . . After he changed his clothes and came in, I made him more weary when I told him what it was that I had come for—that he was to be called as the patriarch to that stake.

The next morning in conference he bore a remarkable

testimony. Then afterwards we went to the Manhattan Ward, where I was to ordain him. The office was down in the basement, where there was no natural light. . . .

This is the story as told to me by the stake president's wife: "As you walked over to put your hands on the patriarch's head, I thought to myself, this is a man with whom we socialize; we have gone on trips with him, and he has been in our social group. Now part of his responsibility is to declare in patriarchal blessings the lineage from which each one has come. He hasn't been a student of ancient languages—how is he going to know?

"With these thoughts in my mind, I saw you walk over and put your hands on his head, and a light came from behind you and went right through you and into him. I thought to myself, 'Isn't that a strange coincidence that the sunlight has come in just at this moment.' Then I realized that there was no sunlight; I was witnessing the answer to my question. That light came from somewhere behind you, Brother Lee, and went through you into the patriarch. Then I knew where he was going to get that information: from the revelations of Almighty God."

Address at joint Nottingham and Leicester conference, Nottingham, England, September 2, 1973. (See *Ensign*, February 1974, pp. 18-19.)

———◄—●—►———

HAROLD B. LEE

"Close to Those Beyond"

One day a beautiful, flaxen-haired girl—about ten years of age—came with her mother to the home of her grandparents. The Primary song "I Am a Child of God" had just been sent out through the Church. As the mother sat at the piano and accompanied, this little flaxen-haired beauty sang "I am a child of God. . . . Lead me, guide me, walk beside me, help me find the way. Teach me all that I must do to live with Him some day." (*Sing with Me*, no. B-76.)

The grandparents sat with tears in their eyes as this beautiful little child sang that glorious song. Little did they know that in a few short years, suddenly and without warning, that young mother would be snatched away in just a moment. The pleadings of the grandfather over in the Hawaiian Islands and the piteous cries for the mercies of the Almighty to spare her were unavailing. In the hospital, surrounded by doctors with all the medical skill they could summon, she slipped away.

The children, including this little flaxen-haired girl, were called, and around the lonely table in the family room they sat with bowed heads, sobbing their hearts out. The grandfather was summoned to come home, and that night all the family were at the airport to meet him. Then, with arms surrounding that little family, the grandfather said, "I do not know how you can be so brave. Grandfather is crying his heart out, and you stand here with your arms around each other, seemingly with no tears." One of them said, "Grandfather, we have no more tears to shed. We have cried our tears away all day long."

That night this little girl had a dream, one so vivid that, as she slept in bed by her aunt, she awakened and gripped her aunt and said, "I have had a visit from Mother. We were in the family room and she came and I said to her, 'Mother, you are not dead; you are still here.' And Mother said, 'Yes, my darling, I am not gone. You won't be able to see me, but all through your life, Mother will be very close by you. Mother will not always be seen, but you can know that she won't be far away.' "

Years pass, tragedies come, risks, responsibilities, and the inevitable tragedies of life—grandfathers, grandmothers, husbands and wives snatched from each other. The experience I have just related was a drama that was enacted right here in this community. I was the grandfather who pleaded, "Please, God, don't let her die." But it was as though the Father was saying, "I have other plans," and all the faith that could be mustered was unavailing.

But let me tell you something, you parents. The greatest comfort that I have had in having a companion snatched away from me was to know that during the thirty-nine years of married life, I couldn't recall one ugly episode that ever transpired.

Address at the Brigham Young University Sixth Stake quarterly conference, April 27, 1969. (See also *Stand Ye in Holy Places*, pp. 13-14.)

"Unseen Hands to Bless"

May I impose upon you for a moment to express appreciation for something that happened to me some time ago. I was suffering from an ulcer condition that was becoming worse and worse. We had been touring a mission; but my wife, Joan, and I were impressed that we should return home as quickly as possible, although we had planned to stay for some other meetings.

On the way across the country, we were sitting in the forward section of the airplane. Some of our Church members were in the next section. At a certain point en route, someone laid his hand upon my head. I looked up but could see no one. That happened again before we arrived home; again the same experience took place. Who it was, by what means or what medium, I may never know, except that I was receiving a blessing that I came a few hours later to know I needed most desperately.

As soon as we arrived home, my wife very anxiously called the physician. It was now about 11 o'clock at night. He asked if I could come to the phone, and then wanted to know how I was. I said, "I am very tired. I think I will be all right." But shortly thereafter there came massive hemorrhages which, had they occurred while we were in flight, I wouldn't be here today talking about it.

I know that there are powers divine that reach out when all other help is not available.

General conference address, April 1973, in *Ensign*, July 1973, p. 123.

HAROLD B. LEE

"My Record Is Written in the Hearts of the People"

Again, in the mighty demonstration of this solemn assembly [October 6, 1972] I am moved with emotions beyond expression as I have felt the true love and bonds of brotherhood. There has been here an overwhelming spiritual endowment, attesting, no doubt, that in all likelihood we are in the presence of personages, seen and unseen, who are in attendance. Who knows but that even our Lord and Master would be near us on such an occasion as this, for we, and the world, must never forget that this is His church, and under His almighty direction we are to serve! Indeed, I would remind you what He declared in a similar conference of Saints in Fayette, New York, and undoubtedly would remind us again today: "But behold, verily, verily, I say unto you that mine eyes are upon you. I am in your midst and ye cannot see me." (D&C 38:7.)

On the sacred occasion when President Joseph Fielding Smith passed away and I began to sense the magnitude of the overwhelming responsibility which I must now assume, I went to the holy temple. There, in prayerful meditation, I looked upon the paintings of those men of God—true, pure men, God's noblemen—who had preceded me in a similar calling. . . .

Now I stood alone with my thoughts. Somehow the impressions that came to me were, simply, that the only true record that will ever be made of my service in my new calling will be the record that I may have written in the hearts and lives of those with whom I have served and labored, within and without the Church.

Stand Ye in Holy Places, pp. 166-67, 169.

Biographical Sketch

Spencer W. Kimball was ordained twelfth president of the Church on December 31, 1973. He had been sustained to serve in the Council of the Twelve in October 1943, and had been acting president of the Twelve (January 23, 1970, to July 7, 1972) and then president of the Twelve (July 7, 1972-December 31, 1973).

President Kimball was born March 28, 1895, in Salt Lake City, one of eleven children of Andrew and Olive Woolley Kimball. His paternal grandfather was Heber C. Kimball, one of the original twelve apostles in this dispensation and a counselor in the First Presidency to Brigham Young. His maternal grandfather, Edwin Dilworth Woolley, was business manager for President Young.

When Spencer W. Kimball was three years old, his father was sent to the Gila Valley of Arizona, to preside over the St. Joseph Stake, an assignment he fulfilled for more than twenty-six years. He then served ten years as president of the Indian Territory Mission. The family settled in Thatcher, Arizona.

President Kimball received a call in 1914 to serve in the Swiss-German Mission, but the assignment was changed when World War I broke out, and he served instead in the Central States Mission. Upon returning from his mission he attended

355

Arizona State University and then served briefly in the military, just before the Armistice of 1918 was signed.

On November 16, 1917, he married Camilla Eyring, a teacher at the Gila Academy at Thatcher. She was born in Colonia Juarez, Mexico, and had been forced with her family to flee when the Mexican Revolution broke out.

Spencer W. and Camilla Eyring Kimball are parents of three sons and one daughter: Spencer L., director of the research department of the American Bar Association; Andrew, an executive in the foreign department of General Electric; Edward, professor of law at Brigham Young University; and Olive Beth (Mrs. Grant M. Mack), a homemaker and a member of the Tabernacle Choir. Including children, grandchildren, great-grandchildren, and in-laws, the Spencer W. Kimball family now numbers nearly seventy.

President Kimball was active in Church and civic affairs in Arizona before his call to the Council of the Twelve in 1943. A businessman, he was a founder of an insurance company and held many positions in civic groups. At age twenty-nine he became a counselor in the St. Joseph Stake, then was called to be first president of the Mt. Graham Stake when it was divided from the St. Joseph Stake in 1938.

As a General Authority, he has long been associated with missionary work. He served for many years as chairman of the executive committee of the Church's Missionary Committee, and since becoming president of the Church, there has been considerably increased emphasis on missionary efforts worldwide. For a quarter of a century he was chairman of the Church's Indian Committee and helped institute the successful Indian placement program. As president, he has presided over the Washington D.C. Temple dedication, area general conferences in Europe, South America, and the Orient, and has traveled extensively to nearly every corner of the world. He is the author of two widely read books, *The Miracle of Forgiveness* and *Faith Precedes the Miracle*.

SPENCER W. KIMBALL

"That First Tithing Receipt"

When I was a little boy in Thatcher, Arizona, my father, desiring to teach his children industry, thrift, and tithing, turned over to my sister Alice and me a patch of potatoes that he had planted.

I hoed the weeds and helped to irrigate the potatoes until they were ready to dig. Then Alice and I dug and cleaned and sorted them. We took the larger ones of uniform size and put them in a box and loaded them in my little red wagon. Then, after putting on clean clothing, we pulled the little red wagon with its contents to town. We sold our merchandise to some of the neighbors, but a kindly sister who operated the hotel was our best customer. She looked them over and bought from us regularly through the season.

After selling our first load we were so happy we could hardly wait to get home to tell our parents of our success. Father listened to us count our money—a very great amount, it seemed to us. Then he said, "That's capital! Now what will you do with your money?"

We thought of ice cream cones and candy and Christmas presents we could buy. Then in his characteristic and impressive way, our father said, "Now you haven't forgotten the bishop, have you? The Lord has been kind to us. The earth is his. He sent the moisture and the sunshine and all we did was plow and plant and cultivate and harvest. One-tenth we always give back to the Lord for his work. When you have paid your tithing to the bishop, then you may use the balance as you wish."

I think I still have in my keepsakes that first tithing receipt.

Children's Friend, April 1947, p. 147.

SPENCER W. KIMBALL

"Read the Bible from Cover to Cover"

Let me tell you of one of the goals I made when I was still but a lad. When I heard a Church leader from Salt Lake City tell us at conference that we should read the scriptures, and I recognized that I had never read the Bible, that very night at the conclusion of that very sermon I walked to my home a block away and climbed up to my little attic room in the top of the house and lighted a little coal-oil lamp that was on the little table, and I read the first chapters of Genesis. A year later I closed the Bible, having read every chapter in that big and glorious book.

I found that this Bible that I was reading had in it 66 books, and then I was nearly dissuaded when I found that it had in it 1,189 chapters, and then I also found that it had 1,519 pages. It was formidable, but I knew that if others did it, I could do it.

I found that there were certain parts that were hard for a fourteen-year-old boy to understand. There were some pages that were not especially interesting to me, but when I had read the 66 books and 1,189 chapters and 1,519 pages, I had the glowing satisfaction that I had made a goal and that I had achieved it.

Now I am not telling you this story to boast; I am merely using this as an example to say that if I could do it by coal-oil light, you can do it by electric light. I have always been glad I read the Bible from cover to cover.

Ensign, May 1974, p. 88.

━━◆━━

SPENCER   W.   KIMBALL

"The Seven Goblets Were Still Full"

May I tell you another goal that I set when I was still a youngster.

I had heard all of my life about the Word of Wisdom and the blessings that could come into my life through living it. I had seen people chewing tobacco, and it was repulsive to me. I had seen men waste much time in "rolling their own" cigarettes. They would buy a sack of "Bull Durham" tobacco or some other brand, then some papers, and then they would stop numerous times in a day to fill the paper with tobacco, roll it, bend over the little end of it, and then smoke it. It seemed foolish to me and seemed such a waste of time and energy. Later when the practice became more sophisticated, they bought their cigarettes readymade. I remember how repulsive it was to me when women began to smoke.

I remember as a boy going to the Fourth of July celebration on the streets of my little town and seeing some of the men as they took part in the horse racing as participator or as gambler, betting on the horses, and I noted that many of them had cigarettes in their lips and bottles in their pockets and some were ugly drunk with their bleary eyes and coarse talk and cursing.

It took a little time to match the ponies and arrange the races, and almost invariably during this time there would be someone call out, "Fight!" "Fight!" and all the men and boys would gravitate to the fight area, which was attended with blows and blood and curses and hatreds.

Again I was nauseated to think that men would so disgrace themselves, and again I made up my mind that while I would drink the pink lemonade on the Fourth of July and watch the horses run, I never would drink liquor or swear or curse as did many of these fellows of this little town.

And I remember that without being pressured by anyone, I made up my mind while still a little boy that I would never break the Word of Wisdom. I knew that when the Lord said it, it was pleasing unto him for men to abstain from all these destructive elements, and the thing I wanted to do was to please my Heavenly Father. And so I made up my mind firmly and solidly that I would never touch those harmful things. Having made up my mind fully and unequivocably, I found it not too difficult to keep the promise to myself and to my Heavenly Father.

I remember once in later years, when I was district governor of the Rotary Clubs of Arizona, that I went to Nice, France, to the international convention. As a part of that celebration there was a sumptuous banquet for the district governors, and the large building was set for an elegant meal. When we came to our places, I noted that at every place there were seven goblets, along with numerous items of silverware and dishes; and everything was about the best that Europe could furnish.

As the meal got underway, an army of waiters came to wait on us, seven waiters at each place, and they poured wine and liquor. Seven glass goblets were filled at every plate. The drinks were colorful. I was a long way from home; I knew many of the district governors; they knew me. But they probably did not know my religion nor of my stand on the Word of Wisdom. At any rate, the evil one seemed to whisper to me, "This is your chance. You are thousands of miles from home. There is no one here to watch you. No one will ever know if you drink the contents of those goblets. This is your chance!" Then a sweeter spirit seemed to whisper, "You have a covenant with yourself; you promised yourself you would never do it. With your Heavenly Father you made a covenant, and you have gone these years without breaking it, and you would be stupid to break it now." Suffice it to say that when I got up from the table an hour later, the seven goblets were still full of colorful material that had been poured into them but never touched.

_____
Ensign, May 1974, pp. 88-89.

◆━━◆

SPENCER W. KIMBALL

_____

"Seven Little Boys"

Long years ago when I was in the presidency of the St. Joseph Stake in Arizona, one Sabbath day I filled an assignment in the Eden Ward. The building was a small one, and most of the people were close to us as we sat on the raised platform about a foot and a half above the floor of the building itself.

As the meeting proceeded, my eye was attracted to seven little boys on the front seat of the chapel. I was delighted that they were in this ward conference. I made a mental note, then shifted my interest to other things. Soon my attention was focused on the seven little boys again.

It seemed strange to me that each of the seven raised his right leg and put it over the left knee, and then in a moment all would change at the same time and put the left leg over the right knee. I thought it was unusual, but I just ignored it.

In a moment or two, all in unison brushed their hair with their right hands; then all seven boys leaned lightly on their wrists and supported their faces by their hands, and then simultaneously they went back to the crossing of their legs again.

It all seemed so strange, and I wondered about it as I was trying to think of what I was going to say in the meeting. And then suddenly it came to me like a bolt of lightning: These boys were mimicking me!

That day I learned the lesson of my life—that we who are in positions of authority must be careful indeed, because others watch us and find in us their examples.

Ensign, November 1974, p. 79.

SPENCER W. KIMBALL

"The Breaking of Day Has Found Me on My Knees"

My beloved brethren, this is the great day of my life. [President Kimball had just been sustained to the Council of the Twelve.] I have seen hands raised many times in my life, but never have they meant quite so much as they meant today when you raised your hands to sustain and support me.

I feel extremely humble in this calling that has come to me. Many people have asked me if I was surprised when it came. That, of course, is a very weak word for this experience. I was completely bewildered and shocked. I did have a premonition that this call was coming, but very brief, however. On the eighth of July, when President J. Reuben Clark called me, I was electrified with a strong presentiment that something of this kind was going to happen. As I came home at noon, my boy was answering the telephone and he said, "Daddy, Salt Lake City is calling."

I had had many calls from Salt Lake City. They hadn't ever worried me, like this one did. I knew that I had no unfinished business in Salt Lake City, and the thought came over me quickly, "You're going to be called to an important position." Then I hurriedly swept the thought from my mind, because it seemed so unworthy and so presumptuous. I had convinced myself that such a thing was impossible by the time I heard

President Clark's voice a thousand miles away saying: "Spencer, this is Brother Clark speaking. The brethren have just called you to fill one of the vacancies in the Quorum of the Twelve Apostles."

Like a bolt of lightning it came. I did a great deal of thinking in the brief moments that I was on the wire. There were quite a number of things said about disposing of my business, moving to headquarters, and other things to be expected of me. I couldn't repeat them all; my mind seemed to be traveling many paths all at once—I was dazed, almost numb with the shock; a picture of my life spread out before me. It seemed that I could see all of the people before me whom I had injured, or who had fancied that I had injured them, or to whom I had given offense, and all the small, petty things of my life. I sensed immediately my inability and limitations and I cried back, "Not me, Brother Clark! You can't mean that!" I was virtually speechless. My heart pounded fiercely.

I recall two or three years ago, when Brother Harold B. Lee was giving his maiden address as an apostle of the Lord Jesus Christ from this stand, he told us of his experience through the night after he had been notified of his call. I think I now know something about the experience he had. I have been going through it for twelve weeks. I believe the brethren were very kind to me in announcing my appointment when they did so that I might make the necessary adjustments in my business affairs, but perhaps they were more inspired to give me the time I needed for a long period of purification, for in those long days and weeks I did a great deal of thinking and praying and fasting and praying. Conflicting thoughts surged through my mind—voices seeming to say, "You can't do the work. You are not worthy. You have not the ability"—and always finally came the triumphant thought: "You must do the work assigned—you must make yourself able, worthy, and qualified." And the battle raged on.

I remember reading that Jacob wrestled all night, "until the breaking of the day," for a blessing; and I want to tell you that for eighty-five nights I have gone through that experience, wrestling for a blessing. Eighty-five times, the breaking of the day has found me on my knees praying to the Lord to help me and strengthen me and make me equal to his great responsibility that has come to me. I have not sought positions nor have I been ambitious. Promotions have continued to come faster than I felt I was prepared for them.

I remember when I was called to be a counselor in the stake presidency. I was in my twenties. President Grant came down to help bury my father, who was the former stake president, and to reorganize the stake. I was the stake clerk. I recall that after I had been chosen, some of my relatives came to President Grant, unbeknownst to me, and said, "President Grant, it's a mistake to call a young man like that to a position of responsibility and make an old man of him and tie him down." Finally, after some discussion, President Grant said very calmly, but firmly, "Well, Spencer has been called to this work, and he can do as he pleases about it," and, of course, when the call came, I accepted it gladly, and I have received great blessings therefrom.

Conference Report, October 1943, pp. 15-16.

◄━━►◄━►

SPENCER W. KIMBALL

"Brother Kimball, Have You Ever Been to Heaven?"

More than once I have repeated an experience I had in getting my portrait painted. On the fourth floor of the Salt Lake Temple is the room of the Council of the Twelve Apostles, with large chairs in a semicircle. Here important meetings of that body are held, and around its walls are portraits of the Brethren. When I came to this service, I looked upon them with admiration and affection, for these were truly great men with whom I was associated.

Sometime later authorization was given by the First Presidency for my portrait to be added to the others. Lee Greene

Richards was selected as the artist, and we began immediately. I sat on a chair on an elevated platform in his studio and tried very hard to look handsome, like some of the other brethren. With paints, brushes, and palette ready, the artist scrutinized my features and daubed on the canvas alternately. I returned many times to the studio. After weeks the portrait was exhibited to the First Presidency and later to my wife and daughter.

It did not pass, and I was to submit for a redoing.

The angle was changed, the hours—many of them—were spent, and finally the portrait was near completion. This particular day was a busy one like most others. I suppose I was daydreaming, and quite detached from this world. Apparently he had difficulty translating my faraway gaze onto the canvas. I saw the artist lay down his palette and paints, fold his arms, and look straight at me, and I was shocked out of my dreaming by the abrupt question: "Brother Kimball, have you ever been to heaven?"

My answer seemed to be a shock of equal magnitude to him as I said without hesitation: "Why, yes, Brother Richards, certainly. I had a glimpse of heaven just before coming to your studio." I saw him assume a relaxed position and look intently at me, with wonder in his eyes. I continued:

"Yes. Just an hour ago. I was in the holy temple across the way. The sealing room was shut off from the noisy world by its thick, white-painted walls; the drapes, light and warm; the furniture, neat and dignified; the mirrors on two opposite walls seeming to take one in continuous likenesses on and on into infinity; and the beautiful stained-glass window in front of me giving such a peaceful glow. All the people in the room were dressed in white. Here were peace and harmony and eager anticipation. A well-groomed young man and an exquisitely gowned young woman, lovely beyond description, knelt across the altar. Authoritatively, I pronounced the heavenly ceremony which married and sealed them for eternity on earth and in the celestial worlds. The pure in heart were there. Heaven was there.

"When the eternal marriage was solemnized, and as the subdued congratulations were extended, a happy father, radiant in his joy, offered his hand and said, 'Brother Kimball, my wife and I are common people and have never been successful, but we are immensely proud of our family.' He continued, 'This is the last of our eight children to come into this holy house for temple marriage. They, with their companions, are here to participate in the marriage of this, the youngest. This is our supremely happy day, with all of our eight children married properly. They are faithful to the Lord in church service, and the older ones are already rearing families in righteousness.'

"I looked at his calloused hands, his rough exterior, and thought to myself, 'Here is a real son of God fulfilling his destiny.'

" 'Success?' I said, as I grasped his hand. 'That is the greatest success story I have heard. You might have accumulated millions in stocks and bonds, bank accounts, lands, industries, and still be quite a failure. You are fulfilling the purpose for which you were sent into this world by keeping your own lives righteous, bearing and rearing this great posterity, and training them in faith and works. Why, my dear folks, you are eminently successful. God bless you.' "

My story was finished. I looked up at the portrait artist. He stood motionless in deep thought, so I continued: "Yes, my brother, I have had many glimpses of heaven.

"Once we were in a distant stake for conference. We came to the unpretentious home of the stake president at mid-day Saturday. We knocked at the door, and it was opened by a sweet mother with a child in her arms. She was the type of mother who did not know there were maids and servants. She was not an artist's model, nor a society woman. Her hair was dressed neatly; her clothes were modest, tastefully selected; her face was smiling; and though young, she showed the rare combination of maturity of experience and the joys of purposeful living.

"The house was small. The all-purpose room into which we were welcomed was crowded and in its center were a long table and many chairs. We freshened up in the small bedroom assigned to us, made available by 'farming out' to the neighbors some of the children, and we returned to this living room. She had been very busy in the kitchen. Her husband, the stake president, soon returned from his day's labors and made us welcome and proudly introduced us to all of his children as they returned from their chores and play.

"Almost like magic the supper was ready, for 'many hands make light work,' and these numerous hands were deft and experienced ones. Every child gave evidence of having been taught responsibility. Each had certain duties. One child quickly spread a tablecloth; another placed the knives and forks and spoons; and another covered them with the large plates turned upside down. (The dishes were inexpensive.) Next came large pitchers of creamy milk, high piles of sliced homemade bread, a bowl at each place, a dish of fruit from storage, and a plate of cheese.

"One child placed the chairs with backs to the table, and without confusion, we all knelt at the chairs facing the table. One young son was called on to lead in family prayer. It was extemporaneous, and he pleaded with the Lord to bless the family and their schoolwork, and the missionaries, and the bishop. He prayed for us who had come to hold conference that we would 'preach good,' for his father in his church responsibilities, for all the children that 'they would be good, and kind to each other,' and for the little cold shivering lambs being born in the lambing sheds on the hill this wintry night.

"A very little one said the blessing on the food, and thirteen plates were turned up and thirteen bowls filled, and supper proceeded. No apologies were offered for the meal, the home, the children, or the general situation. The conversation was constructive and pleasant. The children were well-behaved. These parents met every situation with calm dignity and poise.

"In these days of limited families, or childless ones, when homes often have only one or two selfish and often pampered children, homes of luxury with servants, broken homes where life moves outside the home, it was most refreshing to sit with a large family where interdependence and love and harmony were visible and where children were growing up in unselfishness. So content and comfortable were we in the heart of this sweet simplicity and wholesomeness that we gave no thought to the unmatched chairs, the worn rug, the inexpensive curtains, the numbers of souls that were to occupy the few rooms available."

I paused. "Yes, Brother Richards, I glimpsed heaven that day and many days, in many places." He seemed uninterested in his painting. He stood listening, seemingly eager for more, and almost involuntarily I was telling him of another flight into heavenly situations.

"This time it was on the Indian reservation. While most Navajo women seem to be prolific, this sweet Lamanite wife in their several years of marriage had not been blessed with children of her own. Her husband was well employed. These new converts to the Church were buying their weekend groceries. As we glanced at the purchases in the large, well-filled basket, it was evident that only wholesome food was there—no beer, no coffee, no cigarettes. 'You like Postum, do you?' we asked them, and their reply touched our hearts: 'Yes, we have had coffee and beer all our lives, but since the Mormon missionaries told us about the Word of Wisdom we use Postum, and we know it is better for the children and they like it.'

" 'Children?' we asked. 'We thought you were a childless couple.' This brought from them the explanation that they had filled their home with eighteen Navajo orphans of all ages. Their hogan was large but their hearts even larger. Unselfishness—the milk of human kindness! Love unfeigned! These good Indians could shame many of their contemporaries who live lives of selfishness and smugness."

I said to the artist: "Heaven can be in a hogan or a tent, Brother Richards, for heaven is of our own making." I was ready to return to the picture but apparently he was not so inclined. He stood and listened intently.

"This time I was in Hawaii in the beautiful little temple at Laie. It was a missionary group. The spirit was there; the proselyters could hardly wait their turns to bear testimony of the Lord's gospel. Finally, the little Japanese missionary gained the floor. By the pulpit in her stocking feet she knelt reverently, and with a heart near bursting with gratitude for the gospel and its opportunities, she poured out her soul to heaven.

"Heaven was there, my brother, in that little room, in that sacred spot, in that paradise of the Pacific with those sweet, consecrated young soldiers for Christ."

I continued: "Heaven was in my own home, too, Dr. Richards, when home evening was held. Through the years the room was filled with our children, when each, eager for a turn, sang a song, led a game, recited an Article of Faith, told a story, and listened to faith-promoting incidents and gospel teaching from parents who loved them.

"Again, I found heaven in Europe:

"Elder Vogel was a local convert German boy of great faith. His parents refused to assist him in the mission which he so desired to fill. A kind American member helped with a monthly check to assist with the mission expenses. He enjoyed his work and all went well for a year and a half. One day a letter came from the wife of his sponsor, advising that her husband had been killed in an auto accident and it would be impossible to send any more money.

"Elder Vogel kept his disappointment hidden and prayed earnestly for a solution. As he and his American companion, Elder Smith, passed a hospital one day, a solution to his financial problem was born in his mind. The next day he made an excuse and was gone for a time. When he came back he said little but went to bed early. When asked the reason, he said he was a little extra weary. A few days later Elder Smith noted a small bandage on the arm of the German brother, but his question was passed off lightly.

"Time passed and Elder Smith became suspicious of the periodical bandages until one day, unable to keep his secret longer, Elder Vogel told him: 'You see, my friend in America is dead and can no longer give support to my mission. My parents are still unwilling to help me, so I visit the blood bank at the hospital so I can finish my mission.' Selling his precious blood to save souls! Well, isn't that what the Master did when he gave his every drop in the supreme sacrifice?

"Do you believe in heaven, Brother Artist?" I asked. "Yes, that is it. Heaven is a place, but also a condition; it is home and family. It is understanding and kindness. It is interdependence and selfless activity. It is quiet, sane living; personal sacrifice, genuine hospitality, wholesome concern for others. It is living the commandments of God without ostentation or hypocrisy. It is selflessness. It is all about us. We need only to recognize it as we find it and enjoy it. Yes, my dear brother, I've had many glimpses of heaven."

I straightened up in my chair and posed again. The artist picked up his palette and brushes and paints, did some touching up of the portrait, and sighed contentedly as he said, "It is completed."

In due time it was placed with those of others of the Brethren in the Council of the Twelve room on the fourth floor of the Salt Lake Temple, where it hangs this day.

The gospel of Jesus Christ teaches men to live righteously, to make the family supreme, the home inviolate. It moves the characters of its adherents toward faultlessness. It is the true way. If lived rightly it will ennoble men toward Godhood.

Conference Report, October 1971, p. 152-56.

SPENCER W. KIMBALL

"I Wanted to Spend the Day with Him"

As told by Elder Boyd K. Packer.

After his call to the Twelve, President Kimball suffered a series of heart attacks. The doctors said that he must rest. He wanted to be with his beloved Indians. Brother Golden R. Buchanan took him to the camp of Brother and Sister Polacca, high in the pines of Arizona, and there he stayed during the weeks until his heart mended and his strength returned.

One morning he was missing from camp. When he did not return for breakfast, Brother Polacca and other Indian friends began to search. They found him several miles from camp, sitting beneath a large pine tree with his Bible open to the last chapter of the Gospel of John. In answer to their worried looks, he said, "Six years ago today I was called to be an apostle of the Lord Jesus Christ. And I just wanted to spend the day with Him whose witness I am."

Ensign, March 1974, p. 4.

SPENCER W. KIMBALL

"This Is No Ordinary Man"

As told by Elder Boyd K. Packer.

In 1957 throat problems developed, to be diagnosed as cancer of the vocal cords. This, perhaps, was to be his Gethsemane.

He went east for the operation. Elder Harold B. Lee was there. As President Kimball was prepared for surgery he agonized over the ominous possibilities, telling the Lord that he did not see how he could live without a voice, for his voice to preach and to speak was his ministry.

"This is no ordinary man you're operating on," Elder Lee told the surgeon. From the blessings and the prayers, an operation a bit less radical than the doctor recommended was performed.

There was a long period of recuperation and preparation. The voice was all but gone, but a new one took its place. A quiet, persuasive, mellow voice, an acquired voice, an appealing voice, a voice that is loved by the Latter-day Saints.

In the intervening time he could work. During interviews he tapped out on the typewriter answers to questions and spent his time at the office.

Then came the test. Could he speak? Could he preach?

He went back home for his maiden speech. He went back to the valley. Anyone close to him knows it is not a valley, it is *the* valley. There, in a conference of the St. Joseph Stake, accompanied by his beloved associate from Arizona, Elder Delbert L. Stapley, he stood at the pulpit.

"I have come back here," he said, "to be among my own people. In this valley I presided as stake president." Perhaps he thought that should he fail, here he would be among those who loved him most and would understand.

There was a great outpouring of love. The tension of this dramatic moment was broken when he continued, "I must tell you what has happened to me. I went away to the East, and while there I fell among cutthroats. . . ." After that it didn't matter what he said. Elder Kimball was back!

Ensign, March 1974, p. 4.

———◆——◆———

SPENCER W. KIMBALL

"The Mobile Office"

As told by Elder Boyd K. Packer.

The family and the friends and associates of President Kimball know that he is never still. There has always been a restlessness about him to get things done. He is up early and works long hours and gets a little rest along the way. A time or two each day he will stretch out on the floor—perhaps in the bishop's office or the high council room if he is at a conference—and sleep for ten minutes. He bounces back with renewed energy to continue his thorough, detailed work.

I passed them on the highway once, up near the Idaho border. They were heading north to conference. Sister Kimball was driving, with Brother Kimball in the back seat, his little typewriter in its accustomed place on his lap, papers on either side of him, for this was an opportunity to work, to do more to help others. This mobile office, as those who have traveled with him know, is characteristic of his dedication.

Ensign, March 1974, p. 6.

SPENCER W. KIMBALL

"Don't You Touch Me"

As told by Elder Boyd K. Packer.

He makes those around him happy. His abundant humor is always in good taste.

On one occasion he was returning from Canada with one of his associates. The stewardess on the flight offered them all kinds of refreshments that are not proper for Latter-day Saints. After failing with coffee, tea, and alcoholic beverages, she asked, with some concern, "Isn't there anything I could get for you?"

"I would like some lemonade, if you have some," President Kimball replied.

"I'm sorry," she said. "We don't have any aboard."

She turned to go down the aisle and then no doubt remembered that lemon slices are often served with alcoholic beverages. She had some lemons aboard, for she turned and said, "But perhaps I could squeeze you a little."

Brother Kimball threw up his arms good naturedly as a barrier and in an expression of mock concern replied, "Don't you touch me!"

He is happy and positive and always reassuring to be around. His handshake is hearty and warm and sincere, and he is ever alert to reach out to those who otherwise might be overlooked or ignored. Those who meet him for the first time are impressed at once with his courtesy.

Ensign, March 1974, p. 6.

————◆—◆————

SPENCER W. KIMBALL

"Why Don't You Ask Him to Give You Your Blessing?"

I was down in Toquepala, Peru. We were dedicating a chapel. Many of the men who were employed in that mining town were Americans. After the dedication they had a dinner at one of the homes. As we moved around in the home, a young boy came to me and said, "Brother Kimball, I'm thinking about a mission. Would you give me a blessing?"

I said, "Why, of course. I'd be very happy to give you a blessing, but isn't that your father I met in the other room?"

He said, "Yes, that's Dad."

I said, "Well, why don't you ask him to give you your blessing?"

"Oh," he said, "Dad wouldn't want to give a blessing to me."

So I excused myself. I went out and found the father, and I said, "You have a wonderful boy there. I think he would like to have a blessing from his father. Wouldn't you like to give him a blessing?"

He said, "Oh, I don't think my boy would want me to give him a blessing."

But as I mingled among these people and saw the father and the son a little later, close together, I could understand that they had come together in their thoughts and that the boy was proud to have his father bless him, and the father was delighted to be asked.

I hope you boys in this audience will keep that in mind. You have the best dad in the world, you know. He holds the priesthood; he would be delighted to give you a blessing. He would like you to indicate it, and we would like you fathers to remember that your boys are maybe a little timid. They know you are the best man in the world, but probably if you just made the advance, there would be some glorious moments for you.

Ensign, May 1974, p. 89.

◆—▶

SPENCER W. KIMBALL

"Guests of the Lord"

Beloved students [of Brigham Young University], you are guests here—guests of the Lord, whose funds pay in large measure for your education. You are guests of the

Lord, his church, his leaders, his administration, his people. You and your parents make a smaller but necessary contribution.

In a faraway land to the south is an old man, somewhat crippled, untrained. The children, several, are ragged; their clothes are hand-me-downs, and winter or summer they trudge barefooted to a little primitive school. The home is tiny—two small rooms, one under the other with a ladder connecting. The little mother makes baskets and sells at the public market. The father makes chairs and tables out of the native jungle trees and, on his calloused, leathery bare feet, walks long distances, carrying his furniture those miles to market, hopefully. The middle man or the bargaining buyer leaves him very little profit from his honest labor; but because he is a faithful member of the Church, he takes his tithing to his branch president. And it finally reaches the treasury house, and part of it is allocated to the Brigham Young University.

This dear old man, this deprived little mother, and these gaunt little children, along with their fellow members and numerous others who are tithepayers, become host to you—the guests—and supply a goodly percentage of the wherewithal for land and buildings and equipment and instructions.

The boy working in the cornfield in India is your host, for he returns his ten percent.

The rich man living in his luxury who pays his tithing is your host.

The widowed mother with several hungry children is your hostess.

The custodian of your meetinghouse is your host.

The Navajo on the desert following his little band of sheep trying to find enough grass—he is your host. His dollars are few, his tithing is meager, but his testimony of the gospel, his dreams for his children, and his love for his fellowmen and his Lord induce him to send in his little tithing. He also becomes a joint host for you.

As guests we have opportunities and responsibilities. Our rights are few. Our demands should be fewer. As guests we gratefully accept the favors of our hosts and hostesses.

Would a guest attend a banquet uninvited? Would he dress in fatigue clothes when the host had set it up as a black-tie affair? Would he respect the host and his position? Would he say disparaging things about his host even while accepting of his hospitality? Would he declare his freedom to eat with his fingers, laugh raucously, tell evil stories about his host?

Would he come early or stay too late? Would he take with him the host's treasures? Would he monopolize the conversation and disregard the wishes of the host? Would he ill-behave himself, ignore the wishes of the host, or defy his requests?

Would he march or riot or demand? Would he criticize— the house too small, the temperature not right, the cook ugly, the waitresses inefficient? Because other guests have been known to be unruly, would he take license therefrom? Because other guests at other houses of hospitality destroy the property of their host, lock the doors, sit in or sleep in, would these guests follow suit?

Would guests come ill-clad? unbathed? unwashed? Would a guest belittle his host or embarrass him? Would guests declare their independence, forget their opportunities, or demand their supposed rights?

The greatest of all universities is our joint blessing. Let us all together keep it the pleasant oasis in the desert, where there is water and coolness when the desert sands blast in their fury.

Let us keep it an island of beauty and cleanness in an ocean of filth and destruction and disease. Let us keep it as a spring of pure cool water though surrounded by sloughs and stagnant swamps of rebellion and corruption and worldliness outside.

Let us keep it a place of peace in a world of confusion, frustration, mental aberrations, and emotional disturbances. Let us keep it a place of safety in a world of violence where laws are ignored, criminals coddled, enforcement curtailed, buildings burned, stores looted, lives endangered.

May we keep this glorious place a home of friendships and of eternal commitments, a place of study and growth and improvement, a place where ambition is kindled and faith is nurtured and confidence is strengthened, and where love for God and our fellowmen reaches its highest fulfillment. Let it continue to be a place of confidence and common admiration and understanding, with students and instructors and staff all people of confidence, affection, and serenity.

Let us not regard this as just another university—not just classrooms and professors, students and books, and laboratories.

May we enjoy the privileges and opportunities of this great institution, profit by our rich experience here, and extend our continued gratitude to the Lord and the joint hosts and hostesses in their gracious and generous hospitality.

My beloved young folks, stay true. Live the gospel. Love the Lord, I beg of you, in the name of Jesus Christ. Amen.

"In the World But Not of It," *BYU Speeches of the Year*, May 14, 1968, pp. 12-14.

◄━━━►

SPENCER W. KIMBALL

"He Is a Prophet of the Lord"

For Dr. Arturo de Hoyos, now a faculty member at Brigham Young University, President Kimball is a very special man. Dr. de Hoyos writes: ·

"In the winter of 1947, I was a freshman at BYU and had come to school from Mexico after I finished a fulltime mission. My roommate, Alfonso Rodriguez, also from Mexico, was also a returned missionary. We had found a room on the back of a house which had no heat other than a gas stove and no refrigerator. The snow was a new experience to us. Apart from a few small problems like not having winter clothing, not knowing English, and other such minor details, we were full of enthusiasm and were enjoying being at BYU. We were making adjustments. To save money for books, we had decided to eat only when absolutely necessary.

"This particular Sunday we had gotten up early. Among other things, we had been discussing the best way to go about defrosting some chocolate milk in a carton we had left outside on the window sill. It had frozen during the night. As it was the only food we had, all the alternatives had to include saving the milk. As we considered the matter, we even thought of fasting again and perhaps leaving the milk for Monday, which would get us one day closer to our next parttime paycheck late in the week.

"But we were not discouraged. True, we were getting kind of thin, but we were still very happy to be alive and at BYU. We also reasoned that there were spiritual compensations. We figured that we had fasted enough that semester to cast off any type of bad spirit that we might encounter.

"As we were considering what to do with our frozen milk, we heard a knock on the door. I opened the door and the visitor said, 'Hi, boys. I am on my way to stake conference in Sanpete County and I thought I would stop and say hello and see how you were getting along.' As he spoke, a thousand thoughts went running through my mind, most of them in Spanish: 'Shall I ask him to come in? . . . No, the room isn't very nice. . . . *Buenos dias*. . . . I wonder why he is here? . . . How do you do? . . . Perhaps we should invite him to have breakfast with us . . . Frozen chocolate milk for three? . . . How did he know we were here? . . . An apostle of the Lord in our room! . . .' Finally I said, 'Come in, Brother Kimball.'

"He came in and shook hands, and somehow we never felt embarrassed. Alfonso said something like, 'We are fine and happy.' We just looked at him and said little and, as I remember, we did not even invite him to sit down. But from the beginning he had made us feel at ease. As he talked he looked at us with that marvelous look of his that always conveys peace, concern, care, joy of life, complete knowledge of suffering, unselfishness, a deep desire to do good, and plain, simple love.

" 'Your mission president told me you were in Provo,' he said, 'and the other day I called the university to find out where you lived.'

"The previous June, during mission conference in Mexico City when Alfonso and I had been released from our two years of service, he, Spencer W. Kimball, had been the visiting authority. And he had remembered us, had called to find our address, and had stopped to see us; and now he was here in our room visiting us!

"He did not stay long. But it was long enough to lift our spirits up in a way that would be impossible to forget. And not only our spirits. For as he left and shook hands with us I found a $20 bill in mine! 'God bless you,' he said. 'Let me know how you get along.'

"Alfonso and I stood there in the middle of our room. We did not say much for a long time. I opened my hand and showed him the $20.

" 'I wonder how he knew,' I said, just to say something.

" 'He is a prophet of the Lord,' Alfonso said, 'and he knows.' "

Ensign, March 1975, p. 12.

Biographical Sketch

EZRA TAFT BENSON

President Ezra Taft Benson was ordained and set apart as prophet, seer, revelator, and president of The Church of Jesus Christ of Latter-day Saints in a special meeting of the Council of the Twelve Apostles held in the Salt Lake Temple on Sunday, November 10, 1985. The membership of the Church sustained President Benson in a solemn assembly held in the Tabernacle on Temple Square on April 6, 1986. President Benson had served as a member of the Council of the Twelve since October 1943 and as president of the Council since December 30, 1973.

From 1933 to 1937, President Benson was a member of the Boise Stake presidency in Boise, Idaho. When the stake was divided in November 1938, he was called as president of the Boise Stake. He served in that capacity until the spring of 1939 when he moved to Washington, D.C. to accept the position as executive secretary of the National Council of Farmer Cooperatives. In June 1940 he was called as the first president of the

Washington Stake. He occupied this position until he was called to the Council of the Twelve in October 1943.

President Benson is a great-grandson of the apostle Ezra T. Benson, one of the first company of pioneers who entered the Salt Lake Valley with Brigham Young on July 24, 1847. President Benson's parents were among the early settlers of southern Idaho, where in the small town of Whitney he was born August 4, 1899. As a young man, he was active in Scouting, priesthood work, and in the Church auxiliary organizations. He attended the Oneida Stake Academy in Preston, Idaho and later Utah Agricultural College (now Utah State University) in Logan, Utah.

From 1921 to 1923 he served as a missionary in the British Mission. Following his return home, he continued his education at Brigham Young University in Provo, Utah, graduating with honors, and subsequently he received a scholarship to Iowa State College in Ames, Iowa. There he received his M.S. degree, graduating with honors as well as being inducted into Gamma Sigma Delta, the National Honor Society of Agriculture. He later did additional graduate work at the University of California in Berkeley.

From 1929 to 1930 President Benson worked as a county agricultural agent in his native Idaho and a year later was asked to head the newly organized department of agricultural economics and marketing at the University of Idaho.

In that capacity he helped organize the Idaho Cooperative Council and served as its first secretary. In the spring of 1939 he was appointed executive secretary of the National Council of Farmer Cooperatives, a federation of 4,600 cooperative groups nationwide. He subsequently served on several advisory committees and national boards in the fields of agriculture and Scouting. He has also served as a director of several commercial business firms and is a member of the Board of Trustees of Brigham Young University.

On January 15, 1946, President Benson was appointed president of the European Mission of the Church with headquarters in London. The European Saints, under local leadership, had been carrying on during the war under distressing circumstances. Elder Benson was sent to attend to the spiritual affairs of the people, to reopen the missions so that active proselyting and organizational activities might be resumed, and to alleviate suffering among members by distributing food, clothing, bedding and other needed supplies among the Saints. President Benson was one of the first civilians to travel throughout war-torn Europe. He was released from this calling on December 11, 1946.

President Dwight D. Eisenhower, recognizing President Benson's outstanding administrative ability as well as his years of experience in agricultural affairs, appointed him to the United States Cabinet as Secretary of Agriculture in 1952. One of only two Cabinet members to serve the full eight years with Ike, President Benson returned to full-time Church service in 1961.

On September 10, 1926, Ezra Taft Benson and Flora Amussen were married in the Salt Lake Temple. They are the parents of six children (two sons and four daughters) and thirty-four grandchildren. President and Sister Benson have a goal for their family, that in this life and in the next there will be "no empty chairs." They are striving for all chairs to be filled, for all family members to be present.

It is a joy for members of the Church to sustain and follow the thirteenth president of The Church of Jesus Christ of Latter-day Saints. Ezra Taft Benson is a trusted, proven, faithful servant.

EZRA TAFT BENSON

"Father Called on a Mission"

A rich blessing for the entire family came as a complete surprise to all. It was during the time, many years ago, when sacrament meeting was held at 2:00 P.M. in the rural wards. We usually went to meeting in the white-top buggy, which would hold the entire family. But at this particular time there was an epidemic — chicken pox, I believe — in the ward. Parents were to attend sacrament meeting, but the children were to stay home. So Father and Mother went to meeting in the one-horse buggy.

As Father and Mother returned from sacrament meeting and we all gathered around the buggy, we saw something we had never seen before in our home. Both Father and Mother were crying at the same time — and they had just returned from sacrament meeting. Being the oldest, I asked what was wrong. Mother assured us everything was all right. "Then why are you crying?" we asked. "Come into the house and we'll tell you all about it."

As we gathered around the old sofa in the living room,

they explained why there were tears. When sacrament meeting was over, the storekeeper opened the store just long enough for the farmers to get their mail, as the post office was in the store. There was no R.F.D. in those days, and opening the store briefly saved a special trip to the post office.

As our parents proceeded homeward, Father driving and Mother opening the mail, there was a letter from Box B in Salt Lake City. This was a call to go on a mission. No one asked if you were able, ready, or willing to go. The bishop was expected to know and the call came without warning.

Then Mother explained that they were happy and grateful that Father was considered worthy to fill a mission. Then Father explained, "We're crying a bit because we know it means two years of separation, and your mother and I have never been separated more than two nights at a time in all of our married life, and that has been when I've been in the canyon for poles, fence posts, or derrick timbers."

Father went on his mission, leaving Mother at home with seven children. The eighth was born four months after he left. In preparation, the small dry farm was sold to finance the mission. A family moved into part of our expanded farm home to rent the row cropland. We children, under Mother's day-to-day encouragement and Father's letters of blessings, took care of the dairy herd and the hay and pastureland.

You can well imagine who had the hardest end of that mission. But not once did we ever hear a murmur from Mother's lips as she would sing at her work the ballads of youth and the songs of Zion she and Father had enjoyed so much in the ward choir. In fact, my first baby tending—we call it sitting now—I remember was as a boy of seven years tending my younger brothers and sisters while Father and Mother went to choir practice on Wednesday evenings.

It was hard work, but a rich two years. Letters from Father from what seemed to us far away—Davenport, Iowa; Springfield, Illinois; Chicago; Cedar Rapids; etc.—coupled with family prayer and unity brought into that home a spirit of missionary work that never left it. Later, seven sons went on missions from that home, some of them on two or three missions.

Many years later at the bedside of that noble mother, who, as Father confided to me as the oldest child, had only a few weeks unless the Lord intervened, I heard her farewell words to her fifth son as he left for his mission. "Remember, George, no matter what happens at home, I want you to stay and finish your mission." A few weeks later a telegram from the First Presidency to President LeGrand Richards of the Southern States Mission told of her passing. And a year later a second telegram told of the passing of Father. But true to the wish of his mother and the missionary spirit of that true Latter-day Saint home, George stayed and finished his mission, and a summer later he returned to his old field of labor on a short-time mission. In the brief will, first call on the modest assets was provision for missions for the two younger sons.

My father, who as a young man had helped to support several of his twelve brothers and sisters on missions also, was spoken of by a prominent citizen, state senator, and nonmember of the Church in these words: "Gentlemen, today we buried the greatest influence for good in Cache Valley." How grateful we eleven children are for parents who always, by word and example, were faithful to the great missionary call of the Master.

Ezra Taft Benson, *God, Family, Country* (Deseret Book Co., Salt Lake City, 1974), pp. 52-55.

EZRA TAFT BENSON

"I Was Almost Walking On Air"

Father, how old do you have to be to receive a patriarchal blessing?" asked an Aaronic Priesthood youth at the end of a Sunday School class in which two returned missionaries had made brief reports of their missions.

The rural Whitney Ward was blessed with a bishop who loved the young people and the great missionary cause. Often from the pulpit and in classes he would quote from the Bible the Lord's counsel to his ancient apostles: "Go ye into all the world, and preach the gospel to every creature." (Mark 16:15.) And then he would emphasize the great responsibility placed upon the Church in our day to "share the gospel with others" and "our duty to preach the gospel to all the world." As a true "missionary bishop," he expected every boy to be ready for a mission.

As a means of stimulating interest, the bishop had each returned missionary make a brief report of his mission in the Sunday School to the children and a more complete report in the sacrament meeting later in the day. This particular morning two missionaries had reported. Although it was sometimes difficult to understand how it could be "the happiest two years of my life," as they would conclude after recounting their hardships of opposition, we early got a desire to go on a mission.

This was the desire that prompted the question I had asked my father that Sunday morning. He told me he knew of no age requirement, but one should be old enough to understand what it means, and of course one must be worthy. I asked him if I was worthy. He informed me that he thought I was, but he was not the one to say because "that is the responsibility of the bishop. Why don't you ask the bishop if you might receive a recommend for a patriarchal blessing?" This I did. After a careful but brief interview in one corner of the chapel—because fifty or sixty years ago many chapels didn't have bishops' offices—he gave me a signed recommend.

As I proudly showed it to my father, he pointed to a tall, white-haired man and said, "Brother Dalley, our stake patriarch, is visiting here today. Why don't you present the recommend to him and ask when you might receive a blessing?" The patriarch responded kindly by putting his hand on my shoulder and saying, "If you'll come with me, we'll walk up the road to the home of my son-in-law, Brother Winward, and I'll give you the blessing right today."

Up the road, arm-in-arm with this godly man, we went to the farm home. In the parlor, a room used on special occasions, with Brother Winward as scribe, this noble patriarch placed his hands upon my head and gave a clear answer to a boy's prayer. I was promised, if faithful, of course, that I would go on a mission "to the nations of the earth, crying repentance to a wicked world." Filled with happiness and assurance that this and other promises in the blessing would be fulfilled, it seemed that I was almost walking on air during the mile walk to our farm home, where I broke the glad news to the family.

God, Family, Country, pp. 51-52.

EZRA TAFT BENSON

"The Truthfulness of the Book of Mormon"

One of Ezra's greatest mission experiences occurred when he and his companion, Elder James T. Palmer, were invited to speak at the South Shields Branch. "We have a number of friends who don't believe the lies being printed about the Church, and we feel certain we will fill our little chapel, if you'll come," branch leaders wrote.

The elders fasted and prayed about the meeting. As promised, the little chapel was filled to capacity. Elder Palmer recorded in his journal what happened: "Elder Benson was assigned to speak on the apostasy. . . . He mentioned that he was humble and nervous about speaking. But he was impressed by the spirit . . . and gave a strong and impressive discourse of the truthfulness of the Book of Mormon, never once remembering that his subject was to be of the apostasy."

Ezra later recalled, "I spoke with a freedom I had never experienced. Afterwards, I couldn't recall what I had said, but several nonmembers surrounded me and said, 'Tonight, we received a witness that Joseph Smith was a prophet of God, and we are ready for baptism.' It was the experience of a lifetime. The Lord sustained me. I couldn't have done it otherwise. It was the first experience of that kind I'd had, where I knew that the Lord was with me." The inspiration to speak on the Book of Mormon would be a recurring theme throughout his life.

Sheri L. Dew, *Ezra Taft Benson, A Biography* (Deseret Book Co., Salt Lake City, 1987), p. 55.

EZRA TAFT BENSON

"The Power of Prayer"

On Sunday evening the elders, dressed in black suits and bowlers, began their open-air assembly near the railway station in Sunderland [England]. As the meeting progressed, attendance increased steadily. Some persons became rowdy, and when the pubs closed, a large group of men, many inebriated, swelled the audience. In order to make themselves heard, the elders turned their backs to each other and shouted their message. Some persons on the periphery began to yell,

"What's all the excitement?" Others shouted back, "It's those dreadful Mormons." With increasing pandemonium, the shout went out, "Let's get 'em and throw 'em in the river!"

The elders became separated, with the crowd pushing Ezra down one side of the railway station and his companion down the other. As he was pushed along in a man-made circle some ten feet in diameter, Ezra began to pray silently for help. "When it seemed that I could hold out no longer," he reported, "a big husky stranger pushed his way through to my side. He looked me straight in the eye and said in a strong, clear voice, 'Young man, I believe every word you said tonight.' As he spoke a little circle cleared around me. This to me was a direct answer to prayer. Then a British bobby appeared."

The policeman escorted Ezra home with strict instructions to stay put. But when his companion didn't return, Ezra disguised himself in an old English cap and jacket and set out to find him. An onlooker who quickly saw through the disguise told Ezra that the elder's head had been "mashed in." Ezra started off in a sprint to find him and ran into the same policeman, who confirmed that the elder had had a nasty blow, but that he, the policeman, had helped him safely home.

"I went back to the lodge and found my companion disguising himself in order to go out and look for me," Ezra wrote. "We threw our arms around each other and knelt together in prayer.... Resorting to prayer in such a time of crisis was not born of desperation. It was merely the outgrowth of the cherished custom of family prayer with which I had been surrounded since earliest childhood."

Ezra Taft Benson, A Biography, pp. 62-63.

—•——•——

EZRA TAFT BENSON

"We've Decided to Accept the Call"

At a stake presidency's meeting in Boise, Idaho, years ago, we were trying to select a president for the weakest and smallest elders quorum in the stake. Our clerk had brought a list of all the elders of that quorum, and on the list was the name of a man whom I had known for some years. He came from a strong Latter-day Saint family, but he wasn't doing much in the Church. If the bishop made a call to do some work on the chapel, he'd usually respond, and if the elders wanted to play softball, you would sometimes find him out playing with them. He did have leadership ability; he was president of one of the service clubs and was doing a fine job.

I said to the stake president, "Would you authorize me to go out and meet this man and challenge him to square his life with the standards of the Church and take the leadership of his quorum? I know there is some hazard in it, but he has the ability."

The stake president said, "You go ahead, and the Lord bless you."

After Sunday School I went to this man's home. I'll never forget the look on his face as he opened the door and saw a member of his stake presidency standing there. He hesitantly invited me in; his wife was preparing dinner, and I could smell the aroma of coffee coming from the kitchen. I asked him to have his wife join us, and when we were seated, I told him why I had come. "I am not going to ask for your answer today," I told him. "All I want you to do is to promise me that you will think about it, pray about it, think about it in terms of what it will mean to your family, and then I'll be back to see you next week. If you decide not to accept, we'll go on loving you," I added.

The next Sunday, as soon as he opened the door I saw there had been a change. He was glad to see me, and he quickly invited me in and called his wife to join us. He said, "Brother Benson, we have done as you said. We've thought about it and we've prayed about it, and we've decided to accept the call. If you brethren have that much confidence in me, I'm willing to square my life with the standards of the Church, a thing I should have done a long time ago." He also said, "I haven't had any coffee since you were here last week, and I'm not going to have any more."

He was set apart as elders quorum president, and attendance in his quorum began going up—and it kept going up. He went out, put his arm around the inactive elders, and brought them in. A few months later I moved from the stake.

Years passed, and one day on Temple Square in Salt Lake City, a man came up to me, extended his hand, and said, "Brother Benson, you don't remember me, do you?"

"Yes, I do," I said, "but I don't remember your name."

He said, "Do you remember coming to the home of a delinquent elder in Boise seven years ago?" And then, of course, it all came back to me. Then he said, "Brother Benson, I'll never live long enough to thank you for coming to my home that Sunday afternoon. I am now a bishop. I used to think I was happy, but I didn't know what real happiness was."

God, Family, Country, pp. 186-88.

EZRA TAFT BENSON

"Good Mormons Live It"

Many years ago, a member of our district council in the mission in Washington was traveling by plane. He had been in Canada, and on the flight back the plane developed trouble and had to land on an auxiliary landing field in Pennsylvania. It was a cold night, and the passengers were told that the plane would probably be on the ground for an hour. They got out and stretched and wandered around a little, and then they noticed over in the brush a light. They walked over toward this light and found a CCC camp, and as they opened the door they got an aroma of hot food. So they got courage and walked in, and they were invited to join the CCC boys at dinner. Now, the member of our district council found himself seated between two CCC boys, and when they brought around the hot coffee our friend, who didn't use it ordinarily, thought, "The coffee is hot and I am cold and there isn't anything else readily available to drink." So he took some and engaged in conversation with the two boys beside him. One of them said, "Where do you come from?" He said, "I come from Washington, but originally I came from Utah." "You don't happen to be a Mormon, do you?" "Yes," he replied, "I am a Mormon." The boy said, "You are not a very good one, are you?" Well, he was a pretty good one, and it was an awful shock to him to hear this comment. He said, "What do you know about the Mormons?" The boy said, "Well, a couple of years ago I was in St. George, Utah, and I attended Mormon services. I know you Mormons have in your church what you call the Word of Wisdom, and that good Mormons live it." Can you imagine how the district councilor felt? It wasn't the cup of coffee—that is not going to destroy anyone—but it was the fact that he hadn't maintained that which he believed in. He hadn't kept the standards.

It never pays to let down your standards in this church. You will be thought more of if you live the gospel, if you will be what you profess to be. You will be happier, you will have a better feeling inside, you will do more good in the world, and you will be more effective missionaries. So live church and missionary standards wherever you go.

God, Family, Country, pp. 62-63.

EZRA TAFT BENSON

"A Day Which I Shall Never Forget"

My beloved brethren of the priesthood, my heart is filled to overflowing with gratitude as I look into your faces this day—a day which I shall never forget.

I am grateful beyond my power of expression for the blessings which have come to me, and particularly for this great honor that has come to one of the weakest of your number. I love this work. All my life I have had a testimony of it and a love for the leaders of the Church and for the priesthood of God. I know that it is true, and no sacrifice is too great for this wonderful work in which we are engaged.

My brethren, I must confess I had no premonition of this call, even of the shortest duration. When passing through Salt Lake and stopping here, just between trains, enroute to Colorado on the twenty-sixth of July, President McKay indicated that the President of the Church wanted to see me a few minutes. Even then such a thought as being called to this high and holy calling never entered my mind. It was only a few minutes later that President Grant took my right hand in both of his, and looked into the depths of my very soul, and said: "Brother Benson, with all my heart I congratulate you and pray God's blessings to attend you; you have been chosen as the youngest apostle of the Church."

The whole world seemed to sink. I could hardly believe it was true, that such a thing could happen; and it has been difficult since for me to realize that it is a reality.

Leon R. Hartshorn, comp., *Outstanding Stories by General Authorities*, vol. 2 (Deseret Book Co., Salt Lake City, 1971), pp. 27-28.

EZRA TAFT BENSON

"A Greater Call"

I know something of the honors which men can bestow, but I know that there is nothing that can compare with the honors which come to us as servants of the Lord through the priesthood of God.

May I be pardoned if I refer to a recent trip during which time I passed through this city and during which time this great call [as an Apostle] was announced. I had been holding a series

of meetings with cooperative and agricultural leaders throughout the southwest, in California, and in the intermountain states.
While in California, I spent Saturday afternoon and Saturday
night at the home of the president of the organization with
which I am associated, the National Council of Farmer Cooperatives. This man is a national figure. He was a member of the
board during President Hoover's administration. He is a friend
of our people. When my fifteen-year-old son and I bade him
and his good wife good-bye on Sunday morning, with one of his
men who was driving us to Bakersfield, he called me to one side
and said: "We know you've had opportunities to go elsewhere,
but we want you to stay with the cooperative movement. All
you need to do is name your figure. Don't become disinterested.
We want you to continue."

I said, "Mr. Teague, I have no desire to leave the fine
group of men with whom I have been associated during the past
four years. I love the cooperative movement — I believe in it. It
squares with my philosophy of life, my religious philosophy."

Then only a few days later this call came. I called this man
on the phone from Grand Junction, Colorado, and said, "Mr.
Teague, the Church has called me to a more important work,"
and then I indicated what the call was, and this good man said,
"With all my heart I congratulate you." From that day until
this, there has been nothing but words of praise and congratulations to me personally, but particularly for the Church and
its fine ideals and standards and the type of manhood which it
turns out into the world.

I carried in my pocket as I went through Salt Lake a note
to call to my attention a matter which I proposed to discuss
with some of the brethren. I had an opportunity for almost a
year to go elsewhere at a figure that shocked me, running into
tens of thousands of dollars, an offer to go into the active man-
agement of a great cooperative corporation. It would mean
leaving the Washington Stake, and I had hoped to have an
opportunity to confer with the leaders of the Church. But now
there was no need of conferring, for in the meantime this call

came, a call greater than any call that can come from men —
that can be offered by the men of the world.

Reed A. Benson, comp., *So Shall Ye Reap* (Deseret Book Co., Salt Lake City, 1960), pp. 11-12.

EZRA TAFT BENSON

"We Need More of That Spirit in Our Home"

I was seated in my office in Salt Lake City when I received a telephone call from a man in New York, a multimillionaire and one of our great industrialists. He had a son in a camp just outside Salt Lake City who had been expecting to be shipped overseas, and then the war had ended and so the servicemen were crowded into that camp. This boy was discouraged and his father was worried about him, so he called and said, "Would you please call him on the telphone and see if you can cheer him up a bit." I said, "Of course, I would be happy to." And so I called him and said, "Wouldn't you like to come into the office for a little visit?" He said, "I surely would."

He was a bit delayed coming in and I was just ready to leave for home when he arrived. I said, "Wouldn't you like to go out to the house with me and take pot luck with the family? My wife doesn't know you are coming, but you will be welcome." He said, "I can't imagine anything I'd rather do tonight than that." So he went with me and we had our dinner and we had our prayer. Then we gathered around the piano afterward and enjoyed ourselves in some singing. After we visited for a while,

I drove him down to the bus. In a few days, I got a letter from his father. And you know, you would have thought I had saved the boy's life! In the letter, the father quoted a letter from his son in which the son had said, "Father, I didn't know there were any people in this world who lived like that."

Yes, we take it all for granted. Here was a man worth millions of dollars, who could buy his son anything that dollars could buy and never miss the dollars, and yet this simple thing of prayer and devotion in the home had passed him by. We need to be more grateful. I think there is no true character without gratitude. It is one of the marks of a real strong character to have a feeling of thanksgiving and gratitude for blessings. We need more of that spirit in our homes, in our daily association, in the Church, everywhere. It doesn't cost anything, and it is so easy to cultivate. It is so easy also to be dissatisfied and to be envious of other people.

God, Family, Country, pp. 201-2.

EZRA TAFT BENSON

"I Think You Should Stay"

I have many happy memories associated with my brethren in the Council of the Twelve. There were eight years when I was not able to meet with them often, and how I missed being there! But I felt that I had received a call from our prophet when, on learning of the possibility of my being appointed Secretary of Agriculture in President Dwight D. Eisenhower's Cabinet, President David O. McKay said, "My mind is clear, and if the invitation comes in the right spirit, I feel you should accept."

I remember leaving with a promise of staying two years, and then at the end of two years, the insistence of President Eisenhower that I stay another two years, and then four years more.

One morning I received in my office in Washington a call from the White House. The appointment secretary on the other end of the line said, "We have a man here by the name of David O. McKay from Salt Lake City who has asked to see the President. Do you know him, and do you think we should have him see the President?" I said I was sure the President would feel honored to see David O. McKay.

After his interview with the President, President McKay came over to my office and said, "Brother Benson, I didn't even tell my counselors that I was leaving this morning. I just received the impression to get on the plane and come back here to see the President and ask if he wouldn't release you now that the 1956 campaign is over and he has been reelected. You have been here four years."

I said, "President McKay, I hope you were successful."

He said, "No, I was not. Of course they can't force you to stay, but I think we have an obligation to our country and that we should accede to his wishes. I think you should stay on."

But there were very few weeks while I was in Washington that my thoughts didn't turn to the Salt Lake Temple on Thursday, because I knew that on that day of the week the members of my quorum, whom I love most deeply, would be on their knees with the First Presidency, and then they would be gathered around the altar, dressed in the robes of the holy priesthood, and on that day I would be especially remembered.

God, Family, Country, pp. 69-70.

EZRA TAFT BENSON

"A Spiritual Experience in Moscow"

From the time he arrived [in Russia], Ezra repeatedly requested that he be taken to visit one of the two Protestant churches in Moscow. Finally, as his party was being taken to the airport for their departure, he again asked to stop at a church. Reluctantly, his driver swung into a narrow alley behind an old stucco building—the Central Baptist Church. It was raining, but the chill left as the Secretary's party entered the church which was filled to overflowing with mostly middle-aged and elderly people. Ezra understood that Soviet citizens attended these services at some risk; anyone who looked to a career of any kind avoided the slightest suspicion of belief in Christianity.

The American group caused an immediate stir in the old church. A newsman present described the scene: "Every face in the old sanctuary gaped incredulously as our obviously American group was led down the aisle. They grabbed for our hands as we proceeded to our pews which were gladly vacated. . . . Their wrinkled old faces looked at us pleadingly. They reached out to touch us almost as one would reach out for the last final caress of one's most-beloved just before the casket is lowered. They gripped our hands like frightened children."

Surprisingly, the minister invited Secretary Benson to speak. Knowing there was some danger, Ezra turned to Flora and asked if she thought he should do it. Without pause she answered, "You bet, T!" And he made his way to the pulpit.

Never had he stood before an audience like this. As he scanned the crowd of anxious faces, it took some moments for him to control his emotions. These were good people, he felt immediately, subjected to a society that deprived them of unrestricted worship. The emotional impact was almost more than he could bear. Then he began to speak about hope and truth and love. As he talked about the Savior and the hope of life after death, tears flowed freely throughout the church.

"Our Heavenly Father is not far away," the Secretary promised. "He is our Father. Jesus Christ, the Redeemer of the World, watches over this earth. . . . Be unafraid, keep His commandments, love one another, pray for peace, and all will be well."

Women took out their handkerchiefs and nodded vigorously as they moaned, "Ja, ja, ja!" He looked down at one elderly woman, her head covered by a scarf and with a shawl about her shoulder, and spoke as though directly to her: "This life is only a part of eternity. We lived before we came here. . . .We will live again after we leave this life. . . . I believe very firmly in prayer. I know it is possible to reach out and tap that Unseen Power which gives us strength and such an anchor in time of need." He concluded, "I leave you my witness as a church servant for many years that the truth will endure. Time is on the side of truth. God bless you and keep you all the days of your life."

By this time tears were streaming down Ezra's face. When his entourage finally filed down the aisle, men and women waved handkerchiefs and grasped the visitors' hands in an action that spoke more than words. Spontaneously they began to sing "God Be With You Till We Meet Again." The language was foreign, but the tune was unmistakable. The Americans entered their cars with not a dry eye among them. Finally a newsman broke the silence, commenting, "I believe they were the only really happy people we saw in Russia."

"I shall never forget that evening as long as I live," Elder Benson later wrote. "Seldom, if ever, have I felt the oneness of mankind and the unquenchable yearning of the human heart for freedom." Others felt similarly. Cynical newsmen who had complained about "going to church with Ezra" stood and wept openly. . . .

When they reached the airport, nearly all the newsmen traveling with Ezra told him it had been the greatest spiritual experience they had ever had. He was profoundly grateful for the circumstances that had allowed him to leave his testimony with those people. He knew he would never forget the experience.

Ezra Taft Benson, A Biography, pp. 342-45.

EZRA TAFT BENSON

"A Father's Blessing

A young man came to my office a short time ago for a blessing. He had problems — not moral problems, but he was neurotic; he was confused; he was concerned and worried. And so we talked for a few minutes and I said to him, "Have you ever asked your father for a blessing?" "Oh," he said, "I don't know that Dad would do a thing like that. He is not very active." I said, "But he's your father." "Yes." "Does he hold the priesthood?" "Yes, he is an inactive elder." I said, "Do you love him?" And he said, "Yes, I love him. He is a good man, he's good to the family, good to the children." I said, "Do you ever have family prayer?" He said, "It has been a long time since we had family prayer." I said, "All right, would you be willing to go home and watch for an opportunity, and ask your father if he will give you a blessing? And if it doesn't work out, you come back, and I will be glad to help you."

So he left, and in about three days he came back. "Brother

403

Benson, this has been the sweetest thing that's happened in our home," he said. "Mother and the children sat there, my younger brothers and sisters, with my mother wiping tears from her eyes. She expressed her gratitude later. Father gave me a lovely blessing." He added, "I could tell it came from his heart."

There are a lot of fathers who would enjoy giving their own children blessings, if they had a little encouragement. As patriarchs of their families, that is one of their obligations and duties, responsibilities, and, of course, opportunities.

God, Family, Country, p. 184.

EZRA TAFT BENSON

"They Have Come At Last"

I know that the Lord can touch the hearts of men behind the iron curtain. I have seen it happen. I have been very close to it. I remember very well our efforts to get to Warsaw, Poland, in 1946 and my desire to get up to Selbongen in East Prussia where we had one congregation, the only congregation in Poland and the only Church-owned building in Germany at that time. There was one plane going, taking supplies to the American Embassy, but no passenger service. We had to get permission from the Russians and the Poles to get into Warsaw. Brother Fred Babbel, who was with me, had tried to make arrangements without success, and then I had tried, and we still weren't successful. But our plane was to leave in two days, and so we did some fasting and praying. At last I went to see the Russian general who was in charge of the Poles and finally, after about two hours in his office with him, he signed the document to permit us to go. Then we made arrangements to ride on the plane with the Americans who were carrying supplies to the American Embassy. I learned later that this general lost his commission because he had given permission for an American to go into Poland, and I always felt that the Spirit worked on this man, because he had previously turned us down.

In Warsaw there was only one hotel that was even partially intact, and that was the Polonia Hotel. I shared one room with seven other men, most of them members of the press. We got the Americans to loan us a jeep, and we drove up to Selbongen. It took us all day to drive there on Sunday, through two rain-storms and with no cover on the jeep. When we drove into the little town of Selbongen we found the name had been changed to Zelback, because the Poles had changed all the names throughout the area. There was no one on the street because it was Sunday, and as we approached our little chapel, we saw a woman running away from us. She had seen this military vehicle and had thought it meant more trouble, because the people had been persecuted and their homes had been ran-sacked.

Well, we stopped the jeep and I jumped out. When the woman saw we were civilians, she turned around and came walking toward us. Then she recognized us—I guess from a picture, I don't see how else—and she screamed, "Oh, it's the Brethren! They have come at last!" She ran to us with tears in her eyes and then guided us to the home of the branch president. I think I never saw so many tears shed by a small group as we saw that day, as the word spread and the people came into the branch president's home. Then we held a meeting. I said, "Haven't you had your meetings today, yet?" They said, "Yes, we have had our meetings—priesthood, Sunday School, and sacrament meeting—but now that you are here we want another meeting." It was five o'clock, just starting to get dusk, and so we set the meeting for six and sent the members out to notify the Saints. At six o'clock the little chapel was filled.

During the service, as I was speaking near the time of closing, two Polish soldiers came in the front door and took a few steps into the building. I motioned for them to come forward. There were only two vacant seats, on the front row. Then, through the interpreter, I told them why I was there and on what authority and something about our work. I went ahead speaking to the people after the soldiers had taken seats at my invitation. I could tell the people were frightened of them, because as they came down the aisle the women would push away from the aisle. As we came to the end of the service and were starting to sing the closing song, they left the meeting place.

We had planned to close the meeting, but three or four people stood up immediately and asked, "Couldn't we have another meeting? This was not like a real meeting with soldiers here." One lady said, "I have a candle at home I have been saving for a special occasion [there were no lights in the building]." She said, "I will go get it if you want to read from the scriptures." And so we held another meeting for an hour and a quarter with these wonderful people.

God, Family, Country, pp. 71-73.

EZRA TAFT BENSON

"I Never Heard of a People with Such Vision"

I thought of our first interview with General McNarney, the top general in the American forces. It was in the I. G. Farbin building in Frankfurt, which had been spared by "pin bombing," because the Americans expected it would be their headquarters when the war was over, as it was.

We had driven our little jeep up to the building, parked it, and gone in to see if we could get an appointment with the general. We had been in Europe just a few days. We wanted to get permission from him to make our own distribution of our welfare supplies to our own people through our own channels. In those days, of course, everything was being distributed through the military. We were told by the colonel at the desk that we couldn't get an appointment for three days. The general was very busy, with important delegations coming to see him. We returned to our car and had a prayer together, then went back in. In the meantime, the secretary at the desk had been changed, and, in less than fifteen minutes, we were in the presence of General McNarney.

Then I saw the Spirit operate on that man. I heard him say, "Under no conditions can you have permission to distribute your own supplies to your own people. They must come through the military." And, of course, we recognized immediately that if we had to go through the military, our Saints wouldn't get much of the supplies. And so we started telling him about the program of the Church, and when he saw we were somewhat determined, he said, "Well, you go ahead and collect your supplies, and probably by the time you get them collected the policy will be changed." I said, "General, they are already collected; they are always collected. We have ninety warehouses full of supplies. Within twenty-four hours from the time I wire our First Presidency in Salt Lake City, carloads of food, bedding, clothing, and medical supplies will be moving toward Germany." When I said this, he said, "I never heard of people with such vision." And before we left him we had written authorization to make our own distribution to our own people through our own channels, and from that moment on we had wonderful cooperation.

So I know that the Spirit can operate on nonmembers of

the Church in high positions when it is in the interests of the work of the Lord. I have seen it with my own eyes.

―――

God, Family, Country, pp. 73-74.

―――◆―◆―――

EZRA TAFT BENSON

"Twenty-Two People Were Living in One Room"

Probably the saddest part of our mission [in 1946] was with our refugees. These poor unwanted souls had been driven from their once happy homes to destinations unknown. They came with all their earthly possessions on their backs, but after organizing them into branches and calling them into meetings, they sang the songs of Zion with a fervor I am sure has never been surpassed. We visited some of their homes—their shacks—where as many as twenty-two people were living in one room—four complete families! And yet they knelt together in prayer night and morning and bore testimony to us regarding the blessings of the gospel.

Now, just a word about the Welfare Program. I bring to you, my brothers and sisters, the deep gratitude and thanksgiving of the Saints in Europe. The spirit of the Welfare Program was there long before we arrived. The Saints in various countries had sent help to their less fortunate brothers and sisters in other nations. Welfare gardens had been planted. We found them among the bombed-out buildings. We ran on to many instances where, following bombings, branches had joined together and pooled all their remaining supplies, food, clothing, and household articles, and turned them over to the priesthood for distribution according to need.

It was a great joy when the welfare supplies came through. It was also a great surprise to the military authorities and others to learn with what dispatch the supplies arrived from Zion. . . .

I have faced congregations of more than a thousand Latter-day Saints where it was estimated by the mission president that more than eighty percent of the total clothing worn was clothing from Zion, sent through the Welfare Program. My brethren and sisters, do you need any further evidence of the need for this program and the inspiration back of it? I wish you could have spent a few days with me in Europe during this past year. I tell you God is directing this program. It is inspired! Had it not been so, there would have been many, many hundreds more of our Latter-day Saints perish with hunger and die of cold because of the lack of simple food commodities and clothing.

Outstanding Stories by General Authorities, vol. 3, pp. 33-34.

◄━◆━►

EZRA TAFT BENSON

"People Who Have Never Seen Us"

As Elder Benson and his associates drove toward Keil, Germany, they saw dozens of people combing the ditch banks. He described the scene in a letter home: "Some take ordinary grass and weeds and cut it up to mix with a little chicken feed and water which is their meal. I noticed between meetings some would take out of their pocket a little cup partly filled with chicken feed or cereal and water which they would eat cold. . . . I didn't intend to write all this sad picture. I have tried to spare you at home most of the heart-rending scenes in Europe today. But somehow I just couldn't hold it this morning. It's terrible to contemplate. . . .

When the first shipment of welfare supplies arrived in Berlin, Elder Benson took acting mission president Richard Ranglack to the battered warehouse that, under armed guard, housed the precious goods stacked nearly to the ceiling. "Do you mean to tell me those boxes are full of food?" President Ranglack asked. "Yes," Ezra replied, "food, clothing, bedding, and a few medical supplies." To prove his point, he pulled down a box of dried beans. As Ranglack ran his fingers through the contents, he broke down and cried. Ezra opened another box, this one filled with cracked wheat. Ranglack touched a pinch of it to his mouth. When he could finally speak, he said, "Brother Benson, it is hard for me to believe that people who have never seen us could do so much for us."

Ezra Taft Benson, A Biography, pp. 218-19.

EZRA TAFT BENSON

"A Circle of Light"

There came to my mind an experience my wife, Flora, had when she was on a mission in Hawaii.

She had been officiating part-time in the temple while on her mission, and this particular night the session had run a bit late, and she had been delayed for some reason. So when she got to the door she found that it was locked. She was in and everyone had gone, and she was alone in the temple. The mission home in those days was situated across a stile, over a fence, and through some trees. When she found she was locked in, she tried the door and said, "Yes, I can open it from the inside." But she said a prayer that she would be protected, because in those days there was a camp in the trees just off the trail to the mission home, and there had been some incidents, so she was worried. She prayed to the Lord that she would be protected, and then she started toward the door. As she stepped outside the door, there was a circle of light all around her person and that circle of light accompanied her all the way to the mission home — over the stile, through the trees, to the door of the mission home.

God, Family, Country, pp. 70-71.

Index

413

414